NATURE-GUIDED THERAPY

Brief Integrative Strategies
for Health and Well-Being

George W. Burns

BRUNNER/MAZEL

Taylor & Francis Group

NATURE-GUIDED THERAPY

USA	Publishing Office:	BRUNNER/MAZEL *A member of the Taylor & Francis Group* 325 Chestnut Street Philadelphia, PA 19106 Tel: (215) 625-8900 Fax: (215) 625-2940
	Distribution Center:	BRUNNER/MAZEL *A member of the Taylor & Francis Group* 1900 Frost Road, Suite 101 Bristol, PA 19007-1598 Tel: (215) 785-5800 Fax: (215) 785-5515
UK		Taylor & Francis Ltd. 1 Gunpowder Square London EC4A 3DE Tel: 0171 583 0490 Fax: 0171 583 0581

NATURE-GUIDED THERAPY: Brief Integrative Strategies for Health and Well-Being

1 2 3 4 5 6 7 8 9 0   B R B R   9 0 9 8

This book was set in Times Roman. The editors were George Kendall, Edward Cilurso, and Greg Edmondson. Cover design by Joe Dieter.

A CIP catalog record for this book is available from the British Library.
∞ The paper in this publication meets the requirements of the ANSI Standard Z39.48-1984 (Permanence of Paper)

Library of Congress Cataloging-in-Publication Data

Burns, George (George William)
    Nature-guided therapy: brief integrative strategies for health
and well-being/George Burns.
        p.   cm.
    Includes bibliographical references and index.

    1. Nature, Healing power of.   2. Nature—Psychological aspects.
3. Mind and body therapies.   4. Mental health.   I. Title.
R723.B86   1998
615.5—dc21   97-44772
                                                                            CIP

ISBN 0-87630-850-7

This book is dedicated to Leah, Jurien, and Thomas.

Could I but teach the hundredth part
Of what from thee I learn.

William Wordsworth
from *Anecdote for Fathers*

CONTENTS

Part II
A MATTER OF SENSE

Part III
NATURE-GUIDED STRATEGIES

PART V
NATURAL WELLNESS

Preface

Oikos is a Greek word. It means household or living place. It has a sense of intimacy, of interconnectedness between person and place. Probably for this reason Ernst Haeckel, seeking to broaden the concept of biology to include the interrelationships between organisms and their environment, used it to coin the term *ecology* in 1873.

A special part of my own childhood living place was a treehouse built by my father in an old eucalyptus tree that dominated our backyard. From it I could peer into neighbors' properties, look out over grassy paddocks, or watch soft, swirling clouds dancing above the tree's proud branches. It was to here that I would retreat if I felt out of sorts with the world. I quickly forgot the hassles of the school day, the scolding I'd had from my mother, or the falling out with my sister. It was a safe and secure place to be alone.

As a child, I simply experienced those times; it never occurred to me to ask why I felt such enjoyment in nature. I didn't stop to question whether watching a trail of ants working their way up and down the trunk we both shared, or listening to the serenade of a bird that had landed on a branch within touching distance, could alter my state of affect. I just knew that it did. If I wanted to feel happier or calmer I would climb into the gentle motion of the tree's branches, listen to the soft song of its leaves in the breeze, or await whatever unexpected delights it might bring my way.

Neither such experiences nor their environmental contexts were addressed during my training in psychology. I was brought up in a psychoanalytical school that saw insight as the basis of therapy and considered change a long-term process achievable only after destructuring, shuffling, and reconstructing a person's intrapsychic dynamics. But when I sat down with clients in my first job, I was meeting people with problems for which they were seeking practical solutions rather than an academic understanding. Without realizing it, they were launching me on a career-long search for therapeutic methods that would provide the means to best help them achieve their goals.

The search led into client-centered therapy, hypnotherapy, behavior therapy, Gestalt therapy, transactional analysis, cognitive therapy, Ericksonian therapy, psychobiology, brief therapy, solution-oriented therapy, and several other schools of treatment. Each has contributed, with varying levels of significance, to my professional evolution. Yet when I asked clients what had previously helped them change thoughts, feelings, or behaviors, I found they described processes not usually mentioned in the therapeutic literature. It was often nature-based experiences that facilitated relaxation, happiness, and wellness. As a consequence, I developed the Sensual Awareness Inventory to access these client resources (see Chapter 4).

Colleagues, in informal discussions, related similar stories about what they did for their personal happiness and well-being or about what had helped them through periods of difficulty. For fun or relaxation, they usually hike, scuba dive, sail, travel, garden, or participate in other nature-based activities. But, somehow, there is an incongruence between what they use effectively in their own lives and what they do with clients. Our training often teaches that, for our clients to reach similar goals, they must tread a different path from what we travel ourselves.

The nature-guided therapeutic assignments I began to offer clients were ones I didn't initially discuss with fellow therapists. They didn't fit the usual gambit of conventional therapies. On reading more widely I realized that other disciplines had long been describing and using the person-nature connection. In anthropology I found examples in which boundaries were not drawn among people, environment, and cosmos, in which healers used nature-based healing exercises. Poets, travelers, and writers lyrically recorded their affect-altering experiences with the natural ecology. Biologists, as far back as Ernst Haeckel, had recognized that organisms do not exist as individuals but as intricate, interwoven elements of a system. Environmental psychologists were researching, and scientifically validating, the emotional and physical benefits of nature contact. The results ranged from enhanced relaxation through altered behavioral patterns and physiology to more rapid discharge from the hospital. Among such divergent schools of thought there was a general consensus: The wellness of any organism is based on both the health of its ecology and the well-being of the relationship between the two.

In my exploration of this material I felt a sense of sadness, first, that each body of knowledge has kept its wisdom within its own boundaries, and, second, that psychotherapy has been so tardy in acknowledging that the psyche is not a separate entity but an integral aspect of an ecological whole. Well-being depends not only on the balance of our intrapsychic systems but also on our interactions with both the micro and macro ecology of which we are just one interdependent element.

Attempting to understand the whole rather than simply the parts, this book draws together a variety of usually disparate disciplines: ethnomedicines, environmental psychology, social geography, anthropology, ethology, psychobiology, sociobiology, ecology, and clinical psychology. I am quick to confess that I am not an expert in all of these fields. I am not a researcher, but I have benefited from the research of others whose work is appropriately acknowledged throughout the text. Similarly, I do not see myself as a theorist. In the process of writing, however, I have become aware of how working with the practical applications of nature-guided therapy has brought about a shift in my therapeutic paradigm. My background, training, and interests are as a clinician. As such I am seeking to develop pragmatic approaches that will help clients reach their desired therapeutic goals in the quickest and most effective manner.

With this objective in mind, the book has been structured into five parts. Section 1 begins with an evolutionary history of the developmental relationship of our species with our ecology. A cross-cultural journey into traditional healing disciplines explores their holistic concepts of the person-nature relationship. There is an examination of how clinical data, empirical scientific investigations, and anecdotal accounts all point to the healing benefits of a balanced relationship with the ecology. The second chapter in this section expounds the characteristics of nature-guided therapy.

Because our perceptual faculties are the intermediaries of any interaction with nature, Section 2 travels into each sense modality, examining its mechanical basis, its affect-creating potentials, and the ways in which it can be used therapeutically. For each modality there are examples of how therapists can offer directives for change, and these are illustrated with case vignettes. At the end of this section the Sensual Awareness Inventory is presented as an instrument that can quickly and effectively access client resources for the development of therapeutic strategies.

Section 3 develops more detailed case histories and presents pragmatic, step-by-step procedures for using nature-guided strategies. From the therapeutic benefits of stopping to smell a rose to the challenges of trekking in the Himalayas, ecotherapy assignments range from simple sensate focusing to the construction of more complex experiential metaphors.

Clinical applications of ecotherapy are presented in Section 4. Nature-guided therapy goes beyond a simple symptom-elimination approach. Interactions with nature are more likely to resolve an existing problem by creating a desired positive affective state. To emphasize this, the chapter headings, along with the material presented, focus on creating, developing, and enhancing the client's desired state of well-being.

Section 5 draws together research in the formerly unrelated disciplines of environmental psychology and psychobiology. As environmental psychologists demonstrate that the natural environment has rapid affect-altering abilities and psychobiologists point out that affect has a contingent relationship with our physical well-being, it is logical to propose that there is a direct nature-mind-body connection. On this basis, an ecopsychobiological model is presented with case illustrations in the areas of cancer, pain, and the process of healing.

I do not suggest that nature-guided approaches are necessarily the sole way of working therapeutically. Both the approaches presented in this book and the underlying paradigm are readily adaptable to other theoretical models or thera-peutic modalities. Designed to expand the therapist's repertoire of clinical skills, they can be employed adjunctively with other treatment strategies or used inde-pendently.

To represent the natural ecology in an overly romanticized manner would be unrealistic. So, while acknowledging the existence of beautiful butterflies, soporific whale songs, and awe-inspiring waterfalls, I also acknowledge that our environment is home to health-threatening viruses, fear-inducing reptiles, and destructive hurricanes. Nature-guided therapy is more about being prag-matic than about being romantic. As such it is a potent and important addition to the therapeutic tool kit.

My invitation to you in reading this volume is that you examine the ideas, the stories, the cases, the research, and the therapeutic interventions in associa-tion with your own personal experience and the experiences of your clients. Experiment with the exercises provided and find the things that you can effec-tively use with your own specific client population. I would enjoy hearing the results of your work.

George W. Burns

Acknowledgments

Writing this book has been a fascinating process of discovery. One of those discoveries is that no book is a solo effort. Although only one name may appear on the dust jacket of a book, the turn of each page reveals contributions of many unnamed people not cited in the references. Without their dedication, commitment, and assistance, this volume would not be in your hands now.

Each word has been keyed in by Julie Nayda and then revised, and revised, and revised. Her patience and active involvement have at times exceeded my own. She has juggled my ever-changing thoughts, along with the demands of a busy practice and the management of the Milton H. Erickson Institute of Western Australia's teaching program. Conscious of the additional workload the book imposed on her, I raised the suggestion of a software program that allowed me to dictate directly onto the computer, bypassing her keyboarding skills. She replied, "What, and miss out on all the things I am learning?" With her cheerful nature and endless supply of cheeky jokes, she has kept me positive. Thanks Jules.

Unseen in the text is the encouragement offered by some very special people to publish my ideas: Professor Brian Dibble of Curtin University, Perth; Michelle Anderson of Hill of Content Publishers, Melbourne; my mates Dr. Peter Moss and Dr. Ken Woo, Perth; and Natalie Gilman, who signed me up with Brunner/ Mazel. I deeply appreciate Stephen and Carol Lankton's introduction to Brunner/ Mazel, their support and answers to my many early inquiries. Suzi Tucker, Senior Editor at Brunner/Mazel, offered valued, valuable and constructive recommendations for shaping ideas into a book. The folk at Taylor & Francis had the final challenges of guiding it in publication: Lansing Hays, Alison Howson, and George Kendall. I thank you all.

Michael Yapko, PhD, has been most generous in sharing his ideas and experiences with a novice writer. He, along with Rob McNeilly, MBBS, and Graham Taylor, MA, has challenged my thinking and expression with honest and useful evaluations of the manuscript. Jeff Zeig, PhD, has given support and encouragement not only in this endeavor but in many ways over the past years. Ian Bytheway, PhD, saw what many had missed. And I am deeply indebted to Professor Emeritus Lin Jensen, who has kindly and selflessly offered his personal writings for inclusion.

In each page, too, is the patience of friends and family who, whenever they have wanted things of me over the last 3 years, have become used to the phrase "When the book is finished." Monika, throughout, has blended those uniquely diverse qualities of a caring pal, sounding board for my ideas, ruthless critic of my grammar, and compatible sailing mate. Leah, I thank for the challenge of getting my book completed before her thesis. She won. Congratulations.

This volume has been contemplated and composed in many beautiful places, from the tranquil bays of Rottnest Island to the rugged red gorges of Kalbarri. I thank Judith Buck for her cottage amid California's snow-decked Ponderosa pines; Dave and Ellen Johnson for a retreat with parrots and possums in temperate rainforest on the Southern coast of Australia; Pam Wooding for the sun-warmed verandas of her Victorian farmhouse—and especially for being my sister. These friends have helped me personally put into practice what this work is about.

There are many, many clients who, over the years, have shared their intimacies, hopes, and successes. They have taught me things that I would never have found in a library of psychological texts and alerted me to the effects of nature as a recuperative resource in their own lives. The major cases presented in this text have the consent of the clients concerned. Most have read their own case account and agreed to its publication. To retain anonymity, I have carefully sought to disguise the person while maintaining the essence of the story and treatment.

From early childhood, my parents introduced me to picnicking in the countryside, camping in the desert, building sandcastles on the beach, and constructing cubbyhouses in the bush. I owe them an indefinable depth of gratitude. In their own special ways, they sowed the seeds for nature-guided therapy.

PART I
NATURE-GUIDED THERAPY

Chapter 1

NATURE HEALS

A way of doctoring
Is more than healing.
It is something to do
With life itself.—Ainslie Meares (1985)

"There is now a mismatch between the human mind and the world people inhabit," claim Ornstein and Ehrlich (1989, p. 9). Arguing that industrialization and technology have outstripped our biological evolution, they consider this mismatch as having a negative effect on our personal relationships and our relationships with our environment. It may also, they claim, be a significant source of emotional discontent and physical disease.

Mismatch is a term picked up by a number of researchers and authors to describe, first, the detachment of humans from their natural and evolutionary history, and, second, the consequences of that dissonance on our physical and psychological well-being. Bateson (1980) lamented that most of us have severed the unifying bond between biosphere and humanity. The loss of what he coined "the pattern which connects" is seen by others (Garrett, 1994; Nesse & Williams, 1996) as one of the major causes of disease. According to Nesse and Williams, we now live in an environment so alien to that from which we evolved that "natural selection has not had time to revise our bodies for coping with fatty diets, automobiles, drugs, artificial lights and central heating. From this mismatch between our design and our environment arises much, perhaps most, preventable disease" (1996, p. 9). What they assert, in regard to our physical functioning, seems equally applicable to a psyche detached from its historic milieu and sources of nurturing.

3

Roszak lays the responsibility for this psyche-environment detachment in psychological theory and practice squarely at the feet of Freud. "As much as any other Positivist philosopher of his day, Freud toiled under the influence of one of the most commonplace images in our language: the spatial metaphor that locates the psyche 'within' and the real world 'outside'" (1992, p. 44). In fact, Freud actively steered therapy away from the outer world of nature. He declared, "Nature is eternally remote. She destroys us—coldly, cruelly and relentlessly" (cited in Roszak, 1996, p. 22). This wedge, so actively driven between psychology and nature, led Roszak to conclude, "The result was a psychotherapy that separated person from planet" (1992, p. 44).

"In clinical psychology and psychiatry . . . a powerful proportion of professionals still strictly adhere to person-centered approaches," assert Demick and Andreoletti. They argue that "the unit of analysis in psychopathology might more aptly be conceptualized as the person-in-environment system" (1995, p. 65). For nature-guided therapy, the person-environment relationship is both the unit of analysis and the basis of treatment.

It is from the natural ecology that our species evolved. We are a part of our environment, and, unless we are living in a state consonant with that environment, we can expect neither health nor happiness. According to Pigram, we have a "genetically coded predisposition to respond positively to natural-environment content" (1993, p. 402). Examining how we function effectively in nature—and how we reap restorative benefits from nature—he concludes, "The implication is that everyday, unthreatening natural environments tend to promote faster more complete recuperation from stress than do urban settings" (1993, p. 402).

To examine the therapeutic benefits of the person-nature connection, this chapter begins with a historic and evolutionary exploration of our relationship with nature. It proceeds to investigate the psychological and physical healing powers of nature as evidenced in traditional models of healing, recent scientific findings, clinical applications, and anecdotal accounts.

ORIGINS OF A NATURAL RELATIONSHIP

In the beginning, according to modern creation theorists, a star exploded. Particles were hurled through space. These heavyweight atoms, remnants of that supernova explosion, formed the origins of our planet at least 5 billion years ago. The atmosphere, made up of gases such as methane, ammonia, nitrogen, and helium, was constantly bombarded by energy sources such as ultraviolet radiation, gamma rays, electrical discharges, and meteoric impacts (Maturana & Varela, 1987). These energies initiated movements in the atmosphere that, in turn, resulted in chemical reactions.

At the birth of the original star, there had been a molecular homogeneity; with the process of chemical transformation in the earth's formative years, however, there developed an ongoing diversification of molecular structures. As a result, the first singular celled life form began to emerge around 4,000 million years ago.

The next major step toward life on earth was the emergence of photosynthesis, by which some living organisms were able to convert the sun's energy into complex organic molecules. Photosynthesis resulted in the release of oxygen into the atmosphere and consequently enabled the development of organisms that not only tolerated but, in fact, used this gas for their growth and survival. Oxygen, converted into ozone, began to filter the sun's ultraviolet radiation so that the planet became a more conducive environment for the evolution of our current life forms.

Reanney, a biochemist and microbiologist, described this history as "more fantastic than the strangest dream of the wisest seer" (1994, p. 35). He claims that there is a direct and unbroken line that binds us physically, as well as in our consciousness, to a universe of which we are an integrated part.

Using the example of an atom of iron that resides in our bloodstream, Reanney states: "It was smelted into being in the fiery furnace that was the brilliant core of a giant star; it was flung across space by the violence of a supernova when that star exploded into an apocalypse that had the brilliance of a million suns; it congealed in the rocks of a just-born planet; it was rubbled into soil by wind and water and the action of microbes; it was taken up and made flesh by a plant; and it now lives in a red cell, circling the rivers of your blood, helping you breathe and keeping your consciousness afire, here, now" (1994, p. 35).

The physical interconnectedness of all elements of our ecology is now recognized by many scholars. Suzuki claims, "Every creature alive today can trace his, her, or its, ancestry back to that first primordial cell. All life on earth is truly related" (1990, p. 224). On the other hand, an eon of molecular change that traces the atoms of our being back to a starry apocalypse leads Reanney to conclude that "the profound insight that 'All is One' is the truth of the universe" (1994, p. 36).

EVOLUTION OF A NATURALLY
HEALTHY RELATIONSHIP

According to Bowden, Dovers, and Shirlow (1990), since our ancestors began to explore the open savanna as an environment in which to live and flourish, there have been four distinct ecological phases that reflect the relationships that existed between the human species and the ecosystems of the biosphere.

The Hunter-Gatherer Phase

This phase, the longest of the ecological phases, was characterized by a process of natural selection. This means that the most adapted and best environment-suited individuals were more likely to survive and reproduce. As a result, advantageous genes and acquired learnings were passed on in a dynamic way from generation to generation. By this process our species developed the best biological fit to its ecosystem. Not only were biological characteristics of skeleton and physiology being selectively screened but also characteristics such as intelligence, behavior, and adaptive skills (Nesse and Williams, 1996). Individuals who understood and related with the closest affinity to nature were most successful in overcoming inherent dangers and using natural resources. Such individuals had the evolutionary advantage of surviving longer and reproducing more successfully.

Early Farming Phase

With the beginnings of agriculture in certain regions of the world some 10,000 to 12,000 years ago, humans still needed a close affinity with their ecosystem. They needed to understand the nature and fertility of the soil, the changing of the seasons, the times of rain, the patterns of growth. With this phase we also see an attitudinal change, particularly in the middle to latter stages. Mason (1993) refers to it as the period of "Agri-Culture," splitting the word to emphasize that with farming came a cultural shift that was to have a significant future impact on both humanity and the biosphere.

Early Urban Phase

Urbanization began in southwestern Asia around 5,000 to 9,000 years ago. People gathered together for convenience, for protection, and for satisfaction of cultural needs. Occupations became more specialized as specific trades developed. Urban dwellings began to put different demands on the ecosystems, as evidenced in the first cities of Mesopotamia where the need for construction as evidenced in the first cities of Mesopotamia where the need for construction timber quickly denuded the region's forests. Humans began to lose direct contact with, and accountability to, nature.

High Energy Phase

Although the shortest of the four phases, spanning only the last 150 to 200 years and confined largely to the Western world, this period has been one of high ecological impact.

The relevance of these ecological phases becomes more apparent when we examine them on a comparative time scale in regard to our physical and emotional adaptation. If we consider a human generation as 25 years (Bowden, Dovers, & Shirlow, 1990), it has been more than 100,000 generations since our ancestors moved from the trees to the plains of East Africa. Just 500 generations have passed since the very beginnings of agriculture, and the high energy phase has spanned just six to eight generations, with much technology (for example, television and home computers) arriving in most of our life spans.

What this means is that our historic and evolutionary adaptation has been in an environment different from that in which most of us now reside. We are not only particles of an exploded star; we have also adaptively developed a biological fit to our natural ecosystems. If we are at our optimal levels of consonance in that environment, then it also follows that we are likely to be at our optimal levels of physical and emotional well-being. It is logical to assume that the environment to which we are most adapted will be our healthiest.

Contrary to the common concept that Neanderthals were unhygienic and unhealthy, Bowden, Dovers, and Shirlow argue that our ancestral hunters and gatherers were "for most of the time in a good state of health" (1990, p. 41), probably healthier than we are today. Primeval people were largely free from the infectious diseases that spread so rapidly in high-density living (Garrett, 1994). Cholera, typhus, influenza, and tuberculosis were relatively unknown prior to urbanization. Tuberculosis is now the major killer disease in developing countries, accounting for 26% of avoidable adult deaths. Expanding urban populations have seen an increase in TB rates, such as the 18% rise in the United States since 1985 (Nesse & Williams, 1996).

Technology, too, has been directly responsible for the spread of some infectious diseases. Human hosts, in a matter of hours, can carry new strains of influenza around the globe aboard international flights. Hotel air-conditioning provided the perfect home and means of dispersal for the organism causing staphylococcal concentrations and the potentially fatal toxic shock syndrome (Nesse & Williams, 1996).

Lifestyle problems, such as cardiovascular disease, cancer, dental caries, duodenal ulcers, and diverticulitis, were rare among our ancestors, as were the nutritional problems of malnutrition and obesity. Admittedly, for several reasons, their life span was not as long, but Bowden, Dovers and Shirlow claim that "hunters and gatherers were less likely to be sick than the modern city dwellers" (1990, p. 41).

TRADITIONAL WISDOM ABOUT NATURE'S HEALING POWERS

Traditional wisdom has long held that nature not only promotes health but also heals. Health, according to traditional healers, is a holistic concept, referring to physical wellness as well as to an emotional and spiritual well-being. A oneness of the person with his or her ecology and cosmology, in itself, means wellness. Disruption of that balanced relationship leads to illness, whether physical, mental, or spiritual. Restoration of the balance, by reestablishing open communication with the forces of the universe, restores health.

There are several important characteristics of the close interactions that traditional healing systems have with nature.

Natural Phenomena: Sources of Health and Well-Being

Specially defined natural sacred sites are seen by many cultures as both powerful and therapeutic. Swan, exploring the relationship between such sacred places in nature and transpersonal experiences, noted that "plants, animals, stones and all forms of nature are seen as being messages for spiritual images and information from a world beyond this one." When people visit these sacred places, they often report entering a special "mind space" (1988, p. 22).

Mazumdar and Mazumdar (1993) describe the processes of attachment to sacred places in natural landscapes, giving examples of how the Himalayas for Indian Hindus and Tibetan Buddhists have been venerated as the abode of deities and ancestors, in the same manner as the Shinto and Buddhists of Japan relate to Mount Fuji or Hindu Balinese sanctify Mount Agung. The affectionate term *Ma Ganga* (Mother Ganges) is a metaphor for subcontinent Hindus of the relationship between river and believer.

Cross-cultural similarities in revering the "cosmic mountain" and "world

Cross-cultural similarities in revering the "cosmic mountain" and "world tree" in the cosmology of shamanism are provided by Eliade (1989), who also describes how natural settings can be sanctified by the occurrence of a miracle, a healing, a vision, or a significant event in the life of a religious leader (Eliade, 1959).

For the Temair people of Malaysia, like most other non-Western cultures, "illness agents come from the mountains, fruits, and river rapids; from the same origins come the spirit guides that can effectively engage them" (Roseman, 1991, p. 130). For these indigenous people health and medicine are intricately interwoven with music, dance, culture, and environment.

Interactions With Nature

Well-being has long been seen as an interactive process between the person and the environment. A shaman may direct his patients to engage in interactive rituals such as journeying to a particular natural site, be it a revered tree, cave, or thermal pool, and communicating with that place through offering sacrifices, meditation, or prayers. Hammond-Tooke, referring to such processes in South African traditional medical practices, comments that "because the sickness they are suffering is sent from the ancestors, its curing depends not on medicines but on rituals" (1989, p. 107).

"One bargains with nature, apologizes for intruding upon it, begs pardon of the animals one hunts and kills, tries to make good the losses one has brought about, offers sacrifices and compensation. Sanity is just such a matter of balance and reciprocity between the human and not-human. The very idea that the two can be segregated, that the human world should or even *can* be treated as autonomously self-contained, would be the very height of madness for a traditional psychiatry. The connection between the two is not simply a matter of survival but of moral and spiritual well-being" (Roszak, 1992, pp. 79–80).

The shaman seeks, through rituals and prescribed assignments, to establish and maintain the vital connectedness between human and nature so that the two are interacting in an ongoing, healthy dialogue.

Natural Medicines

Nature may offer what humans need for healing, and humans, through their healer, must acknowledge and reciprocate the environment's generosity in much the same way as one would a gift from a friend. For nature has been a most generous friend. Bolivian healers have access to some 600 different medicinal herbs. In northwestern Amazonia the Indians make use of at least 1,300 plant species for a variety of medicinal purposes, while Southeast Asian forest dwellers access around 6,500 different plants for treating diseases that include malaria, syphilis, and stomach ulcers. Of the 18,000 flowering plants in India, 2,500 provide medicines (Peterson, 1989).

Apart from indicating how traditional people have relied on nature's therapeutic agents, these figures also have a poignant message for Western medicine. The majority of these traditional medicines from tropical rainforests have not yet been investigated by Western medical science, even though some 75% of prescription drugs are already said to have their origins in traditional ethnomedical systems (Knudtson & Suzuki, 1992).

Peterson (1989, pp. 160–166) gives a comprehensive account of the history of the discovery of certain major pharmaceuticals from rainforests. He asks, "How many other powerful anti-cancer drugs are yet to be discovered in the tropical rainforests? Latin American rainforests alone contain roughly 90,000 different plants, of which only 10,000 have been examined for possible use as anti-cancer compounds. The world should have the opportunity to consider the remaining 80,000" (p. 165). He argues, "In a larger sense the health of the world's tropical forests could sustain the health of humankind, since the tropical forests' genetic reservoirs contain a great many natural occurring pharmaceuticals" (p. 160).

Traditional healing systems, however, are not limited to the pharmaceutical properties of a plant. Such properties are but a part of the ritual interaction with nature. Tibetan doctors, for example, still trek into the mountains to find, identify, and gather fruits and plants, herbs and minerals (Donden, 1986; Khangkar, 1991). In fact, in Tibetan medicine there is no differentiation between physician and pharmacologist. This system is not alone in its close involvement with nature and use of natural products from the local ecology for the prevention and curing of disease. It is used as an example to illustrate the way in which interactions with nature are perhaps an even more important element of traditional healing disciplines than the pharmacological substances.

Interconnectedness of Person, Spirit, and Universe

The integrative nature of traditional medical systems has been well summated by Dr. Tenzin Choedhak, the chief medical officer at the Tibetan Medical Institute and personal physician to the 14th Dalai Lama: "Based on the holistic Buddhist concept of mind-body, Tibetan medicine is a system of psycho-cosmo-physical healing" (Clifford, 1984). The holistic philosophy he describes, while not limited to Tibetan medicine, illustrates how traditional healing methods see well-being as a balance among the mind, the body, and the universe.

In traditional shamanic practice, medicine is not used for the purpose of avoiding death, as tends to be the concept in Western traditions. To lose one's soul is of far greater consequence than to lose one's body, since without a soul life itself is meaningless. Traditional ethnomedicine is more about empowerment, for the loss of personal power means that one is more susceptible to being struck by an arrow, an evil spirit, or an illness. Consequently the first task of the healer is to restore the ailing person's sense of empowerment. Counter-acting the power of the illness-producing agent is a secondary factor (Achterberg, 1985).

In Taoism, for example, "Human beings are just one very delicate part of the whole picture. Humanity is considered to be a minuscule part of nature, and the key to understanding ourselves and the world we live in is through the understanding of nature" (Tsui-Po, 1994, p. 54). Contravening nature leads to individual suffering through physical or emotional illness.

Because Taoism accepts the principle that humans affect the cosmos and are in turn affected by it, the universe is seen as a holistic unit. The conversion of these beliefs into day-to-day practice is aimed at developing actions and interactions basically designed to maintain harmony with fellow beings, the world of nature, and the universe as a whole. Wellness is a state of balance between the individual and all elements of his or her ecology.

The Koyukon Indians of subarctic Alaska interpret this relationship as a spiritual kinship in which every part of the universe—a raindrop, a plant, a rock, an insect, or a human being—has shared origins. The natural world that they cohabit with the rest of creation is as alive and vital as themselves, no more or no less. Their world is aware, is feeling, and is personified. Every element of nature must be treated with proper respect and care because everything is alive and vital. Everything is powerful in its sense of oneness (Nelson, 1983).

CURRENT RESEARCH INTO NATURE'S HEALING POWERS

There is an increasing body of research, especially in the area of environmental psychology, that demonstrates how contact with natural environments can enhance positive affect (Russell & Mehrabian, 1976); reduce levels of stress (Baum, Singer, & Baum, 1982; Ulrich & Simons, 1986); improve parasympathetic nervous system functioning (Ulrich, Dimberg, & Driver, 1991); increase physical health (Reitman & Pokorny, 1974; Wright, 1983); promote more health-oriented behaviors (Russell & Mehrabian, 1976); reduce the length of hospital stays (Jerstad & Stelzer, 1973; Lowry, 1974; Ulrich, 1984); enhance self-concept, self-esteem, and self-confidence (Wright, 1983); improve staff-patient relationships (Reitman & Pokorny, 1974; Ulrich, 1984); and benefit the treatment of the mentally ill (Levitt, 1991).

Simply looking through a window upon a natural scene has beneficial effects. A number of studies, such as Stone and Irvine's (1994), have demonstrated how access to a window view can reduce boredom and enhance perceptions of creative tasks. Ulrich (1984) has gone a step further to investigate the effects of natural views on hospital patients recovering from surgery. Comparing patients whose windows overlooked trees from their hospital beds with those who looked out onto brick walls, he found that the former occupied hospital beds for fewer postoperative days, required less pain medication, and were more favorably rated by the nursing staff. Similar examples of the importance of simple visual contact with nature in the preventative and healing processes come from prison populations. When inmates have cell windows with views of nature, they suffer fewer stress symptoms, digestive illnesses, and headaches. The prisoners in such cells also make fewer calls on medical services (Moore, 1982; West, 1986).

Other tests on postexamination students have shown that stress factors such as muscle tension, blood pressures, headaches, and pulse rates are markedly reduced in students shown videos of landscapes in comparison with those shown videos of traffic scenes. Not only are the symptoms diminished in a much briefer period, but the benefits seem to last longer.

Stokols (1992) discusses the benefits of the transactions that take place between people and the health resources in their environment. While he takes a broad definition of the term *environment*, including mental, emotional, social, organizational, and community dimensions, he also covers the physical environment, which includes the natural ecosystem. In these contexts he emphasizes the necessity of examining what he calls "health promotive environment."

Environments that may promote and facilitate healthy recovery from serious injury have been studied in terms of their impact on prognosis after serious illness or injury. Borkan and Quirk (1992), and also Borkan, Quirk, and Sullivan (1991), studied the ambulatory status of 80 hip fracture patients from prefracture to 3 and 6 months after the injury. Among several factors, they found that patients who perceived their problem as related to the external environment, rather than related to an inner self-focus, showed greater improvement in their ambulation at the 3- and 6-month intervals. Those elderly patients in this sample who were walking better at the observed intervals were also noted to have a greater sense of autonomy, independence, and connectedness with the world around them. Quirk and Wapner (1995) conclude that interventions designed to improve outcome after hip fracture should focus on a number of factors, including the patients' past and present experiences in the environment as well as their "world view."

As shown in subsequent chapters, contact with nature provides very real benefits in the recuperative process. Such benefits can be gained simply by looking out the window onto greenery, watching a slide or video of natural landscapes, or participating in outdoor recreational activities. These positive outcomes are not limited to the psychological level but may involve the central nervous system and the psychophysiological concomitants of anxiety.

Benefits of nature contact are found in the treatment of mental illness symptoms, the enhancement of self-esteem, and the promotion of healthier behaviors such as reduced smoking and alcohol consumption. Curiously, these therapeutic gains can be obtained even through a passive view of nature, such as a still photographic representation of a natural scene. There is the suggestion that posters or murals of forest scenes on home and workplace walls can aid in stress reduction, help motivation, and enhance performance. Given this, one may wonder how much more potential gain there may be in multimodal sensory interactions with nature in vivo.

Levitt, in discussing the benefits of therapeutic camping programs for the mentally ill, cautions that "we still do not understand what is therapeutic about camping in a wilderness or wilderness-like setting. The flora and fauna of wilderness, the uniqueness of wilderness, the low level of stimulation of wilderness, the aesthetic or spiritual value of wilderness, the isolation of wilderness from the city, or the ability of wilderness to evoke coping behaviors have been cited as the possible factors that produce therapeutic gains" (1991, p. 167).

Therapeutic gains were further acknowledged in a report on the outdoors commissioned by President Reagan (President's Commission on America's Outdoors, 1986). "The total value of the outdoors for recreation is difficult to describe, let alone price. . . . Price denotes short-term value. . . . A sunset, a rainbow, an ocean wave, a 500-year-old tree are priceless commodities. . . . The real value of the outdoors lies in its vitality . . . the way it enhances our lives. When a sport program keeps a teenager away from drugs, when a neighborhood park offers a friendly gathering place for older people, when families learn to appreciate each other on a camping trip, when a jogger adds years to her or his life, how do we place a price on it? The value is life itself."

CLINICAL RECOGNITION OF NATURE'S HEALING POWERS

Recognition of the healing benefits of nature is a concept that has come slowly to the practice of clinical psychology and is only gradually being incorporated into psychotherapeutic strategies. Freud's intrapsychic journeying reversed the orientation of therapy from the outward focus of traditional healers to one of inner analysis. The path that led us into the deep recesses of the unconscious became a highway followed by generations of therapists, with some exceptions.

Pavlov, Skinner, and other behaviorists explored immediate external stimuli and the behavioral responses they elicited. Unfortunately, with behavior being the only aspect of human personality to fit comfortably into the required measurability of scientific methodology, we were led into overlooking the mental, emotional, and spiritual elements of our being.

With the emergence of family therapy came a move away from the more introspective forms of analysis. Clients were treated in terms of their interpersonal systems. These approaches largely developed out of the work of Milton Erickson, but, in focusing on just one system of influence on the client, they failed to use the broader perspectives that Erickson himself incorporated into therapy. In Erickson's work can be seen the beginnings of many innovations in the psychotherapeutic field. Brief therapies, solution-oriented approaches, family therapy, strategic therapy, Ericksonian psychotherapy and hypnotherapy, psychobiology, and psychoneuroimmunology all find their origins in his uncommon therapeutic practices. It is in Erickson's work that we also discover the embryo of nature-guided therapy.

Erickson often assigned his clients tasks involving an interaction with nature, replicating the model observed in traditional healing practices. He assigned tasks to facilitate clients' contact with their own sensual awareness. An example is the story he told of a woman who hated to leave Phoenix and was reluctant to holiday in Flagstaff. He offered a suggestion to focus her attention on an unexpected "flash of color." She extended her vacation from 1 week to a month after seeing a redheaded woodpecker fly past an evergreen tree. Soon she was traveling throughout the United States and even Europe, looking for further "flashes of color" (Rosen, 1982, pp. 108–109).

Erickson used interventions individualized to each client. At times he reminded his students that to adapt such strategies one had to put aside the learning of textbooks and look at the patient, dealing with the patient in a manner that most befits his or her own unique problem. He did just this in a case of an alcoholic man whose family, on both sides, had a long history of alcohol abuse. Erickson said, "Now, the thing I am going to suggest to you won't seem the right thing. You go out to the Botanical Gardens. You look at all the cacti there and marvel at cacti that can survive three years later without water, without rain, and do a lot of thinking." Many years later he reported that a young woman came to his office to express her thanks. She was the daughter of that alcoholic and said that her parents had both abstained from alcohol after her father had taken his journey to the botanical gardens, observed the cacti, and done a lot of thinking. He changed his job to one involving less alcohol risk and apparently, from the young woman's report, changed the structure of the family into one far more conducive to a healthy upbringing (Rosen, 1982, pp. 80–81).

Another regular interactive exercise that Erickson prescribed for both his students and patients was to climb the highest mountain in the Phoenix area where he lived and worked. At 1,100 feet (335 meters), the strenuous climb of about 1.5 miles (2.4 kilometers) usually takes between 45 and 60 minutes. The path, in the manner of a true Ericksonian metaphor, is not straight but winds up the mountainside, taking many undulations in its way and reflecting the ups and downs that one's journey through life might take. One tends to arrive at the summit with a sense of accomplishment and a new perspective of the world below.

Exercises such as these invite people not only to interact with nature but also to actually adapt to it, to discover how they need to adjust their own pace to their environment, to experience the differences of ascending and descending, to sense the terrain under their feet, to sit on the summit of a mountain, or to look forward to the opportunity to adjust their own time frame of reference into that of the time of nature. In the process they are both contributing to and receiving from the experience. Such nature-based assignments create an interaction likely to enhance a sense of responsibility with the environment and, thus, bear some similarities to the nature-based interactive rituals prescribed by traditional healers.

A number of clinicians have used wilderness and nature experiences in the processes of restoration (Hartig, Mang, & Evans, 1990), in the treatment of mental patients (Jerstad & Stelzer, 1973), and for the improvement of psychological well-being (Kaplan & Talbot, 1983; Scherl, 1989). Haley (1984) devoted a chapter of his book, *Ordeal Therapy*, to using the great outdoors. I (Burns, 1995) have outlined ways of using natural stimuli in the hypnotic treatment of anxiety and depressive conditions as well as in the enhancement of relationships. Forthcoming chapters provide more detail on how the clinician can use nature's healing powers for therapeutic benefits.

ANECDOTAL ACCOUNTS OF NATURE'S HEALING POWERS

Frequently, across a range of literature and in personal accounts, one comes upon individual testimonies to the benefits of nature. The enhancement of psychological well-being is reflected in the words of Yohinobu Shimbo, a 38-year-old man residing on Japan's west coast. After a time of managing a coffeehouse in the big, busy city of Niigata, he decided to retreat to a small village with his wife and daughter to take up onion farming. "I had a steady income, not too many financial worries. My life now is tiring, but psychologically it does me good. The pace is very slow. I see things more clearly. I ride my bike an hour and a half to work in the morning, and I can pay attention to the value of nature" (Smith, 1994, p. 89).

For Bill Miller, a retired California school principal, interacting with nature had, and maintains, direct physical healing. For almost 30 years, he has been a part-time seasonal ranger in America's Grand Teton National Park. Speaking about this mountainous reserve, he said, "It changed my life. I used to have chronic ulcers. They went away my first season here and never came back" (Hodgson, 1995, p. 137).

Many of the world's leading psychotherapists, therapist trainers, and writers on therapy who are known to the author seek their own relaxation and recreation in nature. They enjoy bushwalking, scuba diving, sailing, and cross-country skiing or are seen searching for a park to stroll through during a break in their training workshops. Yet it seems only occasionally that these personally valued recuperative activities are used in their therapeutic strategies.

We have seen how Milton Erickson, in contrast, systematically directed clients into interactive exercises with nature. That nature heals is more than simply implied in his work. It was an integral element in his own recovery from poliomyelitis. He drew upon these personal experiences, recounted them in stories, and translated them into therapeutic strategies for his clients. Perhaps more than any other clinician he has left us with a personal account of the role of nature in his upbringing as a child, his self-initiated treatment for polio, and his interventions in clinical practice.

Erickson, who lived from 1901 to 1980, has been hailed for his perceptive and creative genius in changing the direction of psychotherapy. It has been said that what Freud did for the theory of psychotherapy, Erickson has done for the practice of psychotherapy. Perhaps it was the experience of his own childhood background and the process of his recovery that led him to adopt ecotherapeutic strategies for his patients.

Erickson's life was grounded in nature, even from his early childhood. He grew up in rural environments in Nevada and Wisconsin. The rural lifestyle allowed him direct contact with nature and the opportunity to discover the need for a person's synchronicity and symbiotic involvement with the environment. In turn, he developed an acceptance of what nature brought his way.

Indeed, it was a personal tragedy that at the age of 17 Erickson had his first poliomyelitis infection. However, there seems to have been an acceptance of what had happened, as well as an optimistic attitude of looking to the future, of exploring how the situation could improve. In terms of this orientation and the strategies he determinedly employed for his own therapy, he discovered the value of contact with nature. He said, "I graduated from high school in June 1919. In August, I heard three doctors, in the other room, tell my mother, 'The boy will be dead by the morning.'" Erickson reported how indignant he was that his own country doctor and two specialists from Chicago had the audacity to make such a statement to his mother.

"Afterwards my mother came to the room, bland of face. She thought I was delirious because I insisted that she move the large chest in my room in order for it to be at a different angle beside the bed. She put it beside the bed one way and I kept telling her to move it back and forth until I was satisfied. That chest was blocking my view through the window—I was damned if I would die without seeing the sunset!" (Rosen, 1982, p. 52).

He saw only half of the sunset as he lapsed into unconsciousness and stayed that way for the following 3 days. He continued to use interactive encounters with nature in his own recovery. Haley and Richeport, in their 1993 documentary video on Erickson's life and work, recorded that within 12 months of his diagnosis he could move his upper body and his legs, albeit with great difficulty. In the fall, using what strength he had in his arms, he dragged his legs over the hardened furrows of a fallow field, making contact with the earth and stimulating his legs as much as possible. Advised to exercise his upper body, he again put himself in contact with the natural environment by undertaking a 1,000-mile solo canoe trip. When he started he could neither walk nor portage his canoe across a dam. At the end of the trip, he could swim a mile and walk once more.

Such changes would not surprise Professor Emeritus Lin Jensen, whose own account of nature's therapeutic abilities is presented in Chapter 16. In personal correspondence he wrote, "Unless we humans recognize that our health depends on harmony with the natural world, we shall never be truly well" (Jensen, 1965).

Chapter 2

ECOPSYCHOTHERAPY

I've sent more than one depressed man to go and dig and plant a
flower garden for someone.—Milton H. Erickson (cited in Zeig, 1980)

Traditional wisdom, clinical practice, personal experiences, and a growing
body of research indicate that nature per se is healing. Nature has been used by
therapists such as Milton Erickson and an increasing number of Western health
practitioners who recognize the power and potency of natural stimuli for quick
and effective changes at both psychological and physiological levels of our
being. I refer to this nature-guided approach to therapy as ecotherapy or ecopsychotherapy.

As a term, *ecotherapy* does not fully do justice to the concept that it
seeks to communicate. Therapy in the past has been linked to other words in
basically two different styles. When we speak of psychotherapy or physiotherapy, for example, the "therapy" is linked to "psycho" (mind/soul) or "physio"
(body) to indicate that it is treatment for the mind or treatment for the body.
In this sense the term ecotherapy is misleading, because it is not the ecology that
is the subject of treatment. Indeed, the ecological balance of our world has maintained a dynamic, cohesive, and functional evolution for millennia.

Many conservationists claim that the major threat to nature's well-being is
the human species. According to Aldo Leopold, a pioneer among ecologists,
"The most important characteristic of an organism is that capacity for internal
self-renewal, known as health. There are two organisms whose processes of
self-renewal have been subjected to human interference and control. One of
these is man himself. The other is land. The effort to control the health of the

land has not been very successful" (1949, p. 194). What Leopold does not elaborate in this particular quote is that the health of humanity is directly related to the health of the land.

The other style in which the word *therapy* has been used is not in conjunction with the *object* of treatment but with the *method* of treatment. Here we may use terms such as *art therapy* and *music therapy*. Conceiving ecotherapy in this style again fails to do justice to the concept. Art and music are, at the one time, both specific and static; they are, in themselves, inanimate. They do not have life. They are a creation of humans, offering a limited range of stimuli, and are not interactive.

In some ways the term *nature-guided therapy* expresses well what this approach is about. It defines nature as an initiator of health, healing, and well-being. By health I mean a state of physical wellness. As with all life forms on this planet, health is what ensures our ability to survive and reproduce our species. Healing is the process of rectifying an imbalance of the state of health. It is about fixing a problem or resolving a disturbance to our normal state of equilibrium. Well-being I define as a broader concept than either health or healing. It takes into account the emotional, relationship, and spiritual needs of the human species. Well-being thus includes a state of physical health as well as a mental and emotional state of consonance. Well-being is attained when a person is experiencing an inner state of wellness, exists in a healthy environment, and experiences a harmonious connection with that ecology.

The term *nature guided* also includes a sense of gentleness. It is not authoritative. Just as a guide may know the path and may show the way, the guided has a choice as to whether to follow that path or not. What the nature-guided term does not express is the interactional and integrated elements of the nature-human relationship.

For these reasons I therefore prefer to use the term *ecopsychotherapy*. Ecopsychotherapy includes the concepts of both the human mind and the environment. It assumes that there is a dynamic process taking place between the two, not only for healing but also for an ongoing state of well-being. This process is more along the lines of a conversation: that of a person communicating with nature and responding to the communications of the earth. As with all meaningful communication, it is a process of sharing.

Effective communication does not exist when two entities are in conflict. When a country wages war with another country, they are not sharing in a mutually satisfying and rewarding conversation. Similarly, if we approach nature with a desire for conquest, an attitude of belligerence, or a need to control, we are not communicating in a way that is going to allow mutual benefit. Most of the research shows that the healing to be gained from nature is attained either through passive participation in natural settings or through positive attitudinal interaction. When humans are involved in this ecological conversation, reciprocal benefits flow. Using these benefits for potential mind-body well-being is the core goal of ecopsychotherapy.

Despite my preference for referring to nature-guided therapy as ecopsychotherapy, I shall, throughout the rest of this text, mainly use the term *ecotherapy*, first, because that nomenclature is less cumbersome, and, second, because it is more akin to the terminology of other writers and workers in this field. In general, the words nature-guided therapy, ecopsychotherapy, and ecotherapy will be seen as synonymous. When I use the term *ecopsychotherapy*, it is to emphasize to the reader the importance placed on the nature-mind connectedness of this approach.

Roszak, a historian who has examined the historical, philosophical, and cosmological relationship between people and nature, defines the therapeutic basis of what he calls ecopsychology in the following terms. "Just as it had been the goal of previous therapies to recover the repressed contents of the unconscious, so the goal of ecopsychology is to awaken the inherent sense of environmental reciprocity that lies within the ecological unconscious. Other therapies seek to heal the alienation between person and person, person and family, person and society. Ecopsychology seeks to heal the more fundamental alienation between the person and the natural environment" (1992, p. 320).

Indeed, the restoration of the person-environment relationship and the development of effective communication are essential to the benefit of both person and planet. It is not in the context of this work to examine the environmental issues or to take a stand for conservation, although this is indeed implicit in the issues being discussed. Without readily available access to the stimulation of nature, we would be robbed of a rich resource for health and well-being. As shown in subsequent chapters, human-made milieus can be more stressful, less pleasurable, and more likely to elicit unhealthy behaviors. Thus, people and their natural environment have very mutual goals. Our survival certainly depends on the survival of our ecology and the totality of its biodiversity. This has already been well argued by the environmental movement (Leopold, 1949; Ornstein & Ehrlich, 1989; Roszak, 1992).

One aim of this book, while maintaining a focus on the dynamic person-nature relationship, is to examine what nature can contribute to our well-being.

Implicit, however, is the need to maintain the context so as to be able to achieve what has been described as the "wilderness experience." This need goes beyond the conservation of the environment for our survival. Indeed, it is much more subtle. Health, happiness, and well-being can be the products of the pleasurable sensory stimulation that we derive from nature. In this way we are very directly dependent upon nature for the maintenance of our psychological and physical equilibrium.

While it may be possible for the human species to survive on a planet of depleted resources, by that stage we may have lost the diversity, the quality, and the extent of natural stimulation necessary for pleasure and contentment in life. Then it is not just our individual health, but the health of our society as a whole, that is likely to suffer. Therefore, to discuss the benefits and principles of ecotherapy we must assume the maintenance of rich resources in natural contexts with which we can communicate. This assumption implicitly argues for the preservation of these resources long before it even becomes a question of the survival of our species.

THE CHARACTERISTICS OF ECOPSYCHOTHERAPY

The characteristics of ecopsychotherapy are as follows:

1. Effective
2. Brief
3. Solution oriented
4. Client focused
5. Pragmatic
6. Wellness based
7. Motivation enhancing
8. Encouraging of choice
9. Empowering
10. Enjoyable

Ecopsychotherapy Is Effective

Contact with pleasant natural environments can reduce stress (Baum, Singer, & Baum, 1982; Heywood, 1978; Ulrich & Simons, 1986). Such contact has been demonstrated to increase pleasurable emotional states and reduce the desire to engage in unhealthy behaviors such as smoking and drinking (Russell & Mehrabian, 1976). It has also been shown to bring about positive physiological alterations in indices such as heart rate, skin conductance, blood pressure, and muscle tension as well as being hypothesized to have a direct beneficial parasympathetic system effect (Ulrich, Dimberg, & Driver, 1991).

Wilderness experiences have positive psychological benefits (Kaplan & Talbot, 1983; Ulrich, 1981). West (1986) found that prisoners in cells taking in natural views had fewer stress symptoms and experienced better health than other prisoners. Similarly, in hospital settings postoperative patients healed more quickly (Ulrich, 1984). McDonald (1991) describes what she calls the "wilderness spiritual experience" as a resource for enhancing peak and religious experiences. In the mental health area, Levitt (1991) lists recreational programs that include mixed activities such as arts and crafts, physical exercise, and camping in wilderness areas as effective therapeutic interventions across a number of health-related variables.

With the caution that some studies have shown negative effects of nature-based recreational programs, a well-documented list of effective outcomes is provided by Levitt. This includes improved physical health and fitness along with enhanced self-esteem and self-confidence. Participants in nature contact programs show increased initiative, enthusiasm, and sense of fun. There is usually improvement in their educational attitudes and behavior, as well as a reduction of emotional problems and pathological symptoms. Social interactions improve in terms of their quantity and quality, with the establishment of new friendships and enhancement of patient-staff relationships. New interests and skills are developed. Psychiatric patients participating in these programs of environmental contact are discharged from the hospital sooner and have a lower rate of readmission (Levitt, 1991).

Ecopsychotherapy Is Brief

When one looks at the research, *rapid*, rather than *brief*, is probably a more appropriate term. Russell and Mehrabian (1976) demonstrated effective and positive changes in subjects' emotional states and health-related behaviors after just two sessions of 10-second exposure to slides of pleasant environments. Ulrich et al. (1991) have shown that a range of psychophysiological indicators of stress can be brought back to baseline levels within 4 to 6 minutes of exposure to videotapes of wilderness environments. These rapid modifications of affect, cognition, and behavior can be achieved by clients in either therapist-directed or self-administered strategies.

This is not to claim that ecotherapy necessarily provides a total and immediate modification of a lifetime of personal problems. Rather it is part of the therapeutic tool kit that can be used independently or in conjunction with other therapeutic processes. It should be seen as a part of the overall design of interventions designed to achieve the client's specific therapeutic goal.

Erickson reported single-session case successes using elements of nature, such as the case of the African Violet Queen of Milwaukee (Zeig, 1980, p. 828). Haley, in discussing the rapid change achieved by Erickson, said, "It seems to be based upon the interpersonal impact of the therapist outside of the patient's awareness, it includes providing directives that cause changes of behavior, and it emphasizes communicating in metaphor" (1973, p. 39). Erickson frequently directed clients to interact with nature and used these interactions as metaphors for learning, change, growth, and enjoyment.

Because of the rapid relief from unwanted feelings and the ready acquisition of more desirable states of affect, clients can quickly learn means for achieving their own therapeutic goals. Therapist intervention is thus diminished as the client takes over administration of her or his therapy.

The aim of ecotherapy is to be effective rather than to be brief. As such, it is based on solution and therapeutic outcome rather than on time. While effectiveness, in itself, may mean brevity, the two are not necessarily synonymous, and therapeutic interventions, along with the time required to achieve a goal, will be as individual as the presenting client.

Ecopsychotherapy Is Solution Oriented

As ecopsychotherapy asserts that therapeutic success is concerned more with outcome than origin, it is directed toward the enhancement of problem-solving skills. While respectful of the past, its sights are more on what the client can do to achieve current and future happiness.

The client's goal is usually clear: to change from one undesirable set of experiences to a more desirable set via the quickest and most effective means. In evolutionary terms, our species has survived by this ability to quickly shift from threatening, anxiety-arousing situations to situations of security and calm. Hartig and Evans claim that our ancestral survivors were those individuals who found solutions: "For continued survival . . . selection would have favored protohuman abilities to comprehend extended spatial areas and to plan" (1993, p. 444). Planning involves the ability to look forward and to find solutions.

Historically, such problem resolution was in the context of the natural ecology. A number of studies have looked at the effects of natural settings on problem-solving attitudes and abilities (Hartig, Mang, & Evans, 1990; Rickard, Serum, & Forehand, 1975; Rickard, Serum, & Wilson, 1971). Data analyses of motivation for people engaging in nature-based adventure activities (McIntyre, 1990) have defined six factors, the second of which is problem solving. According to Amedeo, any person-environment interaction requires that individuals "acquire, synthesize and integrate environmental information with internal sources of knowledge" as a basis for experience and behavior (1993, p. 98).

Thus, both the motivation for and the process of relating with the natural environment involve skills essential to problem resolution. The more variety and challenge provided by the natural environment, the greater the need for a solution-based orientation. Knopf, in a literature review, found that a primary factor differentiating natural from urban environments as contexts for behavior was the challenge natural settings, particularly wilderness areas, posed to our "accustomed behavior patterns, resources, and problem-solving styles" (1987, p. 787).

Such challenges can bolster confidence in problem-solving skills, facilitate a solution-focused orientation, and enhance expectations about managing the future. The therapist's expectations may also provide the model for the client's expectations. If the therapist assumes that a solution is possible, that change can and is likely to take place, and that such change can occur rapidly, then those assumptions will almost certainly be communicated to the client and even adopted in a manner that will determine a successful and rapid outcome. Ecotherapy, based on research findings and case examples such as those described earlier and in Chapter 1, can provide the therapist—and, consequently, the client—with appropriate solution-oriented expectations.

Ecopsychotherapy Is Client Focused

Ecotherapy is focused more on the person and the person's relationship with his or her environment than on the problem. It very actively joins people in their language, in their experiences, and in the intimacies of their sensual awareness. The Sensual Awareness Inventory (see Chapter 4) provides a useful vehicle for relating with clients in their world of resources and enjoyment.

As such, ecotherapy is a warm and interactive process. It incorporates a deeply human quality of sharing the things that are meaningful, pleasurable, and important in one's life. In being client focused, it assumes and uses the resources already available within the client to experience feelings of happiness and to achieve a state of wellness.

Feelings of joy and excitement are experienced from an early age and can be rediscovered in our present. In instances in which conditioned patterns of anxiety or depression block the potential within, ecotherapy may help to re-establish these inherent resourceful capabilities in the client.

The focus of ecotherapy on a person's sensory-perceptual experiences (see Chapter 3) allows the therapist to quickly tune in to the client's individually preferred modality. This aids the establishment of rapport and the shaping of therapeutic change. In addition, the ecotherapy model allows the therapist access to the resources a client has in each sensory area, with the aim of using these resources in the direction of change.

Ecopsychotherapy Is Pragmatic

Ecotherapy is a pragmatic intervention because it provides, first, simple, defined steps that are practical to apply for immediate therapeutic gain.

Second, it offers a direct route to the therapeutic goal of enhanced feelings, cognitions, and behaviors. As when driving a car, if you are looking in the direction you want to go, then that is the line you will most likely follow. If you start to look back, shifting your attention away from the goal, then it is easy to veer off course. Ecotherapy does not require this retrogressive shift of attention. It also differs from many other therapeutic models in that it does not require training the client in the therapist's conceptual frame before therapy can really begin.

Third, it is ecotherapy's aim to create a conducive environment for achieving the desired goal-oriented changes. Once a change has occurred, no matter how small, it validates that change is possible. This tends to break the traps that keep people bound in their pathology or illness behavior and reinforces the fact that further positive changes are possible.

Finally, ecotherapy is not as interested in why a problem has occurred as in how it might be rectified. It may be difficult to pinpoint why an individual experiences anxiety symptoms at a particular point in time if genetic defenses are developed over a millennium of generations (Nesse & Williams, 1996). But we do know that nature can be used pragmatically to facilitate problem solving, enhance confidence, modify affect, and facilitate healing (Chapter 1).

Ecopsychotherapy Is Wellness Based

The concept of wellness goes beyond concepts of conflict resolution, problem solving, and illness cure. Much psychotherapy, like surgery, is directed toward cutting out the persistently unpleasant mood, or difficulty in a relationship, as though it were a tumor. Its goal is to return to neutrality: to be devoid of the cancer, to be not depressed, or to have an aconflictual relationship. Given this objective, it is surprising that psychotherapy has ever been effective. First, neutrality is impossible to attain. It is not consistent with human nature. We are continually fluctuating, altering, and changing beings. Second, even if it were possible to achieve, neutrality is not necessarily a desirable target. Who wants to live an existence barren of the full range of human emotions and experiences?

The concept of wellness, through the history of healing disciplines, has been both positive and global. It is positive in that it accepts optimism, self-efficacy, and pleasure as legitimate therapeutic goals. Walters and Havens claim, "As increased optimism and contentment become the focus of therapeutic intervention, not only do we induce healing, but we also feel a sense of self-esteem and purpose" (1993, p. 4). According to Achterberg (1985), this knowledge is nothing new to the discipline of healing. For traditional healers, the intention is not to cure the disease or symptomatically take away the patient's presenting problem. Such issues are secondary to the more positive concept of creating and maintaining well-being.

The wellness approach is also more global than one that simply tackles the presenting problem. In ecotherapy a person is not viewed as a broken leg or an obsessive-compulsive disorder, in the style of reductionistic models. In fact, the wellness model extends the Hippocratic concept that the doctor should look at the person rather than the symptom. It perceives people in terms of a oneness with their environment, a oneness with themselves, a oneness with the other people with whom they interact, a oneness with their senses, a oneness with their surrounding flora and fauna, a oneness with their sense of spirituality. The cornerstone of this approach is the totality of a being's relationship with the universe.

Wellness might thus be seen as synonymous with the concept of happiness. We are beings with an in-built ability to experience happiness. Our senses have evolved not only to alert and protect us but to provide us with pleasure. When we are functioning in a state of wellness we are, most likely, also in a state of happiness, and vice versa. It is hard to imagine a condition in which our bodies are feeling healthy, our minds are being stimulated, our senses are comfortably aroused, and we are in a consonant relationship with our environment while at the same time we are experiencing an emotional disturbance or physical illness. The two seem mutually exclusive.

Ecopsychotherapy Is Motivation Enhancing and Change Oriented

Because ecotherapy joins a client in his or her positive experiences of nature and is focused toward the achievement of desirable objectives, it depotentiates resistance in the therapeutic process. Strangely, we tend to hang onto things that are familiar to us, no matter how nonfunctional or even unpleasant they may be. Symptoms that have become a part of our life may be something we feel reluctant to part with. Clients often say things like "I know my smoking is no good for me, but it has sort of become a friend."

We have this reluctance to surrender that with which we have become familiar. Whether it is a no-longer-desired habit or an unwanted symptom, the emphasis on removing a problem can meet with resistance. In ecotherapy the emphasis is not on giving up the old but, rather, on creating the pleasant, restoring the enjoyable, and gaining new sensations of delight.

Such pleasurable experiences enhance the motivation to seek further natural stimuli for well-being. Schreyer, Williams, and Haggard (1990) described wilderness users as self-motivated to seek out nature-based pleasures. McIntyre (1990) found participants in nature-based adventure activities such as rock climbing to be motivated by a variety of factors, but the physical setting, with its opportunity to experience the wilderness and a proximity to nature, was the most highly valued. A number of studies have suggested that when an individual enters and participates in activities within the natural environment, meaningful changes are likely to occur within the individual's self-perception and self-concept (Newman, 1980; Scherl, 1989; Pigram, 1993).

The positive emphasis on achieving a desirable goal diminishes the focus on what is being relinquished. By joining the client in pleasurable nature-based experiences, lowering resistance, and enhancing motivation, the foundation is laid for a person to bring about changes toward his or her therapeutic goal.

Ecopsychotherapy Encourages Choice

Ecotherapy actively permits and encourages clients to find new options and make their own choices. It is based on the assumption that clients have the ability to make the best choice for themselves at any given moment (Lankton & Lankton, 1983).

Ecotherapy aims at opening up a range of therapeutic choices. In the subsequent examination of the Sensual Awareness Inventory (see Chapter 4), we will discover an instrument that can provide a client with up to 120 potential choices to alter cognitions, affect, and behavior.

The role of the therapist is to encourage the client in exploring her or his own range of choices, creating the directives to make those choices, and setting the context for the therapeutic options to be implemented. Clients themselves make the decision about whether they will engage in a new choice, what that choice will be, and how they will put it into practice.

Ecopsychotherapy Is Empowering

Because the relationship is essentially between the client and nature, the responsibility to engage in wellness activities rests with the client. Thus, the primary relationship, unlike the case in psychoanalytic therapies, is not between the client and therapist. The therapist serves a role perhaps more akin to a traveler's guidebook, offering suggestions, opening up possibilities, looking at potential options. The choices as to where travelers want to go and how they want to go are indeed their own. The experiences gained and the results achieved are a direct product of individuals' own search, interaction, and discoveries.

Empowerment of the client is an intrinsic aspect of each of the characteristics of ecotherapy. Newman (1980) demonstrated that structured wilderness programs promote attributes such as mastery, competence, and self-esteem. Self-enhancement, at several different levels, is among the personal benefits derived from wilderness contact (Scherl, 1989, 1990). One's self-concept is likely to be strengthened as self-sufficiency and self-control develop, with the opportunities for challenge and self-testing. Learned helplessness, according to Newman (1980), is alleviated by these attributes of personal empowerment.

The effectiveness of nature-guided empowerment is based on what the client does rather than what the therapist does. Because clients can make rapid therapeutic responses when exposed to natural environments (Russell & Mehrabian, 1976; Ulrich et al., 1991), the therapeutic process does not provide the temporally or structurally inherent characteristics of long-term therapy, which can lead to dependency or transference.

The focus is not on the competence of the therapist to innovate change for the client but, rather, on the client's own ability and resources, along with the outcome that the client is capable of achieving. Because choices rest with clients, their wellness is their own individual responsibility. Each step along that process, no matter how small, is a confirmation of their ability and a further ratification of their personal power.

The objective is for clients themselves to learn and engage in not only what is therapeutic but what is preventative and, consequently, to discover their capabilities for pleasure, well-being, and self-worth.

Ecopsychotherapy Is Enjoyable

I recently sat with a client who suffers the debilitating and potentially fatal disease asbestosis. Several of his family and friends have died prematurely from the same disease, and he himself was no longer able to work. He suffered a constricting lack of breath and, consequently, energy. He experienced intense and constant pain through his rib cage. Because of this pain, he was no longer able to lie down to sleep at night but, rather, had to prop himself up in a vertical position. He felt a great sense of powerlessness. His medical specialists had advised him that he had a 35% chance of developing the fatal condition mesothelioma.

To adopt a therapeutic process that focused on exploring his history and his powerlessness would have most likely reinforced this personal sense of inadequacy, as well as heightened his feelings of depression. In such a process it would be very easy for the therapist to also become trapped in his helplessness, for the therapist is equally as powerless as the client to bring back his loved ones or change the course of his disease.

When I inquired "What do you do for fun?" the responses sounded depressive. "I *used* to play a lot of sport. I *was* a keen athlete, but I now no longer have the physical energy to play golf, to coach kids in football, or even have a social game of cricket on the beach with my family." Enjoyment was all in the past tense.

When I asked his greatest source of pleasure in the last few weeks, his face, which had been previously lined with pain, began to light up. The lines of anguish slipped away from the muscles of his brow. His eyes brightened and a smile lit his face as he related how, on one particularly calm day, he had gone to sea with some friends in their fishing boat. Even though he had not been able to cast a fishing line or haul in a catch, he had simply enjoyed the experience of being out on the water on a pleasant summer's day with a group of mates.

In comparing this with his usual daily routine of sitting at home alone in pain while his wife was at work, he attributed the differences to natural stimuli: the salty smell of the sea, the colors in the water, the warmth of the sun, the blue of the sky, the sight of the dolphins they passed on the way out. The change of stimuli had resulted in a change of affect and physical symptoms. He commented, "It's funny, when I was out there fishing, and now in relating it, suddenly I am no longer so aware of the pain and discomfort."

Suddenly, too, there was a change in affect in our therapeutic relationship. He found pleasure in talking about a situation that was beneficial and helpful for him. And, as a therapist, I now had some resources that we could mobilize for his well-being.

Conclusions

The enjoyable context and content of ecotherapy offer a constructive and positive learning environment for brief and effective therapeutic interventions. Oriented toward change and maximizing clients' choices, it draws on individual resources that can be pragmatically used in the achievement of wellness. It is focused on the client and directed toward positive outcomes.

If nature's soporific ambience soothes our heart rate, blood pressure, and muscle tone, these responses are incompatible with the arousal experienced in a state of stress. Similarly, if our senses are being positively stimulated by a variety of natural perceptual sensations, it is difficult to remain depressed. Our sensory organs are what put us in touch with nature, transducing the information via chemical or mechanical means to alter our affect and even our physiology. The senses, as the intermediary that makes possible the nature-mind-body connection, are the subject of the next chapter.

PART II
A MATTER OF SENSE

Chapter 3

SENSUAL AWARENESS

My heart leaps up when I behold
a rainbow in the sky;
So it was when my life began
so it is now I am a man;
So it shall be when I grow old,
or let me die!"—William Wordsworth

Modern-day psychology is a relatively recent emergence from the discipline of philosophy. As early as the fourth and fifth centuries BC, Greek thinkers such as Socrates, Plato, and Aristotle were posing fundamental questions about the accuracy and mechanics of our sensory perceptions. It was these philosophers who defined the five basic senses.

René Descartes, Hermann Helmholtz, and Wilhelm Wendt, along with many others scientists (Dell, 1985; J. J. Gibson, 1966, 1979; E. J. Gibson, 1969; Greeno, 1994; Maturana, 1983, 1987, 1995) over the years, have developed a variety of perceptual theories. Core to all of these theories is the fact that the senses are the means for knowing our environment. As such, they serve two primary functions. First, they serve as protection. Second, they are a means of pleasure. Vision, for example, provides the essential protective cues to avoid us getting too close to a cliff edge, but it also provides us with a source of enjoyment and inner peace as we sit atop the cliff watching the fiery ball of sun set across the ocean, dazzling the sky with a kaleidoscopic range of colors. While both of these elements of perception serve essential functions, nature-guided therapy is about developing the latter element to facilitate greater enjoyment of life, ease emotional disturbances, and promote good health. As a result, this chapter focuses on the senses as a source of pleasure, with therapeutic exercises for accessing that pleasure and illustrative case vignettes for applying nature-guided strategies.

Sense modalities respond to, and in fact thrive on, the changes and contrasts in our environment. Continuing, stimulating variations keep them—and, consequently, us—alert and alive.

If, on the other hand, our senses are overloaded, we may experience feelings of fatigue and confusion, the sort of experience we encounter at a noisy party with lots of people talking over loud background music. This overload can cause exhaustion and anxiety, and these feelings may be converted into somatic symptoms such as headaches.

In nature-guided therapy we are looking at two broad categories of therapeutic resources. Each is rich, each is multifaceted, and each has vast potential for therapeutic change. The first is the natural environment itself. It is an extensive and comprehensive external resource providing an infinite source of constantly changing stimulation. One sunset is never exactly the same as the next. In fact, we revel and delight in the altering, changing, never-ending variations in colors, shapes, and experiences a sunset may provide. Mountains are often described as static, stable, and strong, but our perception of them is infinitely varying as the soft light of sunrise changes to clear bright daylight and is maybe shadowed by the clouds of afternoon before being covered with the last lights of day. At times the mountain may look soft and at times harsh; at times its angles may be abrupt, while at others they may curve gently. Each alteration in perception is a new experience, and each new experience can lead to a new feeling.

In addition, the natural environment provides preferential stimulation, stimulation that we prefer over other sources of stimulation. It gives us the opportunity to discover preferred emotional responses that are as individual as each new cloud in the sky. Some people may express uneasiness about the intensity of a thunderstorm. Others may delight in watching a storm rage across the ocean. Because of these varying experiences available in nature, there is the potential for everyone to discover his or her own preferred therapeutic experiences.

The second category of resource in ecotherapy is our senses. It is our senses that provide us with contact with nature. It is our senses that give us the opportunity to input information that can trigger emotional responses. They are our biggest resource, as they are the means for providing us with all external information and external stimulation. Consequently, they are an infinite source of stimulation and pleasurable sensations.

Because psychological research into the senses has been based predominantly on the mechanisms of knowing, and little on the therapeutic potential of sensory experiences, the remainder of this chapter moves from a description of the mechanics of each sense organ into exploring the experiential qualities and more subjective notions of pleasure. Therapist-directed interventions and case vignettes will illustrate how to assist clients to develop an awareness of their own resources and shift their focus from symptomatology to wellness. In communicating with a client about pleasurable nature-based sensations, maybe relating experiences from her or his own personal background, the ecotherapist can begin to elicit the client's search for naturally pleasurable experiences.

SIGHT

Vision is such a significant sense modality that its satisfaction may override other senses. Aldous Huxley, while visiting the Carribean, described enjoying the flavors of fruits that, solely for their appearance, never reached the European or North American markets. He commented, "The appeal of bright colors, symmetry and size is irresistible. The sawdust apple of the Middle West is wonderfully red and round; the Californian orange may have no flavor and a hide like a crocodile, but it is a golden lamp; and the roundness, redness and goldenness are what the buyer first perceives on entering the shop" (1984, p. 9).

We prize, and actively seek, pleasurable visual images. We travel to enjoy new scenery: the Victoria Falls in Africa, the Grand Canyon in Arizona, or the active volcanoes of Hawaii. We go "to see" how other people live on the Pacific Islands, in the jungle villages of the Amazon, in the mountain monasteries of Nepal, or in the outback of Australia. We cherish those visual memories and usually bring home visual records in the form of photographs. We purchase paintings of scenery to hang on our walls. We enjoy a house with a view out onto a garden, park, ocean, or mountains.

So important is our visual sense in providing pleasurable stimuli that the tourist industry is heavily dependent upon it. Mercer (1991) claims that the major resources of tourism include landscapes and natural environments as well as flora and fauna. For Krippendorf (1992), the desire that we have to view unspoiled, natural landscape is "the basic raw material" of tourism. Indeed, the satisfaction of visual senses is very much at the center of ecotourism, an example being the highly specialized birdwatching tours to various international destinations described by Valentine (1984).

Travel writer Paul Theroux, in an essay on Africa titled *Cerebral Snapshot,* described watching a spectacular sunset with about 10 gangly giraffes silhouetted against the red sky. His traveling companion photographed furiously, but later, as they began to talk about it, it was apparent that Theroux had really seen and enjoyed the giraffes, whereas his friend, busy with the camera, missed many of the sights. While his friend had gained the photographs, Theroux concluded he was the one with the cerebral snapshot.

He said, "When you see a sunset or a giraffe, or a child eating a melting ice-cream cone, there is a chemical reaction inside you. If you really stand as innocent as you can, something of the movement entering through your eyes, gets into your body where it continues to rearrange your senses" (1985, p. 17). In this statement Theroux captures much of the essence of ecotherapy. Perception can create chemical or physical changes. It alters affect, becoming a physical process that can be used for the creation of both psychological and physical well-being. As his statement implies, if we allow ourselves time to absorb aesthetically pleasing stimuli, we can experience a rearrangement of senses, emotions, and physiology.

The benefits of such experiences have been incorporated into therapeutic strategies in a variety of ways. Therapists have, for example, used visual imagery as the basis of several treatment models. In relaxation therapy, a person may be required to imagine her- or himself walking down steps into a tranquil garden scene or to recapture an image that previously was uniquely and individually calming. Covert systematic desensitization approaches similarly use hierarchies of imagery to help alleviate fears and phobias that might have been previously contingent on certain objects or activities. And, indeed, in the area of sport psychology there has been research to show that mental rehearsal may be as effective as, if not more effective than, the actual physical participation in training.

In ecotherapy the therapeutic directives are usually offered to the client in overt rather than covert exercises and can be either therapist initiated or client sourced. Therapist-initiated directives simply refer to those in which the therapist is the agent who assigns the client a task of sensual awareness with a therapeutic objective. The therapist thus chooses the type of experience deemed to be desirable. Client-sourced tasks of sensual awareness are those that are derived from what the client her- or himself deems to be a pleasurable or enjoyable experience.

For each sense modality, a case vignette is used to illustrate the application of therapist-initiated directives. It is not presented as a detailed case history. The therapeutic rationale for choosing nature-guided interventions is not offered for each case. More comprehensive case studies follow in subsequent chapters. Here I wish to look primarily at the process of applying eco-therapeutic directives.

Chapter 4 examines the Sensual Awareness Inventory as a means for providing client-sourced stimuli. The applications discussed throughout this book are primarily based on such client-sourced therapeutic interventions.

A Case Vignette Illustrating a Visual Therapist-Initiated Directive

Emma, a woman in her late 40s, was referred by her physician for psychotherapy because she was considered depressed. She said she felt unloved and unwanted by the people she cared about. For some years she had seen an analytically oriented therapist and more recently had been treated with some cognitive behavior therapy, both of which had offered little assistance. She had been prescribed antidepressant medication but ceased taking it of her own volition after a few weeks, commenting that she disliked the side effects, the lack of progress, and the feeling that she wasn't in control of her own destiny.

Her first concern was about her relationship with her daughter. Emma had wanted to see her daughter have the "right type of wedding." Instead she had formed a de facto relationship with a man 17 years her senior. He was unemployed and had several children to former de facto relationships. Emma couldn't stand him. She said that he lacked social graces, and the final straw came when, according to her, he forced her daughter to have an abortion. By avoiding contact with him, however, she was also missing out on seeing her daughter. She complained that the only time her daughter initiated contact was if she wanted something. As a result Emma felt that she had failed in her role as a mother.

Her second area of concern was her second marriage of 20 years. She and her husband were experiencing a number of relationship problems, and they had received marriage counseling but had not come any closer to a resolution. Emma had been thinking of divorcing her husband but was restrained by two factors: the fear of living on her own and the sense of failure that would ensue with a second broken marriage.

At work, she was also experiencing problems. She had fallen out with a female coworker and, on top of this, was feeling somewhat unwanted in that her opinions hadn't been sought in the company's plans to move to new premises.

She had no interests, hobbies, or recreational pursuits. Her entire life seemed to be overwhelmed with worries about her relationships. Nature-guided therapy was thus seen as the treatment of choice.

First, it was a fresh approach to problems that had been resistant to other interventions. Second, it was likely to provide some rewarding stimulation in her rather stimulus-deprived existence. Third, it was likely to put a sense of control and empowerment back into her hands. Fourth, if Emma could experience a comfortable unity with her environment, it was less probable she would feel unwanted. And, finally, once her affect started to improve, it was considered that she would view her problems less emotively and more constructively, thus putting her in a better position to reach resolutions.

Therapist-Initiated Visual Awareness Directives

The steps for administering a therapist-initiated sensual awareness directive were followed. In assessing the availability of natural resources, it was discovered that Emma lived within a short distance of a scenic river.

She was thus offered the therapist-initiated directive of setting her alarm before dawn one day over the next week. When the alarm went off she was to arise, go down to the riverbank, and watch a sunrise. She was asked to focus on the visual stimuli of this experience and report to me at the next consultation the details of what she had seen.

When she arrived, there was a noticeable shift in her emotional state. She described herself as "certainly much better." She continued to regularly watch sunrises without further therapeutic directives. The experience allowed her to take some control over what was happening in her life and started to provide her with pleasurable stimulation. On her sixth and last consultation, she said that after telling her daughter what she had been doing, her daughter suggested joining her for a sunrise picnic breakfast. Together they shared the experience. Emma later described it as "the best sunrise of my life."

Therapist-initiated sensual awareness directives follow several steps:

1. Assess the desired therapeutic goal.
2. Assess the availability of natural resources.
3. Offer therapist-initiated directive.
4. Focus sensual awareness.
5. Focus on therapeutic response.

The first step, assessing the desired therapeutic goal, usually involves a solution-oriented approach, looking more at what clients want to achieve in regard to their thoughts, feelings, and behavior rather than focusing on the problem.

Second, the therapist will want to know the availability of natural resources within the client's milieu that may facilitate movement toward that therapeutic goal. Here it may be appropriate to discover whether clients live within a commutable distance of the beach, whether there is an urban park near their residence, or whether there is a national park to which they may be able to take a weekend day trip. It is useful to have information such as whether they can engage in a lunchtime walk from their place of employment to a park, along a river, or around a lake.

Third, the therapist will offer a directive or exercise that is aimed at bringing about the therapeutic goal. The task may focus on sensual awarenesses that are tranquil or soothing for clients who want to learn to relax or may be directed toward increasing stimulation for clients who want to change a state of depressed affect.

The fourth stage should invite the client to focus on the particular sensual stimuli that the directive presents. To focus on visual stimuli, a client may be asked to specifically be aware of a variety of colors, such as the variations of green on the leaves of a particular tree. Clients may be invited to visually observe in that environment the different shapes and shades, the shadows and silhouettes, or the visual cues of movement or stillness.

Finally, clients are asked, following the completion of the directive, to focus on what ways that experience may have facilitated the movement toward their therapeutic goal: how, having engaged in the task, they may be thinking differently, feeling differently, or doing things differently.

Some examples of visual therapist-initiated directives are watching a sunset or a moon rise, observing a stream, looking at a seascape, studying a natural panorama, looking at a forest, watching a waterfall, looking at a park, watching animals in nature, and observing a starry night sky.

SOUND

Have you ever allowed yourself the opportunity of sitting in a forest with your eyes closed to enjoy the multitude of sounds around you? If you haven't,

I would encourage you to afford yourself the opportunity, both for your own experience and to discover what this experience may be able to offer your clients. Notice what you hear in terms of the calls or songs of birds, the rustle of the undergrowth as perhaps a small animal is making its path through the bushes, the babbling of a nearby stream, the sounds of the winds in the leaves, the creaking of limbs. And as you do, note the effect that this experience has on your state of feeling and state of physiology.

As a comparative exercise, try the same thing in your place of work, at home, in a shopping mall or beside a city street. Be aware of the sounds of voices, the sounds of traffic, the busy sounds of the household, or the sound of the television in the background. Again note what effect this has in terms of both your emotional and physical sensations.

It is this affect-altering ability that makes auditory stimulation a useful resource in nature-guided therapy. An indication of the commercial and general population awareness of this is the proliferation of compact discs with natural sounds that can be used for meditation and relaxation. These sounds vary from the songs of whales, the lapping of waves, and the calls of forest birds to the rustle of wind in the leaves.

Therapist-Initiated Auditory Awareness Directives

Therapist-initiated sensual awareness directives for sounds follow the same steps described earlier for visual directives. At Step 3, however, the therapist will want to direct the client into auditory experiences. Such directions may invite the client to sit by a mountain stream, perhaps close his or her eyes, and be aware of the sound of the water. The client may be asked to listen to the sounds of waves as they crash against rocks or be directed to notice the variety of bird calls in a nearby park. He or she may be requested to listen to the falling patter of rain and to observe the differences among hearing it on a tin roof, in the backyard garden, or on his or her own body.

At Step 4 the focus of sensual awareness will be on the observations clients may make about the tones, pitches, rhythms, and undulations of sounds. They may be invited to focus on the variations between soft and loud or quiet and busy, or they may be asked to observe whether sounds are regular or intermittent.

Once having participated in such therapist-initiated directives of auditory awareness, clients may be requested to observe what difference that experience made in terms of their thoughts, feelings, or behavior. Here of course the therapist, along with the client, is interested in what therapeutic directions can be gained from participating in such an exercise (Step 5).

Examples of auditory therapist-initiated directives are listening to ocean waves, to the wind in the trees, to birds, to a stream, to rain on a roof, to the silence of snow falling, to the sounds of night, to animals in nature, to a storm, and to the laughter of children.

Auditory Awareness Directives: A Case Vignette

The sounds of teenage neighbors, late-night parties, and rock music were proving unduly stressful for Ernest. He would have been happy to move to another neighborhood, but his wife didn't want to vacate the family home; he was also concerned that if they relocated, they would encounter a similar problem.

He described a long history of stress, particularly stress related to sounds. As a child, he remembered the fearful sounds of the German bombing raids over England. This had been so stressful that it had caused his mother to suffer a "nervous breakdown," resulting in her spending 6 years in a psychiatric hospital.

Two months before Ernest was to migrate to Australia, his younger sister died in a motorcycle accident, and he felt guilty about leaving his family at such a time. His guilt was soon to be exacerbated. Within 3 months after Ernest had arrived in his new country, his father unexpectedly died of a heart attack, and his mother committed suicide by firing a shotgun at her head. Ernest was admitted to a psychiatric unit himself and placed on medication.

He recovered from his symptoms of guilt, grief, and depression, and over the years he maintained a reasonable stability in his work and family life—that is, until a family of teenagers moved into the house next door.

His therapeutic goal was very specific. He brought with him a typed letter detailing the problems and concluding, "What I need is somehow to cope with the situation: to find a calmness, not to get so uptight, and to reduce this sensitivity to other people's sound."

In assessing the availability of natural resources, it was discovered that his route home from work each night crossed a river. By taking a short diversion, it was possible for him to park by the river and walk along its embankment.

Given the fact that he was experiencing difficulties with sound, he was offered an auditory therapist-initiated directive: to take a 20-minute walk along the river and listen to the sounds that he found pleasurable.

He returned to his next consultation with a list. He had identified the voices of a variety of birds: ducks, parrots, and willy-wag-tails. He reported how he had observed the sounds of lapping water, of crickets chirping, of the rustle of the wind in the grass and the trees. He described how the sounds were amplified in the stillness of the evening, saying that he felt so relaxed he could have stayed there forever.

Interestingly, he had also noted on his list the sounds that he didn't enjoy. He was conscious of vehicular noises in the background, the sound of an outboard motor as a boat made its way down the river, and also the sound of a low-flying helicopter. He described these latter sounds as unpleasant, and when asked what he did about them, he replied that he switched them off and stayed with the good sounds. This provided the therapeutic opportunity to ratify his ability to tune in to more positive auditory sensations and tune out undesired sensations.

He was asked to continue his exercise of stopping by the river each night on his way home. When last seen, he reported that he was coping better with his neighbors and was successfully able to use his new strategies.

SMELL

Smell has the ability to bypass cognitive processes. It is not mediated by thought, language, or rationality. Fragrances take the shortest and most direct route to state-dependant learnings. Aromas are accurately able to evoke long-hidden memories without cognitive searching.

Contrastingly, the senses of vision and sound are rich with illustrative language. We may say that the sky is blue and the leaves of a tree are green. These words are descriptive and nonemotive. They could even be a dark blue or a lighter shade of green, but they are still cognitive-like and affect-free descriptive terms. With smell, however, we don't have the same availability of words. Smell is like an arrow that flies straight to the emotional bullseye, with full psychophysiological effects. We may find that the smell of a bakery elicits pangs of hunger. We may begin to salivate at the aroma of coffee brewing. The olfaction of cotton candy at a carnival may trigger childhood emotions.

We speak of smells being "yucky" or "yummy," "sickening" or "soothing," "repulsive" or "pleasing." In other words, they are represented in feeling language, either physical or emotional, rather than in objective descriptions of the stimuli.

A Case Vignette of an Olfactory Awareness Directive

An example of the intense and direct way that smell can affect us, both physically and emotionally, in a problematic manner is illustrated in this case of a woman in her early 50s. She presented with typical phobic symptoms, indicating that she became very anxious and panicky whenever faced with the prospect of having to leave home. On buses, in shopping centers, at cinemas, and at other public places, she was overwhelmed with anxiety and feelings of nausea. Consequently she avoided all such situations whenever possible.

Her symptoms began around the time she and her husband separated, about 25 years previously. When I inquired further, she told me she had suspected that her husband was having an affair. He had been coming home late at night, and his clothes often smelt of female perfume. She decided that she would work at the relationship, hoping that she was wrong in her suspicions and that she would be able to win back his attention. One night when he arrived home late, instead of being angry, she sought to offer affection. She initiated foreplay, including fellatio, which she knew he enjoyed. As she started to participate in this activity, she became aware of what she described as the mixed smell of female deodorant and seminal fluid in his pubic hairs. She was overcome with a sense of panic by the smell. She experienced an intense feeling of nausea and had to run to vomit in the bathroom.

Since that time, the smell of perfume and deodorants had elicited the same intense emotional and psychophysiological responses. She was terrified to get on a bus, enter a shopping centre, or even have coffee at a friend's house for fear that somebody might be wearing perfume. Even the thought of walking down the street tended to trigger her sense of anxiety.

Nature-guided therapy was offered in conjunction with several other therapeutic steps. First, she was taught self-hypnosis to help her manage her experiences of anxiety. Second, she was invited to examine the functional elements of her symptoms and how they had served a protective purpose. She was asked to thank that protective part of her each night just before she went to sleep and also to examine whether she needed the protection anymore. Finally, because she was so hypersensitive to negative olfactory experiences, she was offered therapist-initiated directives to create a more positive sensual awareness of smell. Initially this involved exploring the various fragrances in her own back-yard garden, to discover which she liked the most. She was next asked to walk around the block in her neighborhood, and then through a neighborhood park, again noting her most favored smells.

This process goes beyond simply desensitizing her former anxiety. It is resensitizing to more positive and pleasurable sensual experiences. After three sessions of treatment she was progressing well and was able to leave home, visit shopping centers, and travel on public transport.

Therapist-Initiated Olfactory Awareness Directives

In offering directives for olfactory awareness (in accord with the steps out-lined earlier), therapists ask clients to focus on the smell, the fragrance, the aroma, or the perfume of particular stimuli. Examples of olfactory directives are smelling a pine forest, a garden, the salt air at the beach, freshly mown grass, the rain, the dry summer ground, trees in blossom, a young baby, and a favorite flower. Clients may be asked to notice the strength or subtlety of the fragrance and become aware of other such characteristics. As with the case de-scribed earlier, the client should also be directed to focus on the new emotional response elicited by the sensual awareness.

TASTE

Taste, along with its context, is a creator of experiences, an elicitor of emo-tions. It is so important that many people spend their lives fine-tuning the sense. Chefs are constantly attempting to develop new sensual experiences to tempt their customers. Wine connoisseurs note carefully where the fluid falls on their tongue, where flavor contacts the palate, and which of 10,000 gustatory re-ceptors are being stimulated. In consequence, they have developed a language for describing their gustations that far exceeds the four basic tastes scientists say we are able to experience.

While scientists debate whether there is a direct connection between the foods we consume and the emotions we experience, both folklore and personal experience tend to confirm that there is a food-mood link (Esquivel, 1993). There seems to be evidence that some foods may stimulate the morphine-like endorphins that lead to feelings of comfort and calm. Chocolate is popularly perceived as a comforter when we feel anxious, blue, or in need of a little tender loving care. Kellogg, in his delightful and rather puritanical work *The Home Book of Modern Medicine* (1907), lists a variety of foods that may elicit sexual arousal and cautions against their use. Aphrodisiacs have long been known, or at least hoped, to produce sexual excitement (Vernon, 1982). Certain foods have been variously associated with feelings of depression, hyperactivity, arousal, and other emotional states. And we know that foods can directly contribute to illness or facilitate health and well-being.

A Case Vignette of a Gustatory Awareness Directive

Roberto had been a successful businessman managing his own company with a staff of 250 employees. He became increasingly aware of breathlessness, chest pains, fatigue, and an inability to cope with the physical demands of work, even though most of his activities were restricted to the office. Not long after he turned 50, he was diagnosed as suffering with asbestosis and forced to retire.

Thirty years before, as a young Italian immigrant, he had obtained a job as a laborer in an asbestos mine, shoveling dirt and dust away from the ore crushers. The company allegedly knew of the research and evidence about the dangers of blue asbestos fibers but failed to ensure adequate protection for its employees. As a result more than 2,000 men, women, and children who worked or simply lived in the asbestos mining town are dying from the disease (Hills, 1989).

Roberto watched former workmates and family members die painful deaths from the same illness. His own symptoms included stabbing pains in his chest, fatigue that made it necessary for him to rest for lengthy periods during the day, and sleep apnea, which caused him to stop breathing at times when he was resting at night.

His desired therapeutic goals were to gain assistance with pain management, develop more acceptance of the diagnosis of a potentially terminal illness, and acquire help in enjoying, as he put it, "each day at a time." One objective that he had was to visit relatives in Italy. For a man to whom even watching television was a physical effort, he realized the difficulty that he would have in traveling halfway around the globe. He had organized his trip in three stages, allowing several stopovers at cities along the way where he was planning simply to spend his time in a hotel recuperating sufficiently for the next stage of the flight.

I explored with him the availability of natural sources of sensual awareness in the environment where he would be staying in Italy. He recalled a pleasurable childhood experience of sneaking into a neighboring cherry orchard to steal and savor the forbidden fruit. As his trip was planned for the cherry season, it was practical to offer a directive that he actually seek out a cherry orchard where he could purchase and savor the fruit. The directive deliberately required that he find an orchard rather than simply purchase cherries in a supermarket, it being considered that the former would give him the opportunity for other sensual awareness (for example, the sights, sounds, and smells of being in a rural area). The sense of direct focus, however, was that of taste.

The simple offering of the directive began to change his experience. During the last consultation prior to his departure, his attention was not so much directed toward his symptoms or the anticipated difficulties of travel. Instead, he said, with a smile on his face, "I am looking forward to eating cherries."

Therapist-Initiated Gustatory Awareness Directives

The model for therapist-initiated gustatory awareness directives again follows the steps described earlier. In terms of the focus on sensual awareness, the client is invited to take notice of the various experiences of taste, whether the item they are tasting is bitter or sweet, salty or sour, dry or moist, smooth or crunchy. The client is directed toward detecting the flavor or the location of the stimulated receptors on the tongue or palate. Examples of gustatory directives are tasting water from a clean stream, the salty air at the ocean, a young eucalyptus leaf, a fresh garden vegetable, a fresh garden fruit, durian fruit, and a lover's kiss.

A useful way of helping to develop awareness of taste may be to join a wine-tasting course at which the art of this particular sensual awareness is cultivated with finesse. Such a focus on developing sensual awareness may heighten the experience not only of tasting wine but also of enjoying food, chewing on a fresh young eucalyptus leaf, or appreciating the taste of a kiss.

TOUCH

Our skin, the largest of our sense organs, is capable of providing us with an ongoing source of pleasure. We know and create these sensations of enjoyment for ourselves in many ways. How pleasant it is to soak in a warm bath on a cold winter's night, luxuriating in the aroma and soft skin sensations of a pleasant bath oil. How refreshing at the end of a long, hot summer's day to stand on a sand dune and allow your skin to register the caress of a cool afternoon sea breeze, how sensuous the sloppiness of moist clay feels as it is shaped and wielded between your hands in a pottery class.

In a most interesting article reported in the British medical publication *Lancet*, 30 patients in a coma were studied. Some had their environment enriched by being spoken to and touched. Each of the 16 comatose patients in the environmental enrichment group recovered. In contrast, 11 of the 14 comparable patients who did not receive the same stimulation died. In other words, talking and touching seemed to be critical stimuli in terms of recovery. It is proposed that the soothing sensations of sound and touch in fact bring about internal, chemical, and neurological changes that facilitate healing (Le Winn & Dimancescu, 1978).

Examples of tactile therapist-initiated directives are feeling a cool breeze, the sunshine, the ocean waters, a rose petal, a baby animal, the bark of a tree, the seaside sand, the snow, a loved one, and a smooth shell.

Tactile Awareness Directives: A Case Vignette

At 15 years of age and in Year 10 of his education, Jethro presented with a self-initiated request for assistance because of feelings of depression and depersonalization. His parents had separated when he was 4 years old. He and his sister resided with their mother until he was 12. And that time hadn't been easy. His mother, who had been diagnosed as schizophrenic, was prone to violence and irrationality. Jethro and his sister went to live with their father as soon as they could legally make the choice.

Jethro was a bright lad with an IQ in the superior range. He was achieving good grades at a private college but complained of poor concentration and a failure to reach his potential. He felt overshadowed by his sister, who was more athletic and more popular with their peers. He had used marijuana in the past but had decided to stop. He smoked cigarettes and occasionally used alcohol. He denied taking any other drugs. There was no evidence in his history of hallucinations, delusions, or other psychotic symptoms.

Step 1: Jethro's stated therapeutic goals were to stop worrying, become more relaxed, and improve his concentration. Previous hypnotherapy had not helped him reach these goals. Sensual awareness directives were considered likely to facilitate the achievement of these three objectives. First, the focus on positive stimuli could help reduce the extent of his worry. Second, pleasant natural experiences were likely to provide a sense of relaxation. Finally, focusing on a specific sensual stimulus is in itself an act of concentration, and this was one of the skills he wished to develop.

Step 2: Assessing the availability of natural resources, I discovered Jethro's only recreational interest was in surfing. He lived reasonably close to the ocean and could access public transport to get himself and his surfboard to a nearby beach.

Step 3: Jethro was given the directive to go surfing at least once before our next consultation. When he did he was to focus on the tactile sensations of the water on his body.

Step 4: At the next session, Jethro reported that he had initially been aware of the coldness of the water as it crept through his wetsuit. He was particularly aware of the cold on the back of his lower legs. He described the sensations of the water rushing over his body as he paddled out against the surf and also as he started his ride down the face of the wave. He had been aware of the pressure of the fins on his feet.

He then exhibited an interesting generalization response often observed in nature-guided therapy. He extended beyond the given directive, focusing on other areas of sensual awareness as well. He related how he had paid particular attention to the rushing sound of the waves and had delighted in the spectacle of watching the sun set across the water as he sat on his board behind the break of the surf. He was fascinated by the celestial hues mirrored in the gentle rippling surface of the sea, something he had not previously paused to appreciate.

Step 5: When I began to inquire about Jethro's emotional reaction, he described it as very relaxing, saying that while he was focusing on the tactile sensations he was not thinking about his other worries. In fact, he was surprised at how trivial his own problems seemed as he became aware of the "big picture." His experience had been grounded in the present and, as he put it, "life was not complicated" when he was focusing his attention on the beauty around him.

At a follow-up session 3 weeks later, Jethro reported that he had been maintaining his focused sensual awareness task. He described himself as feeling good. He was no longer experiencing periods of depression. He was looking forward to the future, planning his subjects for the next school year and beginning to discuss courses he might want to take at the university.

MULTIMODAL SENSUAL EXPERIENCES

Characteristics of Stimuli in Natural Environments

Variety. A great variety of natural stimuli waft through the window by which I sit writing this morning. Young magpies squawk at their mothers for food; parents fly off, return, and stuff food into their offsprings' beaks. Black and white forms mill about for the breakfast ritual. Every so often mothers take time out to sing a chorus of welcome to the morning light. Lime green parrots with black heads, golden necklaces, and dashes of brilliant red just above their beaks tear gum nuts from the eucalyptus trees, chattering noisily as they drop them to the ground in a patter like heavy, slow motion rain. The wind blows through the trees, shaking branches and leaves. There is the soft hiss of the sprinklers on the garden beds releasing the pleasant smell of earthy dampness.

Stimuli offered by nature vary in different ways from those of human-constructed environments. What we build usually follows geometric patterns. The walls of our house tend to be painted the same color and tend to form regular shapes. The pictures or photographs that hang on them are static. When windows afford a view into nature, we find our attention being drawn in that direction, because nature provides a much greater variety of multimodal sensual experiences than is usually found in urban buildings.

Intensity. Nature also offers a greater intensity of stimuli. Our fabricated environments generally aim to minimize both variety and intensity, thus maintaining some sort of constancy. We climate-control our offices and cars, for example, whereas nature provides seasons with varying intensities of wet or dry, hot or cold. The range of tactile senses in nature can vary from the softness of the touch of a rose petal to the course and crusty feeling of the bark of a tree. While in buildings our feet tread mainly on carpet or linoleum, in nature we may experience the soothing, damp softness of seaside sand underfoot or gingerly move barefooted over craggy limestone rocks.

Motion. Nature further provides far greater stimuli of motion than is found in static, stereotypical buildings. The clouds, the sun, the stars are constantly in motion as they appear to circle the earth. Perhaps no greater evidence of our desire to see nature in motion is the extent to which people will go to observe moving water. The developers of ecotourism are well aware of how we save our weekly wage packet to spend our holidays, journeying halfway around the world to watch water falling over a rift at the Victoria Falls in Africa or the Iguazu Falls in South America.

Anticipation. In addition to the variety, intensity, and movement in natural environments, there is also a sense of anticipation of the unexpected, the unknown, things that are less in our control. Our structured milieu, conversely, is designed to be under our control, to minimize the unexpected. Yet we vacation in a new area in anticipation of seeing or experiencing something different. Ornithologists await the unexpected, rare sighting. Seasiders delight at a passing pod of dolphins. We never quite know how the next sunset will present itself or what other stimuli nature will next bring our way.

Biological Fit. A fifth characteristic of natural stimuli is what we might call biological fit. Our evolutionary history, as described in earlier chapters, has been one of adaptation to the natural environment. In the natural environment we experience a better biological and emotional fit than with constructed milieus. The morning chorus of magpie songs is more pleasant to our senses than the sirens of emergency vehicles through the city. The panoramic view from the summit of a hill can be more emotionally satisfying than the sight of an urban alleyway. The fresh smell of the sea breeze can sit more comfortably with us than the inhalation of rush hour exhaust fumes.

The characteristics of nature-based stimuli are associated with pleasure and enjoyment, as well as with empowerment and healing. While there have been a number of experiments to test these effects, clear illustration comes from research done by Russell and Mehrabian (1976). Russell and Mehrabian conducted two experiments showing interesting correlations among the perceived pleasantness of our environment, our feelings, our thoughts, and our behaviors. University undergraduates rated 240 photographic slides on dimensions of pleasure, arousal, and dominance.

Pleasure was measured on a continuum examining the degree of happiness, pleasure, or ecstasy derived from the slide. Arousal explored the alertness and

Characteristics of Stimuli in Natural Environments Versus Human-Constructed Environments

Natural Environments	Constructed Environments
More variety	More similarity
More intensity	More uniformity
More movement	More static
More anticipation of unexpected	More controlled
Greater historic adaptation	Less adaptation

excitement derived from the stimuli, while dominance measured the control a person felt over the situation as opposed to feeling influenced by the environment. The photographs were taken from a wide variety of physical settings covering urban, suburban, rural, and wilderness areas in the United States, Africa, Europe, the Middle East, and Central America. Some included people, while others did not. There were scenes of interiors and exteriors of buildings, and climatic zones ranging from deserts to snow-covered forests were included.

Studies of environmental preference have almost universally shown people choose natural over human-made scenes (McAndrew, 1993). Even the labeling of a slide, the cognitive context that one attributes to it, can influence the way it is perceived and the amount of pleasure derived from it. Anderson (1981) showed subjects the same slide, referring to it on one occasion as a "wilderness area" and on another occasion as a "commercial timber stand." Greater scenic quality was attributed to the former descriptive label.

Russell and Mehrabian, in the second part of their study, selected 60 slides that were shown to their subjects in sets of 5. Each set had similar emotional qualities (for example, high on pleasantness but low on arousal and dominance). The subjects were asked to imagine themselves spending a couple of hours in each of the five different settings and, particularly, to imagine "the kind of mood or emotional state that you are in." Each slide was shown for 20 seconds, after which subjects answered written questions assessing their desire to affiliate, to explore, and to stay in that particular setting. Behavioral measures were also assessed with reference to the subjects' desire to smoke or to drink alcohol in that context.

The results show that the physical environment has definite power to influence the way we feel and, in turn, to systemically influence the way we behave. For example, when people rated high their desire to stay and explore the environment, the desire to smoke diminished significantly. The desire to drink followed a similar pattern in that it was high after unpleasant or nonarousing circumstances but low in stimulating and enjoyable natural contexts.

If these results are obtained from brief experimental exposure to a photograph and imagining oneself in a natural environment, we may well ask how much greater the effects would be if the person had that experience in reality. How much more benefit could be obtained by enjoying nature for an extended period with the input of multiple sensory modalities? In nature our senses are contacting biologically, ecologically, and historically relevant stimuli that are compatible with our total sense of being. It is only relatively recently in our history that we have had contact with human-made stimuli: concrete, plastics,

TV images, and so forth. In the wilderness we see, hear, taste, touch, and smell stimuli to which we have a long evolutionary history of adaptation. These sensory-perceptual inputs have been with us as a species for millennia upon millennia. They provide us with a biological fit, and as such they are intrinsically rewarding.

It thus appears that there is a qualitative difference in the stimuli provided by natural versus constructed environments. It is perhaps for such reasons that we seek out natural environments so readily. North Americans consistently rate their favorite leisure activities as outdoor pursuits in wilderness contexts, such as fishing, hiking, and camping. Australians also prefer leisure pursuits like fishing and gardening that involve contact with nature. Ask any advocate of these pursuits and one will readily be assured that a person feels different in that context, more peaceful, more rested, less anxious, happier, more at one. It has even been proposed that, in such contexts, our information processing is enhanced because less effort and less concentration are required.

Imagine yourself lying on the lawn, under a cloudless sky on a warm summer's night, or better still take the time to create the experience in reality. You may feel the firmness of the ground, the spots where it presses against the curves of your body. You may be aware of the soft prickle of the grass through your clothes or be more sensitive to its feel against the bare skin of your legs and arms. Perhaps you are aware of the warmth of the summer's night or the refreshing gentleness in the evening breeze. You notice the sounds about you, the rustle in the leaves, the nocturnal songs of birds. There may be an awareness of passing traffic, wafting strains of music or human voices. You may smell the freshness of mown grass or the dampness of the evening dew in the garden. Above, twinkling, glittering myriads of stars fill the sky. It is possible to notice the difference in their size, the varying colors in their glow, and the degree to which they twinkle, move, and dance in the sky. You may observe a satellite on its defined path through the stellar spectacle or watch how a soft cloud allows the starlight to gradually fade, disappear, and reemerge. And when you have given yourself the time to experience these sensations to your satisfaction, you might like to note how you are feeling, whether your present feelings differ from those that you had before you lay on the lawn and started to look into the sky. If those feelings are different, what changes have you experienced? Do those changes feel good? And, if so, how can you recapture that experience?

Preceding sections have explored each individual sense in turn. As we lie on the grass, however, allowing ourselves to be aware of several different senses, we can note that one sense tends to stimulate another. The increment of one sensual acuity tends to enhance the other. It is for this reason that eco-therapy aims to help clients create multimodal sensual experiences in vivo.

The combination of multiple sensual experiences is not a simple formula like $1 + 1 = 2$. In fact, it is more like $1 + 1 = 22$ or 102. For example, if we stand in front of a waterfall electromagnetic radiations is being inverted through our cornea in waves, striking 130 million receptors before being communicated via the optic nerve to the visual center of our brain. Sound waves are funnelled into auditory chambers reverberating through drumlike skins and the body's tiniest bones before being transmitted along neural pathways and communicated to the auditory center of the brain. But what we experience may be a sense of ecstatic awe.

The perfume of a loved one inhaled by one of our 23,000 daily breaths is scanned by 10 million olfactory receptors capable of detecting approximately 10,000 different odors. Add the caress of that person's finger on the back of a hand, detected by cells of our tactile receptors as a pressure signal. When the waves of electromagnetic radiation from the candle on the dinner table strike the cornea, the response may be an overwhelming sense of love and passion.

Therapist-Initiated Multimodal Directives

At the beginning of this section, I examined five characteristics differentiating natural stimuli from human-constructed environments. These characteristics of variety, intensity, movement, anticipation, and biological fit can be employed in providing clients with directives focused on multimodal sensual experiences. The therapist will thus seek to present the client with an experience in nature that offers these five characteristics. Examples of multimodal directives are finding an isolated beach to go beachcombing, choosing a scenic spot to dine at sunset, walking in a forest, picnicking at a panoramic site, camping in a forest or on a beach, watching a starry night sky away from the city lights, skiing or trekking through snow country, tending a garden, cycling along a riverbank or through country fields, bathing in a country stream, and snorkeling over a sheltered reef.

The client will be directed to focus on the five aspects of natural sensual stimuli. The therapist may, for example, want to inquire about the variety of stimuli the client has experienced, how intense the stimuli might have been, or what the experience of motion felt like. Also, the therapist may explore what unexpected experiences or feelings were encountered and how the person felt during the therapeutic exercise. In following up that directive, the therapist will want to help clients explore their experience of those characteristics and how those features of natural stimulation can continue to be used therapeutically.

Multimodal sensual awareness with attention to these five characteristics helps facilitate the process of interaction with nature. Such therapeutic directives ensure that the client is not an external observer in the manner of a scientist seeking to objectively quantify a process or object of nature. Sensual awareness directives of a multimodal nature similarly are not about simply being *in* nature. They are about being *with* nature, about being part of the process, about experiencing the biological and emotional fit.

THE SENSUAL
AWARENESS INVENTORY

If I could only taste a bird,
a flower,
a tree,
a human face!—Anthony de Mello (1987)

The preceding chapter illustrated how each sense modality provides information for our protection and pleasure. Both of these functions exist for the preservation and well-being of our species. Because our senses are the intermediaries that connect and maintain our communication with the natural environment, they are crucial with regard to our state of health and well-being. I have therefore explored how sensual experiences can be used as therapist-initiated directives, providing examples of their application as well as case vignettes. In the chapters to follow, I examine strategies based more on client-sourced directives.

As a working definition, I consider therapist-initiated directives as those strategies that are defined and offered to the client by the therapist on the basis of his or her therapeutic rationale. Client-sourced directives, on the other hand, are those that are initiated by clients as being indicative of stimuli that provide them, as individuals, with personal satisfaction. This chapter examines the Sensual Awareness Inventory (SAI) as an instrument for obtaining client-sourced material for therapeutic interventions.

The SAI is illustrated in Figure 4.1. There are headings for each of the five senses, along with a category labeled "Activity" to assess things a client enjoys doing. This latter category helps in the construction of multimodal directives. If clients enjoy walking, gardening, fishing, or picnicking, they may be directed to engage in one of these tasks while experiencing the multimodal stimuli available in the environment of the activity.

DEVELOPMENT OF THE SENSUAL AWARENESS INVENTORY

While working as a psychologist in a penal institution, I began to explore the reinforcement preferences of inmates with the aim of using these preferences in behavior modification programs, such as those designed for training controlled social drinking behaviors (Burns, 1974). Many of the preferred reinforcers that inmates listed were nature based. When I moved into my own practice that same year, I developed the SAI to explore client resources that might be used for the facilitation of therapeutically oriented feelings. At that stage I had not formulated my concepts about ecotherapy, but I found that the SAI began to provide me with more information than I had anticipated.

First, I increasingly became aware that the majority of stimuli listed by clients as being pleasurable, enjoyable, or comfortable were nature based. Figure 4.2 provides an example of a typical client response. Certain human-created stimuli such as music, theatre, and movies are recorded on the SAI but tend to represent a minor percentage of the overall responses. Other human-created stimuli are rarely listed. Only twice, over 20 years of using the SAI with my clients, has a client listed watching television as a pleasurable sight or sound experience. As with any rule, there are some exceptions to this. On a few occasions people have recorded that they enjoy, for example, listening to the sound of a Harley Davidson motorcycle. But overall it is an extremely rare phenomenon for people to list stimuli related to traffic, inner-city areas, or work situations as being pleasurable.

A second observation from the SAI is that there is often a dissonance between what clients list as pleasurable and what they actually do. On inquiring about clients' activities, I mostly find that people report that their day is occupied by commuting to work, working, returning home, perhaps engaging in domestic chores, and watching television. These clinical observations tend to be ratified by census data. In 1987 the Australian Bureau of Statistics carried out a survey that showed that, apart from working and sleeping, the most time-

SENSUAL AWARENESS INVENTORY

Under each heading, please list 10–20 items or activities from which you get pleasure, enjoyment, or comfort

SIGHT	SOUND	SMELL	TASTE	TOUCH	ACTIVITY

Figure 4.1

SENSUAL AWARENESS INVENTORY

Under each heading, please list 10–20 items or activities from which you get pleasure, enjoyment, and comfort

SIGHT	SOUND	SMELL	TASTE	TOUCH	ACTIVITY
Rural field in bloom	A variety of good music	Fresh air early in the morning	Good food	Touching people	Pleasant walk
Ocean sunset	Waterfall	Flowers, especially roses	Good wine	Touch of a hug	Dance
Beautiful art	Ocean as it hits the rocks	Perfume	The taste of hot bread	Holding hands	Sitting in front of an open fire in winter
Garden display	Rainfall	Aftershave	Roasted chestnuts	Touch of a kiss	Go out to dinner or a dinner party at home with friends and loved ones
View from the top of a mountain	The silence of snow falling	Aniseed liqueur		Body next to mine	
Waterfall	High-heeled shoes	Fresh baked bread		To stroke hair	
Well-set table	Birds singing	Roasted chestnuts		Breeze on my face	Theater
Lit fireplace	Fire	Aromatic herbs		Rain on my body	Quiet night at home by myself
Morning dew on grass	People talking in the streets of Italy	Artichokes cooking		Mud on my bare feet	Gardening
Animal's body	The beautiful sounds of a baby	All good cooking		Feel the floor with bare feet in summer	Long hot bath
Rain falling	Room full of people I love	Newborn baby		Newborn baby	Personal shopping
Snow falling	Laughter			Silk on my skin	Good movie
People hugging				A caress	
A smile				Good massage	

Figure 4.2

occupying single activity in the life of an Australian was watching television or videos. This accounted for approximately 2 hours per day, as compared with 3 hours working and just 18 minutes spent in sport, exercise, or outdoor activities (Australian Bureau of Statistics, 1988).

When I inquire about how regularly, or how recently, a person has engaged in the pleasurable sensory activities listed on the SAI, the responses often are that such activities are enjoyed only on an irregular basis, if at all. At first I thought this was probably a phenomenon of the clinical population, but census data seem to suggest that it is more widespread. It is thus intriguing that many people engage in a routine style of life that they don't consider enjoyable or pleasurable, yet rarely participate in the activities that afford them the opportunity of greatest happiness. To be doing what is not pleasurable and not doing what is pleasurable creates a state of dissonance leading to a lack of satisfaction, discontent, stress, and, possibly, ill health.

ASSESSMENT VERSUS AWARENESS

The SAI is designed as an awareness- and action-oriented inventory rather than as an inventory for assessment. Psychology has long focused on the assessment of individuals in a variety of ways. Our discipline has developed intelligence quotients, personality measures, diagnostic scales, and a multitude of other instruments to label or categorize an individual. Such assessment tends to be an end within itself. To assess a person as being mentally incapacitated or psychotic may not necessarily be an action-oriented conclusion and is certainly not empowering of a client. This having been said, the SAI may serve some assessment functions.

Figure 4.3 shows an SAI completed by a young man who, in the course of his occupation as a multistory car park attendant, was attacked from behind by a would-be car thief who cut his throat. He was dragged between some parked cars, where he was left to die. Fortunately he was found by a returning car owner, but the incident left him both physically and emotionally scarred. He felt his life had been shattered. He was terrified of anyone approaching him from behind. He was intensely angry toward the attacker (who had never been apprehended), the police, his employer, and society in general. He could not return to the car park, failed at several subsequent jobs, and wasn't making a success of his attempt at a lawn mowing business as a result of his depressed and angry affect. Mostly his time was spent at home listening to Jimi Hendrix songs and complaining to his girlfriend.

SENSUAL AWARENESS INVENTORY

Under each heading, please list 10–20 items or activities from which you get pleasure, enjoyment, and comfort

SIGHT	SOUND	SMELL	TASTE	TOUCH	ACTIVITY
Girlfriend	Guitar	Girlfriend	Beer	Girlfriend	Playing guitar
Jimi Hendrix posters	Wind		Steak		Seeing girlfriend
	Silence				

Figure 4.3

The SAI responses of this young man are indicative of his emotional state, as evidenced by the lack of pleasurable stimuli in his life at the time the inventory was completed.

The SAI may also provide indications of particular areas of sensory deficit that could benefit from development in therapy. Figure 4.2 shows a richness of responses in most sensual areas but a comparatively short list for the sense of taste. It may be therapeutically appropriate to either capitalize on the well-developed senses a client already has or help enhance those senses that perhaps seem somewhat deficient.

Awareness, rather than an assessment, is the primary objective of the inventory. Awareness is seen as action oriented because its end is therapeutic. Indeed, simply completing the inventory may help clients move toward their therapeutic goals.

When I initially saw Lorraine, she was experiencing marital problems and reported feelings of depression. I offered therapist-initiated directives for both her and her husband with the aim of helping to facilitate more positive feelings and interactions in their relationship. As they re-created the joy in their relationship, her feelings of depression diminished.

More than a decade later, she consulted me again. Her father had recently died, and she found that she was struggling with her grief reaction. She discussed how she had never been as close to him as her other two sisters. Perhaps in some ways this seemed to be heightening her sense of grief, as she realized that there was now no longer the opportunity to obtain the father-daughter relationship she had always desired.

She said that, in addition, she had always been torn in her loyalty to her parents. Her mother and father had had an unhappy relationship, so Lorraine felt that if she loved her father, she was being disloyal to her mother. In terms of physical appearance, she was closer to her father and considered this to be a result of negative transference from her mother. When her father died, she felt that the tension between her and her mother was exacerbated in that she was not able to comfort her mother or receive comfort from her. In her grief she had become depressed, tearful, and withdrawn. Her husband wasn't sure how to manage the situation, and she again became frightened about the changes in their marital relationship.

Given her previous response to therapist-initiated directives, I asked her to complete the SAI between consultations with a view to offering client-sourced directives. When she returned for the next appointment she said, "I understand what you are getting at. You are saying that if I start to feel good there won't be any room for the bad feelings. When I was filling out the inventory I realized that if I wanted to feel differently I had to do things differently." She then proceeded to list some of the nature-based activities in which she had engaged during the week between appointments. The administration of the SAI alone had helped her become aware of her potential to feel better and had provided her with a means to begin modifying her emotions.

THERAPEUTIC BENEFITS OF THE SENSUAL AWARENESS INVENTORY

In addition to providing action-based awareness, the SAI offers both client and therapist a constructive tool for treatment.

Extensive Therapeutic Resources

Completion of the SAI provides both the therapist and the client with an extensive list of sensual therapeutic resources. When clients complete the 10 to 20 items required under each of the six headings, they have listed some 60 to 120 different items or activities that bring them pleasure, comfort, or enjoyment. This provides a large range of resources for achieving the client's desired affect or behavior.

Immediate Modification

Because most of the resources listed by the client will already be associated with states of positive affect, they can be used clinically to achieve immediate goal-oriented modifications of thoughts, feelings, actions, and psychophysiology.

Client-Initiated Resources

Because it is the client who is required to complete the form, the responses are indeed client sourced. With the SAI, the therapist is not forced into the position of attempting to use his or her own creativity to provide images or exercises that may or may not be appropriate for the client. Clients are providing the resources they know have worked in the past and are likely to work again in the present and future.

Motivation

Self-sourced responses to the SAI are more likely to facilitate motivation to work with assignments offering these resources. Possible resistance factors are minimized because the initiatives are coming from the client rather than being imposed externally. Motivation is thus stimulated by the fact that the SAI helps to create an awareness of desirable and achievable experiences that already lie within the client's own realm.

Multiple Choices

As mentioned in Chapter 2, one of the characteristics of ecotherapy is to give the client choice. The SAI is about choice. In completing the inventory, clients exercise choice about their preferred stimuli and use the form as a basis for making therapeutically directed choices.

Focus on Solutions

The earlier illustration of Lorraine's case highlights how the completion of the inventory alone can begin to guide a client in the direction of positive experiences with a solution focus. Experiences that are pleasurable, enjoyable, and comfortable are often those that equate with the therapeutic goal set by the client.

Empowerment

It is not uncommon for a client like Lorraine to report that "I know what you meant by giving me that task. You are saying that I have been too negative in my thoughts and need to be thinking more positively. I realized that in filling out the inventory and have consequently made a commitment to do something nice for myself every day." The language of clients tends to be in the first person. In other words, they take the responsibility for becoming aware and starting to modify the experience that has been undesirable. The client is thus seeing the power and responsibility for change resting with her- or himself rather than with the therapist.

MULTIMODAL THEMES

Completed SAIs will often provide multimodal themes linking the various sense modalities. Figure 4.4 provides an example.

SENSUAL AWARENESS INVENTORY

Under each heading, please list 10–20 items or activities from which you get pleasure, enjoyment, and comfort

SIGHT	SOUND	SMELL	TASTE	TOUCH	ACTIVITY
Birds in the garden	Birds singing	Freesias	The first cup of tea in the morning	The soft warm muzzle of a horse	Gardening
Colorful garden	Children laughing	Boronia	Chocolate biscuits	Patting/stroking animals	Singing
Clear blue sky	Most music	The children's freshly washed hair		Holding hands while drifting off to sleep	Dancing
Different colors of the sea at Rottnest Island	Bees humming on a hot summer's day	The first rains in winter		Snuggling up while still half asleep	Cycling on Rottnest Island
Lambs jumping	Lambs bleating	New-mown grass		Soft new towels	Reading
Friendly wink	Church bells	Freshly baked bread			Sitting talking with Tom
Smile	Tom's keys in the door	Tom's aftershave			Cuddling
Red sky at sunset	Water running over rocks				Catherine on my knee when she's just woken up
					Sitting on the patio on a summer's evening awaiting the breeze
					Star gazing
					Watching rugby on TV
					Cup of tea outside before kids get up
					Playing cards or board games with the kids

Figure 4.4

In the case of this female client, there is a gardening theme. She enjoys the sight of birds and a colorful garden. She has listed as pleasurable birds singing and bees humming on a hot summer's day. At the top of her list of olfactory enjoyment is the smell of freesias and boronia. Gardening is also her most highly rated activity. Such multimodal themes tend to be nature based. Human-created stimuli tend not to be listed with the same range of sensual satisfaction, usually being restricted to just one category.

A second theme for this client is one that has an animal or rural basis. She enjoys the sight of lambs jumping, the sound of lambs bleating, and the tactile experiences of patting and stroking animals.

Third, she gains pleasure from the different colors of the sea at Rottnest Island, the activity of cycling around the island, and the smell of freshly baked bread. The following are appropriate client-sourced therapeutic directives she could be invited to engage in: (a) Spend time gardening when the freesias and boronia are in bloom; (b) have a weekend away at a farm when the lambs are still young; and (c) visit Rottnest Island and ride a bicycle to the bakery for breakfast. Therapists are encouraged to look for these multimodal themes that will maximize desired positive feelings.

ADMINISTERING THE SENSUAL AWARENESS INVENTORY

The SAI is generally presented to the client on the first consultation. This may be done as a homework assignment with the client invited to return the completed inventory at the next consultation.

Alternatively, the client may be asked to complete, or at least partially complete, the inventory during the appointment. The advantage is that the therapist is able to provide feedback and start to set client-sourced directives immediately.

A third option for administration is in a less formal, conversational style in which therapists may talk with clients about their preferences rather than requesting that they complete a written inventory.

Follow-up to the administration of the SAI, either at the second consultation (if it is given as a homework assignment) or immediately (if administered in a conversational style), follows a three-step solution-focused and presuppositional approach. This approach has a distinct bias toward clients achieving their specified goals. The therapeutic questions are presuppositional in that they presuppose a goal-oriented outcome. If a person has completed the inventory, something different has occurred, and those changes can be used therapeutically (O'Hanlon & Weiner-Davis, 1989; McNeilly & Brown, 1994). The three steps are as follows:

Step 1: Ratifying *what* learnings were gained from completing the inventory.

Step 2: Determining *how* those learnings can be used for continuing therapeutic gain.

Step 3: Determining *when* those learnings can be put into practice.

These three steps allow maximization of the learnings from the SAI and encourage clients to discover the skills necessary for their ongoing benefit. Just as the SAI itself is considered a means of eliciting client-sourced information, so the three-step follow-up to its administration is designed to encourage clients to search for their own continuing empowerment.

Step 1

To help clients consolidate and explore what they gained in completing the SAI, they may be asked questions such as the following:

- *What* did this exercise teach you about your own experiences of happiness and pleasure?
- As you filled out each section of the inventory, *what* did you discover about yourself?
- In completing this task, *what* did you learn about how to satisfy your senses?
- In thinking about your senses, *what* feelings did you experience?

Step 2

In this step, the questions are designed to facilitate the client's use of the discoveries made. Questions will therefore be along the following lines:

- *How* can you continue gaining from these sensory pleasures?
- Now that you have made that discovery, *how* can you put it into practice for yourself?
- *How* can you use this list for your ongoing happiness?
- *How* can you go about doing things that satisfy a number of your senses at the same time?

Step 3

The third step focuses on *when.* The three steps are all critical elements in any decision-making process. To make a decision we need to know *what* we want, *how* we can do it, and *when* we will put it into practice. To decide to go to work in the morning, for example, we initially need to decide *what* we want. We want to go to work because we enjoy it, because we need the money, and so forth. We then need to decide *how.* We need to roll out of bed, get our body up, and start to do the things that get us to work. But we also need to make a time commitment as to *when* we are going to do it. We decide, for example, to get out of bed *when* the alarm goes off. If the *when* is not resolved, then, despite our best intentions, we may still not achieve that objective. The *when* is thus seen as a crucial step in following up the SAI.

When questions may follow a pattern similar to the following:

- *When* can you start to do these things for your ongoing pleasure?
- *When* will be the first opportunity you'll have to (for example) spend some time in the garden, listening to the birds and smelling the boronia?
- *When* will be a convenient time each day to pause and enjoy one of the pleasures from your list?
- *When* would you like to begin to feel a little happier?

USING THE SENSUAL AWARENESS INVENTORY FOR CLIENT-SOURCED DIRECTIVES

Client-sourced sensual awareness directives follow procedural steps similar to those discussed for therapist-initiated directives in Chapter 3:

1. Assess the desired therapeutic goal.
2. Assess the client-preferred natural stimuli from the SAI.
3. Offer the client-sourced directives.
4. Focus sensual awareness.
5. Focus on therapeutic response.

The major differences between therapist-initiated directives and client-sourced directives are in Steps 2 and 3. At Step 2, the therapist is able to examine the SAI, to observe the client's preferred stimuli, and to note what particular multimodal themes exist.

The third step is for the therapist to offer the therapeutic directive based on the client's responses to the SAI. This takes the responsibility from the therapist and gives a greater sense of empowerment to the client. The therapist will thus be formulating the directive in terms of the client's expressed therapeutic goal and the rationale for choosing that particular directive. Steps 4 and 5 follow those already discussed and illustrated in Chapter 3.

In the subsequent sections of this book, I will be covering a variety of ecotherapeutic strategies and their applications with particular clinical problems. These strategies are a development of client-sourced directives, and in most cases the SAI has served as the basis for formulating the therapeutic interventions.

PART III
NATURE-GUIDED
STRATEGIES

Chapter 5

INSIDE OUT

The illusion of separateness we create in order to utter the words 'I am' is part of our problem in the modern world. We have always been far more a part of great patterns on the globe than our fearful egos can tolerate knowing.—Walter Christie (cited in Roszak, 1995)

I have already discussed how contact with nature can promote health, well-being, and happiness, not only by reducing stress, freeing us from polluting environments, and enhancing our sensual experiences but also through a nature-mind-body link. I have also explored how our senses provide contact with nature, are the vehicle for establishing the person-nature relationship, and can be accessed for developing therapeutic directives.

In this section of the book, I examine the strategies that can shift us from an inner symptom focus to more pleasurable experiences: techniques that can facilitate our life-nourishing energies, assist us toward peak experiences, and promote a sense of health.

Craig was not the sort of guy you would necessarily expect to find in a psychologist's office. He was in his early 50s. His forearms had the strength of tree trunks, and his hands were broadened by the muscles of labor. Yet behind his soft, blue eyes, one felt there was a heart as disproportionately large in tenderness of emotion. He was a farmer and an independent man who had learned to survive on his own wit and initiative. For more than half a century he had dealt with what life had brought him—at times effectively and at times not so effectively—and had survived without seeking any external assistance. He was a man who had done it his way.

It was his wife who had initiated the appointment for Craig to seek therapy. When he sat down in the chair of my consulting room, he said, in a tone he might have used in a confessional, "I don't understand what is happening."

He had recently been overwhelmed with a sense of incredible loneliness. He found that he was awakening in the wee small hours of the morning, experiencing agitated and ruminative thought processes that prevented him getting back to sleep. Consequently, throughout the following day he felt tired and fatigued, lacking both the energy and motivation he usually applied to his farming duties. He had also begun to feel fearful and insecure, reporting an unusual lability of his emotions.

Thirty years back he had begun to date his wife. He had fallen deeply in love with this warm, fun-loving woman who was 7 years his junior. Four years later they married, and they maintained a very close relationship. As with any relationship, it had had its ups and downs. There had been the usual pressures of living in isolation on a large farm, the economic fluctuations, the differences in personal attitudes, and the problems of raising a family. Communication had dwindled over the years, but they sought a practical solution and attended a marital enrichment program. After three decades they were still generally enjoying each other's company and their sexuality.

It had been a longtime, unfulfilled dream that they would travel together on an extended tour through Europe. There had been three children to raise and put through university, and each time when things had begun to look right, wool prices had dropped or a drought had struck. Recently his wife's friend had announced that she wanted to travel and invited Craig's wife to join her. Since they couldn't both afford to go, Craig selflessly sent his wife while inwardly longing to be sharing the experience with her himself. It was in the month she was away that his presenting problems emerged.

They had, in fact, originated many years in the past. He had previously had a dream about a friend's father, following which the friend's father died. It worried him a little, but time passed, and so did the worry. On a later occasion he had a dream about a motorcycle accident. Within a day or two, a neighbor was killed in one.

More recently his son had graduated school and secured a job working on a small Southeast Asian island. During his son's time there, Craig had a dream about a tidal wave striking the island. The next day, one did. His son was not harmed, but Craig became extremely panicky about his offspring's safety. These three events seemed to have convinced him that there was a predictive power in his dreams.

While his wife was in Europe he had a premonitional dream of a serious train crash. He was convinced that this was spelling out the fatality of his wife. When he was unable to contact her by phone for the next 7 days, he became overwhelmed with a sense of powerlessness and hopelessness that escalated into depression.

He began to wonder whether his difficulties in coping with the separation from his wife had some deep-seated basis in his past. His attention started to become more internally focused, not only on his symptoms but also on mulling over what previous traumas might be to blame. His family reminded him that at the age of 2, whilst his father was overseas in the armed services, his mother became critically ill and he was looked after by another family for several months. Was he suffering repressed experiences of rejection?

Other traumas began to flood back into his mind, and indeed there had been several understandably distressing events. At one stage he had been caught in a cyclone while on an outback road in his truck. Fierce winds were twisting and tearing at his truck, ripping trees out by their roots and hurling them along the side of the road. One tree crashed on top of the truck, and Craig feared for his life. At the height of the storm, he had to get out with a chainsaw to clear the timbers off his vehicle, then stop frequently to saw others off the road so as to clear his way home. After several hours in this stressful situation, not knowing whether he was going to be crushed by yet another falling tree, he arrived home in an exhausted state, suffered an anxiety reaction, and subsequently consulted a psychiatrist.

Another incident that he recalled with grief and guilt related to his father. Craig had been in his early 20s and, with the brash urgency of that age, wanted to quickly finish a job so that he could get away for a drinking weekend with his friends. He asked his father to help him load some machinery onto a truck. Under the strain his father suffered a heart attack and died in Craig's arms. From then on he started to treat life with a somber seriousness that focused his attention on work and responsibility. He ceased going out with his friends. He wouldn't take holidays. Their lack of money provided him with an excuse to stay home and work rather than go to Europe with his wife, even though the trip had been a longtime dream.

The absence of his wife and the changes in his own emotions had led him to become increasingly internally focused on his psychological symptoms. The more he did, the more he began to seek out what reasons there were in the past. As so often happens when we turn our attention inward, he became fixated on the negatives. The effect was like a whirlpool: the vortex of the internal attention drew him deeper and deeper inward, trapping him in even more undesirable feelings.

Given the process Craig was going through, an ecopsychotherapeutic approach was considered appropriate. While psychotherapy has traditionally looked within the individual for answers, ecopsychotherapy explores how the answers may be found in our relationship with the natural environment. An egocentric focus often tends to be on negative feelings. People become very introspective when feeling depressed, when experiencing anxiety, or when suffering pain. Turning a client's attention inward to stop the experience of those feelings is likely to be a more difficult task because it focuses on pathology. Shifting awareness outward, via an *eco*centric focus, can more rapidly and effectively lead to the desired therapeutic outcome.

THE EGOCENTRIC ORIENTATION

Inner focus may be caused by a number of factors, such as the historic, ideological basis of our Western society, the language that we use, and the modus operandi of our scientific and educational model. Beforing exploring how ecotherapy can shift focus from an inner negative experience to outer therapeutic experiences, I first explore some of the traps that facilitate an egocentric orientation.

The Historical Trap

Western culture has long followed the Judeo-Christian ethic that has shaped our religious and moral attitudes, in turn forming the basis of our civilization and determining the nature of our interactions with our ecology (McAndrew, 1993; Mason, 1993). The very first chapter of the first book of the Bible lays down the basis for the person-nature relationship. God explicitly gave the human race control over nature; he created nature to serve human needs and commanded that we were to "subdue it" (Genesis 1:28).

As a result of this ideological and historic view, we have seen nature as fearful and as needing to be controlled. Colonists set out to tame new lands. Mountaineers have traditionally spoken of "conquering" a mountain, and indeed the older style of mountaineering was to send a military-like battalion out to base camp, launching wave after wave of assault onto the mountain until it was finally subdued. Engineers build dams to irrigate arid land with the assumption that we can manipulate nature into what we perceive we need rather than adjusting our lifestyle to our particular ecological milieu. Roszak cautions that "there are greater endeavors than conquering nature, more reliable forms of well-being than physical dominance; there is a greater richness than the limitless acquisition of things" (1992, p. 40).

The Judeo-Christian view of life is one that is very linear in direction. It goes from *A* at our birth to *Z* at our death, encourages us to use what nature provides along the way, and offers no accountability because our journey never brings us back on this same path. In the view of Native Americans and Australian Aborigines, humans do not hold the same dominant and independent role. Humans are seen, as already discussed, as part of the whole interactive process of animals, plants, insects, places, and spirits. For Buddhists, life is cyclic rather than linear, beliefs in reincarnation bringing one back time and time again to the same world and the same environment. In one life we may be one form of sentient being, in the next another. With this interrelatedness to other sentient beings—and the interrelationship of these beings with the earth, the air, the trees, and so forth—comes an implicit accountability.

The historic and ideologic trap of our particular cultural background promotes plunder rather than preservation (Kanner and Gomes, 1995), elicits fear rather than fun (Durning, 1995), and encourages us to see the trees for their timber rather than for the essential stimulation they may provide (Greenway, 1995). This historic tradition has the potential to not only undermine the essentials for our survival but also diminish our potential for health and well-being.

The assumption that we have control of our world is a formula for unhappiness. The reality is that we have not been able to subdue nature, and we never will. We are a part of the whole and not exempt from it. Despite millennia of attempts at control, we still eat and get eaten. Humans are devoured by sharks, poisoned by snakes, gored by bulls, consumed by alligators. Our bodies are host to bacteria and viruses that ingest us from within. Our homes are flooded by rivers, shaken by earthquakes, burned by fires. The building up of internal assumptions that are not based on reality is a formula for discontent.

This historic trap is one into which Craig had fallen. As a farmer he had been caught in a 10,000-year-old assumption that he had the control to produce crops, genetically engineer sheep, and commercially use the soil. It was similarly an implicit assumption that he should have had control over the cyclone that buffeted his truck, hurled trees at him, and threatened his life. Nature's sudden dramatic challenge of this egocentric focus resulted in a state of anxiety.

The Language Trap

Language influences the way we think, the way we feel, and the way we behave. This, in turn, affects our language and tends to perpetuate a cyclic pattern, at times with unfortunate consequences. If, for example, we give an experience a negative name, the two tend to become associated. We then anticipate that similar future experiences will also be negative.

Last winter I recall leaving home one day with my grandson in the car. As we pulled out of the carport, the rain hit the windshield, and he lit up with excitement. When I turned the windshield wipers on, he was delighted. He was full of cheer at the sounds of rain on the car roof, the splatter against the windshield, and the rhythmic swish of the blades washing away the water. Excitedly he commented, "I love the rain." At the same time, the radio announcer was saying "What a terrible day." I turned off the radio and continued to listen to my grandson.

If we associate words such as *terrible, horrible,* and *disastrous* with an experience, we do more than simply give the experience a negative label. We change it from the neutrality that it has in nature and attribute to the experience the power to elicit a "terrible" feeling within us. An egocentric focus on such negative feelings may result in our being depressed, down, or blue because the day is "miserable." We may then choose to stay inside, maybe feeling cheated that we cannot do some of the things that we would like to be doing; consequently, we feel even more depressed. The next time it rains, we begin to associate the word *terrible* with it, and once again we begin to experience the emotions conditioned with that word. We don't go out, as the young child may be happy to do, under an umbrella, in a raincoat, or splashing through puddles in rubber boots. Because we allow the word to alter our affect and restrict our behavior, we reduce or limit the pleasurable sensations we might otherwise enjoy.

Indeed, there are many ways in which some of these language traps are conditioned: by the radio announcer, by the attitude of parents, or by the comments of teachers. The fact that they vary as greatly as the polar opposites taken by my grandson and the announcer on that particular winter's morning clearly indicates that they are not an objective reality in themselves as much as an association formed by the person concerned.

Let me extend this idea into the clinical setting. If I invite clients, as a therapeutic directive, to go camping, some might find it an exciting prospect to be out in the bush experiencing the thrill of an adventure. Some might think of it as a tranquil experience to hear the whisper of the breeze in the trees, to watch the stars and moon above; others may immediately think of it as being dirty, difficult, or unpleasant, perhaps frightened of creepy-crawlies, spiders, and snakes. This latter attitude may lead to a sense of fear, with the consequence that the person avoids going camping and thus robs her- or himself of a potentially enjoyable experience.

The language trap not only deprives us of a particular experience at the time but also reduces the stimulation that we might gain from engaging in similar such experiences in the future. Diminished satisfaction is detrimental to our well-being and may even lead to pathology. Dissatisfaction with what we cannot modify causes unhappiness. To then label the unchangeable as "terrible" or "catastrophic" exacerbates that unhappiness.

This indeed was another trap into which Craig had fallen. He had begun to convince himself that it was unpleasant being at home by himself without his wife. He began to develop premonitions of potential danger, which heightened his feelings of anxiety and consequently reinforced the unpleasantness of being alone.

The Why Trap

Craig had begun to ask "Why?" He had regressed to the age of 2, the period of separation from his mother. He wondered about some of the difficult events that had befallen him, as well as about the guilt he felt regarding his father's death. Asking why, however, did not produce an answer, and it did not resolve the problems. In fact, the converse was true. It caused him to spiral downward, like an aircraft in a spin.

The why question has arisen out of our scientific model in which deductive logical reasoning is seen as the main or only means of knowing. We are educated, throughout our schooling and academic training, to ask the question "Why?" But not all scientists concur that this is the best way of learning or of resolving problems. Microbiologist, biochemist, and author Darryl Reanney asserts, "In my view, the basic flaw of almost all science presentation is the dependence on logic. At first sight it seems heresy to question the role of logic since deductive reasoning has been elevated to something near divine status by the sociology of our time. Yet logic is not the only way we know the world and not necessarily the best" (1994, p. 5).

Haley (1969), in a classic article titled "The Art of Being a Failure as a Therapist," describes 12 steps for failing in psychotherapy. At the core is the why trap. He argues that, to be a failure as a therapist, one of the essential steps is to direct clients into why-type questions. "Refuse to directly treat the presenting problem, offer some rationale, such as the idea that symptoms have 'roots,' to avoid treating the problem the patient is paying his money to recover from" (Haley, 1969, p. 692). He goes on to comment, "As a further step to restraining patients who might spontaneously improve, the therapist should focus upon the patient's past" (p. 693).

Haley expanded therapy beyond the concept of the patient being the sole owner and resolver of the problem. He recognized the importance of relationships with significant others in the clients' environment: families, friends, schools, neighbors. He further acknowledged "the great outdoors" as an important ingredient in therapeutic success (1984). "Perhaps the most important rule for therapeutic failure," he asserts, "is to ignore the real world that patients live in and publicize the importance of their infancy, inner dynamics and fantasy life" (Haley, 1969, pp.692–694).

One of the most essential contributions of the innovative therapy of Milton Erickson was his shift from the psychodynamic, pathology-based questions of traditional psychotherapy to solution-oriented treatments. He cited many case examples illustrating how he deliberately shifted clients from asking why to finding solutions.

Clients frequently make comments such as "I want to know why I am feeling this way" or "I want to know why this is happening." My assumption is that they are really asking for ways and means to resolve the difficulty they are experiencing. To discover causes is a culturally developed context for therapy. Indeed, it is perhaps very much stimulated by our own profession on the often false basis that understanding causes will, *ipso facto,* change circumstances.

By focusing on solutions rather than causes, some therapists are avoiding the egocentric why trap (de Shazer, 1985; O'Hanlon & Weiner-Davis, 1989). This approach is summed up in the words of Walters and Havens: "It may be concluded, therefore, when the desired outcome is health, the initiation of healthy attitudes and behaviors may be more beneficial than attempts to uncover and cure illness. When the goal is joy, it would be wise to ignore existing sadness and shift attention towards joyful ideas, activities and events. As a rule, people will be happier, healthier, and more competent if they do things that are associated with happiness, health, and competence, rather than trying *not* to do things that are associated with unhappiness, illness, failure" (1993, p. 10).

AN ECOCENTRIC APPROACH

I would like to point out that I do not see an inner, egocentric focus and an outer, ecocentric focus as two separate or mutually exclusive entities. Our inner psyche and the external reality are not dichotomous entities. Unfortunately, our scientific model has tended to create this schism, seeing the ego as separate from the environment, the self as distinct from its surroundings, the mind as detached from its milieu. Instead I want to propose that the two are very closely related and indeed very interactive. Shifting our attention outward, even if the stimulation and sensual input are not what we might interpret as pleasant, represents a shift of attention away from what might be an inner focus on negative sensations.

It is the premise of this work that nature itself has distinctive affect-altering, behavior-changing, wellness-promoting characteristics. In addition, the process of interaction between the individual and the natural ecology is proposed as a unique, simple, and powerful therapeutic dynamic. The use of these variables in the therapeutic process is explored further in subsequent chapters.

Before proceeding, let me point out the universality of the ecopsychotherapy approach. The Sensual Awareness Inventory demonstrates people's clear preference for sensual experiences based on natural phenomena. Very rarely will people list human-made objects as sources of visual pleasure or describe interactions with machines and instruments of technology as enjoyable. In Chapter 1, we saw how this clinical impression is validated by research demonstrating a global preference for natural environmental stimuli. Even when we have culturally conditioned attitudes about the environment or commercial interests in using the environment, natural preferences remain.

Hoffmann-Williams and Harvey (1995) reported an interesting Australian study in which participants were described as either "green" or "nongreen." "Nongreen" referred to people whose primary environmental affiliation was through timber, mining, and agricultural industries. Also included in this group were four-wheel drive and hunt clubs. The "green" sample included people associated with naturalist or conservation societies.

It was of little surprise that when they measured beliefs about nature, they found marked differences between green and nongreen participants. The two groups were clearly differentiated by their beliefs about the naturalness of human activities in forests, the speed of natural change in forests, and the need to manage nature. When the two groups were asked about their aesthetic appreciation of nature, however, it seemed that there was universal agreement. Both greens and nongreens described logging coups as unpleasant and ugly. According to Hoffmann-Williams and Harvey, "There were themes repeated often enough to support the view of many environmental psychologists that patterns of preference are shared by *all* humans. Rain-forests, particularly the cool rain-forests of Tasmania, were repeatedly referred to as a peak of forest beauty. The red gum woodlands of Northern Victoria are another common theme of praise. Pine plantations and areas damaged by insects or weed infestation were commonly described as unpleasant" (1995, p. 5, italics added).

This is extremely significant work because it seems that, no matter whether we have a "green" commitment or not, there is a basic affiliation that links us all to nature. To appreciate nature and gain its healing recuperative benefits, we need to look outside ourselves and take in natural sensual stimulation. The ability to do so is universal.

So, what are the strategies that can shift us from our inner traps to more pleasurable universal experiences, that can facilitate our life-nourishing energies, that can assist us toward peak experiences and promote a sense of health?

Craig's case illustrates the formula. He consulted me on two occasions. After he had related his history on the initial consultation, we began to explore how he might find more joy in his life. He discussed several activities that helped facilitate this emotional state, including fishing. At his second consultation a couple of weeks later, he reported that he had had "some good days and some bad days." The good days had been better because he had been feeling noticeably more relaxed and at peace with himself. Nonetheless, he was still experiencing feelings of anxiety and fatigue, as well as confusion about why he felt the way he did.

As we started to explore more ways of gaining sensual satisfaction, he told me that a group of his friends were planning a 10-day fishing trip to an isolated offshore island. They invited him to go, but he had declined the invitation. He said that he didn't feel up to it and was anxious about what might happen if, in such a remote area, he developed a panic attack. His desire to participate was obviously present, but it was being bounced up and down as if on a seesaw with fear as its partner.

My therapeutic task was very simple. I added some extra weight to the desired side of the scales and elicited a commitment from him to join his friends on the fishing expedition. My therapeutic rationale was that such an activity would put him into a natural environment that could provide multimodal sensual satisfaction and that such satisfaction would be therapeutically beneficial.

Two months later, he came back to report his experiences. He initiated the conversation by saying that he could have pulled out of the fishing trip. On the long drive up the coast, before boating out to the island, he became extremely panicky. He thought of getting out of the car and catching a bus back home. As he sat in the back seat, wrestling with his emotions, he said to himself, "You are not going to enjoy this if you keep panicking. You made a commitment to George that you would come away for the enjoyment." In relating his experiences on the island, he said, "I forgot all the negatives and simply had a great time." He reported how he realized that the fear of death and sickness that he had been contending with when he first consulted me was an absolute waste of time and emotion. In the process, he had discovered effective and simple tools for altering both emotion and cognition.

STEPS FOR FACILITATING
AN ECOCENTRIC APPROACH

Craig's case illustrates the steps for shifting from an inner symptom focus to an outer source of sensory stimulation.

Anticipation

Encouraging anticipation is helpful in facilitating looking forward to, and thinking about, the pleasure that may be derived in an interactive experience with nature. Craig certainly included this on the want side of the seesaw. The difficulties for him arose when he turned inward and began to focus on possible negative consequences. Anticipation helps direct attention toward possible gains.

Commitment

To be able to have the experience that might facilitate a therapeutic change, it was important for Craig to make the commitment. The commitment gave him permission to be in that environment and, consequently, to gain the benefits from the experience. Without this being elicited by the therapist, the client may continue to wallow in pessimistic introspection.

Enjoyment of Sensual Experiences

Craig was encouraged to focus on his sensual experiences during the trip by using client-sourced directives and sensate-focusing activities. The technique of sensate focusing is described further in Chapter 6.

Interaction With Nature

Craig illustrated how, when he got to the island, he was able to put aside all worries about the past. There he was not plagued with concerns of guilt over his father's death. There he was not terrified that a typhoon was personally venting its anger on him. There he was not suffering with premonitions of death or injury. He was instead able, as he described, to enjoy the tranquillity of the sea, to marvel at its colors, and to sit back in the isolated peacefulness of a shady spot on the island. He found pleasure in the rhythms of the ocean and the warmth of the sun. The fishing provided him an interaction with nature, a challenge, and, on landing a fish on the boat, a sense of achievement.

Permission and Encouragement of Therapeutic Changes

As we encourage clients to engage in an interactive relationship with natural environments, so we will observe a shift in emotions, cognitions, and behaviors. It was very difficult for Craig to think about death while nature was living around him. It is difficult to focus on grief when birds are singing with joy. It is difficult to be anxious about our own well-being when our surrounding cosmos simply is being.

We are a species that habituates to constants. We prefer a homeostasis, like the thermostat on our refrigerator maintaining an even temperature. We desire to have our thoughts, our feelings, and our actions in a state of equilibrium. It feels uncomfortable if there is an imbalance among cognitions, affect, and behavior. By altering what is happening in one or two of these areas, we are likely to bring about a change in the others as we seek to reestablish equilibrium. This is a basic premise of all therapeutic change and a key element of ecotherapy. If an anxious client experiences an emotional shift while watching the soothing, lapping waves on the shore, cognitions and behaviors are also likely to help bring about a more pleasant state of equilibrium. If a depressed client, lying on the lawn at night watching a starry summer sky, has a shift in thoughts about himself and his place in the universe, his body may move a little more energetically as he arises. He may feel a little different.

Although I wasn't present with Craig on his fishing trip, I could imagine the behavioral shifts that may have occurred. I doubt whether he would have been walking as stooped as he was when he first came into my office. I doubt if the muscles of his face would have looked like gravity was trying to drag them off his skull. I think that he would have been stepping out more confidently and that the evening barbecue beside the seaside shack with his friends, on a crisp starry night, would have echoed with the sounds of stories, jokes, and laughter. Indeed, the changes were still apparent when he visited me after the trip.

Ratification

The process of ratification is one of validation and confirmation of goal-oriented changes. Because therapy is about not only creating change but maintaining that change, ratification is seen as an integral part of the process. Helping clients to confirm their achievement is empowering. This stage of ecotherapy should assist clients in acknowledging what they have achieved, exploring the means by which they have been able to do so, and reinforcing the fact that they have the ability to draw on those skills in the future.

To help confirm the changes that Craig had made, I asked him to sum up in a few words how he would describe the experience of his trip. He said, "Extremely enjoyable." I validated with him that he was able to achieve this extremely enjoyable feeling on his own. He had been able to achieve it while away on an isolated island without my presence or that of his wife. I also reflected back to him how he had been smiling and relaxed throughout the consultation, save for discussing the conversation he had with himself on the drive up the coast. His attention was drawn to the fact that he made no reference whatsoever to the other troubles that he had originally brought into my consulting room. Further ratifying the progress for himself, he commented that these problems no longer seemed relevant for him.

Maintenance of Therapeutic Gain

The aim of nature-guided therapy is to help clients develop effective self-management strategies that they can use not only to overcome current problems but to better equip themselves to face future life issues. Once we shift to the positive experiences of our senses, relate with nature, and, ipso facto, modify our thoughts, feelings, and behaviors, we have established a process for creating and maintaining a healthy adjustment between ourselves and our environment. The positive feelings thus created are likely to encourage the search for more healthy, therapeutic, and stimulating experiences. This constructive formula, in turn, can gain its own momentum, rolling forward in the direction of health and well-being.

The therapeutic questions mentioned at the end of Chapter 4 are likely to be helpful in this process. With Craig, for example, I asked, "What can you do now to ensure you continue to allow yourself further such enjoyable experiences?" In conversation, we explored his areas of sensual pleasure with the goal of developing further activities that would help him achieve and maintain his desired state of well-being. The following chapters describe such nature-guided therapeutic activities, their function, and their step-by-step administration.

Chapter **6**

SENSATE FOCUSING

You've got to stop and smell the roses
You got to count your many blessings every day
You're gonna find the way to heaven
is a rough and rocky road
if you don't stop and smell the roses along the
way.—Mac Davis and Doc Severinsen (1974)

If we feel cold, we seek to warm ourselves. If we are hungry, we eat. If we are tired, we sleep. We do not analyze the cold, hunger, or fatigue; instead, we create the desired state of being or the desired action to alter the way we feel. This principle also applies to our emotional needs. If we are feeling down, we need to create an experience that will lift us up. If we are feeling anxious, our natural desire is to create the state of feeling relaxed. Therapy is thus appropriately directed toward helping clients achieve and experience the feelings that they want, the desired goal or the desired state of being. It is this very process that is the basis of sensate focusing.

Sensate focusing is a technique for helping the client tune into the sensations of pleasure, comfort, and well-being. It is a shifting of the focus from the unpleasant and the undesirable into the desirable. It is a redirection from an inner, ruminative, introspective focus to the pleasures that prevail in the natural environment and in one's relationship with nature.

PROCESS OF SENSATE FOCUSING

The steps involved in sensate focusing are as follows:

1. Define the problem that needs addressing.
2. Define the desired outcome.
3. Assess whether ecotherapy is appropriate.
4. Formulate the therapeutic program.
5. Select a relevant sense modality.
6. Create a sensate focusing task.
7. Commit the client to the task.
8. Explore the post-task experience and learnings.
9. Teach ongoing sensate focusing tasks.

These steps are expounded below and illustrated with a case example. The chapter concludes with some variations that can be offered in sensate focusing strategies.

Define the Problem to Be Addressed

Mavis was in her mid-30s when she sought therapy. She was a devoted schoolteacher who had sought to extend her career with extensive postgraduate training and work experience. For the past 5 years she had been a principal and administrator of an independent school of approximately 200 students. Because she had been there from the very founding of the school, it had become as much of her as she was of it.

She was referred by her physician at the end of the third term of the four-term academic year. At this stage of the school's curriculum, she annually suffered a "mini-breakdown." However, this particular year had been exceptionally stressful.

She gave a lot of herself, having high expectations of her ability and a perfectionistic drive to do her best. She tended to perceive life as a constant struggle, saying, "I'm struggling with feeling inferior, accepting compliments, and having other people's conflicts upset me." Even when there seemed good grounds for her to give herself a pat on the back, she still perceived the situation as one of struggle. She said, "I am struggling with learning the piano even though I can hear it's improving. I am struggling with art but I see great results."

These struggles had been particularly prevalent in the current term at school. She was attempting to cope with both her administrative responsibilities and a full-time teaching load. The school did not have an on-site counseling service, and she found that she was frequently involved in counseling students. She had to manage the relationship problems that arose between staff members, as well as the various conflicts that emerged among staff, students, and parents.

Of late, the fee-paying parents had been demanding more say in the direction of the school's educational policy, while the teachers were asserting that it was their right to set policy and standards of education. Mavis was caught in the middle, a position she found particularly repugnant. She commented, "I want to avoid conflict. I hate conflict. It makes my stomach tight and I want to cry. I hate the thought of conflict. Is it my fault? Really, do I feel that I should fix it? Why? Because I sometimes can. Because I have been trained to. Because I am good at it. Good for other people. Not always good for me. It is good for me when it resolves, but if I think that it hasn't really resolved, I carry it. It becomes my problem."

She presented as extremely tense and garrulous. She cried her way through each of the first few consultations. She reported feelings of nausea, headaches, insomnia, and nightmares. The pressures of work and her difficulty in managing them had been taking their toll on her 15-year marriage and her relationship with her three primary-school-aged children.

The problems that needed addressing seemed to fall in several areas. First, she was complaining of immediate symptoms of affective disturbance, including feelings of anxiety and tearfulness. Second, she had somatic disturbances, with nausea, headaches, and insomnia. Third, there were the relationship problems that were affecting her family, and, finally, there were the longer standing problems related to the management of stress and conflict issues.

Define the Desired Outcome

Mavis was very clear that she wanted to change the situation. She said, "I know I need to care for myself." She wanted to relax, free herself of her presenting symptoms, and resume her normal teaching duties.

Assess Whether Ecotherapy Is Appropriate

Mavis had not had any previous psychotherapy. Her own efforts had not been successful. A resolution required something different. Relaxation therapy might have helped relieve her anxiety, but it was not seen as sufficient to address all of her issues. Ecotherapy offered the potential for achieving a quick modification of her current symptoms, teaching her more effective ways of caring for herself, and providing her with opportunities to shift her focus from an inwardly directed to a more outwardly directed perspective.

Formulate the Therapeutic Program

The therapeutic program formulated with Mavis initially aimed at teaching her relaxation strategies to diminish her immediate symptomatology. This was to be combined with solution-focused counseling about managing her occupational and general life situations and strategic ecotherapy assignments to facilitate these processes of change. The assignment work was to include sensate focusing tasks.

Select the Sense Modality

There are three ways that a sense modality may be selected to facilitate sensate focusing. First, the Sensual Awareness Inventory may be offered to the client. From this the therapist can select a modality that may quickly achieve the desired therapeutic gain or a modality that perhaps needs to be developed to facilitate the client's therapeutic response.

The second option is for the client to choose the modality. This may be done in discussion with the client or by inviting the client to choose from her or his SAI responses.

Third, as in Mavis's case, the modality can be selected by the therapist without reference to the SAI. Mavis had given a clue early in therapy. While discussing the buildup of her anxiety she commented, "A chasm of insanity was clear and palpable. It was so close I could taste it."

It seemed, from her comment, that taste was probably a key sense modality for her at this point in time, and currently it was associated with unpleasant experiences such as her fear of lapsing into insanity. To help her modify her experiences in this modality would change her current state of affect, offer a sense of empowerment, and provide a model for managing future situations.

Create the Situation for Sensate Focusing

This step can be either therapist directed or client sourced. Scanning the Sensual Awareness Inventory can help provide not only the modality but the activity and the environment that may be most appropriate for the client to experience. As it happened, Mavis had already made reference to such an opportunity. A couple of sessions after we had started treatment, she was planning on taking a 1-week holiday with a female companion. This provided the opportunity to encourage the planned activity. She would be traveling from the city environment into timber country that was home to one of the world's tallest trees. The coastline was dotted with scenic seascapes, and the hinterland was known for its regional wines.

As we discussed the area she was about to visit, I discovered that she enjoyed sweet white wines. Several vineyards produce a white port, a white-grape-fortified, dessert wine. She was therefore given an assignment of gustatory sensate focusing. She was to visit several vineyards, sampling their current vintage white ports.

Commitment to the Task

To facilitate commitment to the task I asked that she choose a port she thought I would like and bring it to the next consultation, at which point I would pay her for the wine.

In prescribing any therapeutic exercise for a client, it is important to elicit a strong commitment to the task for the simple reason that if nothing is done to bring about a change, no change is likely to occur. The commitment in this case was relatively easy. It was apparent from her history that the client was a caring person who tended to the needs of other people, often neglecting her own needs. This factor was used as a resource to elicit her commitment to the task. The assignment drew on her likelihood to tend to the needs of her therapist while engaging her in a task that was designed for her own therapeutic benefit.

Exploring the Experiences and Learnings

The function of this step is to help heighten the client's awareness of the sense of wellness and well-being in the sensate focusing exercise, to consolidate therapeutic gains, and to maintain and reproduce those gains in the present and future. A useful way of doing this involves solution-oriented presuppositional questions.

Mavis brought a white port to the next consultation. I paid her for the wine, and the gesture offered the opportunity to inquire what she had experienced in the exercise. At first she began with a mild complaint: "You set me a very difficult task. I began to discover the ports that I liked and enjoyed but I had no idea what would suit your taste."

"Then what did you discover for yourself in the experience?" I asked.

"I discovered the wines I liked and those I didn't. But it also made me think. It made me aware of the need to pleasure myself and look after my own needs," she replied.

"And what else did you learn?" I pressed.

A faint smile came to her face, the first I had seen since we met. "I was thinking about it during the four-hour drive home. I wondered what you had really intended, and thought it must have been more than just buying you one bottle of wine. I don't know whether this is what you had in mind, but I began to think that there are many tastes better than the taste of insanity."

Formula for Change

To help maintain progress, the client may be offered a five-point formula for change (see Figure 6.1). Depending on the client's state of affect at the time of administration of this formula, there may be two different sets of responses. First, a client may want to retain her or his current state of feeling. The formula is designed to accommodate this choice. Second, a client may want to change the way she or he is feeling to a more desirable state, and again the formula offers steps for this process. Mavis's case gives us an illustration of how it may be used in both ways.

A "Yes" Response. In Mavis's case, the steps involved were as follows.

Step 1: In exploring the experiences and learnings that Mavis had gained from her sensate focusing task, there was both an acknowledgment and an acceptance of what she had achieved from the experience.

Step 2: She was asked whether that new way of thinking and feeling was what she wanted to be experiencing. Because she answered in the affirmative, Step 3 was omitted, and we moved directly to Step 4.

Step 4: What could she do to continue those goal-oriented changes she had implemented? She appropriately pointed out that she couldn't always be on

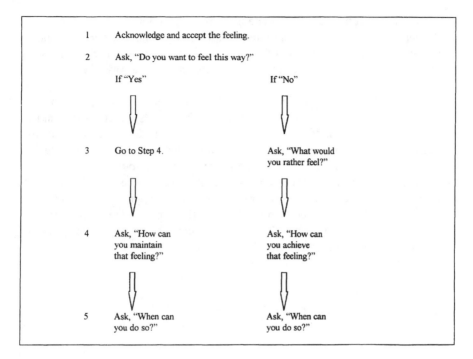

Figure 6.1   Formula for change.

vacation. She did, however, say that whenever she tasted something pleasurable, she would be very conscious that it tasted better than the taste of insanity. Based on the enjoyment she had gained from the bushland areas during her holiday, she had decided to take regular walks in a nearby natural parkland.

Step 5: She was then encouraged to make a time commitment as to when she could put these decisions into practice. She decided she wanted to simply be aware of the taste sensations whenever she became conscious of eating or drinking something pleasurable. Since she was still on leave from work, she decided to commit herself to a daily walk in the woods.

A "No" Response. When I saw her for a follow-up consultation 1 week later, Mavis said that since getting back home she had again become aware of all of the pressures and stresses she had managed to escape while she was away. Although she didn't feel as bad, she was again becoming depressed and tearful.

Step 1: At this point I discussed how her feelings were very normal, that sometimes it is very justifiable for us to experience a sense of grief, sadness, anger, or stress. It may be appropriate not only to feel but to express, in healthy and constructive ways, these emotional experiences. I helped her to acknowledge the feelings by pointing out that, in part, what she was experiencing was a sense of grief. It was a loss of many things that she had always wanted.

She had become a principal. She had become an administrator. She had founded a new school. She had shaped its beginning, its development, and its educational policy. Suddenly other factors, many outside of her control, had brought this dream and achievement to an end. What she was experiencing was a loss, maybe akin to the loss of a partner or friend. In addition to the loss of her career achievements, there had also been a loss of some of the concepts that she held about herself. I discussed with her the appropriateness of these feelings and the natural need to allow herself time for grieving, time for feeling sad, time for being tearful. In this way there was an acknowledgment of her feelings and confirmation that they were acceptable given her current circumstances.

Step 2: I asked, "When you feel you have given yourself appropriate time to grieve, do you want to go on feeling that way?" The response was an emphatic "No!" She said, "I feel I have done enough of that. It is time for me to start to move on."

Step 3: "Then, if you are ready to move on, how would you rather feel?" Because of her recent time away and the exercise in sensate focusing, she had a variety of positive sensual experiences to draw upon (for example, walking through forests, visiting vineyards, and strolling along beaches).

She answered, "I would rather recapture the feelings that I had at times while I was away. There were times when these issues, albeit fleetingly, had left my mind completely, times when I rediscovered my ability to laugh."

Step 4: I then moved on to the next point, asking "Now that you are back home, what can you do to help recapture those feelings more often"? Although Mavis had completed the Sensual Awareness Inventory, we did not need to refer to it. She began to set herself tasks that she could do to help experience more desirable sensations. She was still off work and had the opportunity to continue daily walks in local woodlands. She began to plan weekend picnics with the family. Had she not self-initiated these activities, the Sensual Awareness Inventory would have been a source of information to help stimulate such activities. The therapist may work through the inventory asking clients what items listed are most likely to help them achieve the feeling they want. The therapist can thus use the inventory to set client-sourced directives.

The client may be invited to put the list in a prominent position, such as on the refrigerator door or the dressing table mirror. Each day the client can see it and choose an item or activity of pleasure. It may simply be to stop and smell a flower or to take time out to watch the clouds rolling by in the sky, or the therapist may invite the client to focus on one particular sense area for the week. In such ways the client is provided help in discovering what sensate focusing tasks can best elicit the desired state of affect.

Step 5: Finally, the client must be committed to undertaking the pleasurable sensual activities that will bring about the desired affective modification. Once the activity likely to achieve the desired feeling is defined, this can be followed through with questions such as "If this is likely to be of benefit, when can you begin to put it into practice?" and "When will be the most convenient time for you to start?" Without a time commitment, tasks may often be delayed or never put into practice. As the questions of this five-point formula help clients clarify the practicalities of change, they are taught the formula, enabling them to use it at times when they are experiencing alterations in feelings, thoughts, or behaviors they may not desire at that point in time.

* * *

Mavis's trip had opened up the opportunity for us to work with other sensory interactions with nature. Once we had explored the experiences and learning from her sensate focusing task, and once she had learned to use the formula for change, her affect began to improve, she appeared to be coping better, and she reported feeling happier with herself.

By our seventh session she had suffered a setback. Her employer's insurance company had not been making life easy for her, and in addition to that a meeting of the school committee, regarding the tenure of her position, had left her feeling a failure. She said at that consultation, "I don't deserve to live." Not only was she blaming herself for the current situation, but she began to cognitively regress into incidents from the past about which she still felt guilty. Toward the end of the session she said, "Everything I do turns out bad."

That week I gave her a paradoxical assignment that, while not strictly ecotherapy based, illustrates how ecotherapy may be used adjunctively with other therapeutic strategies. She was asked to do something bad each day. She presented at the eighth consultation with a marked improvement in her affect, announcing she had discovered that "it's not bad to do something for me."

On the first day she had talked to a male friend of whom her husband was jealous. She said that she enjoyed the conversation and, despite having deliberately set up the exercise, concluded that it didn't really feel all that bad. The second day she went out with a female friend, choosing to come home late when she normally would have been there cooking the family meal. She was surprised to discover her husband had started to prepare the meal and was looking after the children. The break in her routine again didn't feel all that bad. She was a "greenie" at heart, zealously caring for every tree and bush in her garden. However, on the third day she decided to cut out a couple of bushes simply for the sake of gaining a better view. She said that she appreciated the view and it didn't seem so bad cutting down the bushes.

The fourth day she again took an unusual step. Normally she protectively cared for her children, never leaving home without them. That night she arranged for them to be babysat by her mother while she and her husband went out alone for the first time in years. They enjoyed themselves so much that leaving the children behind didn't seem bad either. On the fifth day it happened to be her birthday. She went shopping with the intent of buying herself a present and found a lovely casserole dish that she really liked. She rolled the dish over and saw that it was made in France. She was strongly opposed to the French nuclear testing in the Pacific and normally would have avoided products made in that country. However, she said that she really liked it and decided to purchase it for her birthday. Again her enjoyment was such that her action didn't feel so bad.

At that point her face became a little red; she expressed a nervous laugh and said, "But today, I have done something really bad." I asked, "What was that?" She replied, "I have come to the consultation without bringing the checkbook to pay you!" We both agreed that was really bad. I congratulated her on at last achieving what she had been asked to do. And we laughed together.

Mavis continued to make steady progress. There were occasional remissions, usually associated with contact with her former school. However, she maintained the use of sensate focusing exercises and the formula for change. She decided to take her husband on a holiday and share some of the experiences that had signaled the beginning of her progress. She was seen for a follow-up 6 months later, at which point she had returned to part-time work in the education system. She was seen again for a 12-month follow-up, at which stage she was working full time, planning education courses and teaching teachers. She reported that she was coping well, feeling "pretty good" and had regained a purpose in life.

At an interval of 18 months after the completion of treatment, she was still working full time. She was managing her occupational demands as well as her family responsibilities, even though the circumstances had not been easy for her. Her husband had commenced time-demanding postgraduate studies in addition to his full-time job. One son had contracted glandular fever. Her grandfather, whom she loved, was dying, and her sister had announced to their con- servative religious family that she was a lesbian. While these factors may have caused her disruption in the past, she commented that she now felt she had the skills to continue to cope successfully.

VARIATIONS IN SENSATE FOCUSING STRATEGIES

Paradoxical Suggestions

Given Mavis's response to the paradoxical suggestion to do something bad each day, I set up a paradoxical sensate focusing exercise for her the following week. Because it was wildflower season, she was assigned the task of taking a daily walk in nearby parklands and making a note of wildflowers she had not previously seen. To note what she had not seen in the past meant she needed to focus visually on what she had seen and be conscious of what she had not seen.

The main steps involved in paradoxical sensate focusing tasks are those detailed earlier for sensate focusing; instead of being asked to attend to a particular sense, however, the client is asked *not* to notice that particular sensual stimulus. This approach has advantages for resistant clients and in situations in which clients may have already evidenced responses to paradoxical types of suggestions.

Sensory Deprivation

The 1960s studies in sensory deprivation showed that acuity of sensory input tends to be heightened once deprivation is ceased. Depression may be seen as a state in which there is a deprivation of sensory stimulation (see Chapter 12). To deliberately require the client to create a state of such deprivation may have several advantages. First, it replicates and extends what the client is already doing. In this way, it is in line with the client's symptoms and is less likely to alert resistance to change.

Second, to create a situation of deprivation is likely to enhance the experi- ence of the recommended sensate focusing once the deprivation ceases. Exer- cises in such deprivation may include asking the client, for a period lasting an hour or two to a day or two, to stay at home, switch off the radio or television, not make any phone calls, or close the curtains so that he or she cannot even look out the window. Such tasks need to include safeguards to ensure that the activity will not be harmful to the client.

A third benefit of such deprivation is that it is, in fact, a paradoxical bind. Compliance with the suggestion is likely to bring about the benefits of more acute positive sensual experiences. Noncompliance with the task avoids the deprivation and is likely to focus attention on enhanced sensual experiences.

Once the deprivation is established and the time limit is prescribed, the client is then directed to seek natural rewarding experiences that may be selected from the Sensual Awareness Inventory.

The Sensual Journey

Whereas sensate focusing involves concentrating on one sense modality, the sensual journey invites the client to take a journey through a variety of sensual experiences. When possible, it is preferential to make this an in vivo experience so that the client can actually be in contact with a preferred natural environment. Clients may be invited, for example, to sit on a riverbank and allow themselves the pleasure of a journey through the visual, auditory, olfactory, tactile, or even gustatory experiences provided by that environment. Since it may not always be possible for a client to engage in such a real-life experience, the sensual journey may be created at an imagery level, with clients taught ways of replicating the activity for themselves. Although the use of imagery is a viable therapeutic tool, it is not dealt with specifically in this work because research and clinical experience suggest that direct contact with nature has a relationship quality not replicated in imagery.

Chapter 7

NATURE-BASED ASSIGNMENTS

One touch of nature makes the whole world kin.—William Shakespeare

By nature-based assignments, I refer to therapeutically crafted tasks that use natural objects or interactive processes with nature and that have in the past—or are likely to in the present—assisted the client in achieving the therapeutic goal. The Sensual Awareness Inventory, as described here, can elicit resources that either have been or can be potentially useful for goal achievement.

The use of nature-based assignments is not novel in the therapeutic area. We have already seen how traditional healers have used this approach over the centuries and how recent psychotherapists, such as Milton Erickson, have created therapeutic exercises in a variety of natural contexts. What is uniquely characteristic about this current approach is, first, that positive natural experiences are used in a systematic and constructive manner to achieve a therapeutic goal. The natural context is a purposely selected element essential to therapeutic gain.

Second, it is assumed that nature itself can directly result in modification of a person's affective state, thought processes, behavioral patterns, and physical well-being. Third, there is a systematic use of nature's rich resources to exploit their therapeutic efficacy in the most efficient manner.

Nature-based assignments can thus readily be incorporated into most therapeutic models, especially those directed toward brief, effective, strategic, and solution-oriented approaches.

CHARACTERISTICS OF NATURE-BASED ASSIGNMENTS

Broad Learning Options

Nature-based assignments create options that are not available in the clinic or consulting room. Indoor settings tend to provide the context for learning about things rather than learning from the experiences that equip us for living. It is in a classroom that we learn that the Magna Carta was signed in 1215 or that Antarctica is the driest continent on the earth. In the context of a convention room, we learn important things about our profession. The experiences, however, that teach us about life, about survival, and about enjoyment require a much broader learning context. It follows, then, that the more we can expand the learning context for our clients, the greater their potential to learn from important life experiences.

Intrinsic Values

Simply being in the presence of nature has intrinsic values. I have already discussed some of the experimental work demonstrating these intrinsic qualities (Chapter 1). Nature-based assignments aim at using these qualities for the achievement of the client's therapeutic goal. For example, nature can be intrinsically calming, pleasurable, stimulating, challenging, and healing.

Intrinsic Calm. One does not necessarily need the experimental data of the environmental psychologists to know the relaxing and soporific experiences of watching a sunset across an ocean, listening to the regular and rhythmic roll of waves against the shore, or hearing the warbling songs of birds in the bush.

Intrinsic Pleasure. To have a wild parrot alight on your forearm and gently pluck seeds from the palm of your hand, to feed bread to an opossum at dusk, or to see dolphins surfing down the face of a wave are experiences that can elicit instant joy and pleasure.

Intrinsic Stimulation. Researchers have demonstrated how exposure to sensual stimulation in nature can help lift feelings of depression, grief, and sadness.

Nature's rich variations of color, sounds, fragrances, tactile sensations, and taste arouse and alert our senses to new experiences.

Intrinsic Challenge. As we saw in Chapter 1, shamans may assign their clients intrinsically challenging interactive tasks with nature. Milton Erickson used similarly challenging therapeutic assignments, such as sending people to climb Squaw Peak (see Chapter 1). To move out of our usual urban context into a different environment presents us with a new challenge, be it climbing a mountain, crossing a stream, or surviving in a different context.

Intrinsic Healing. People with views of nature from a hospital window are discharged quicker than if they viewed a brick wall. There appears to be a direct nature-mind-body connection that intrinsically links our health to our environment at both physical and emotional levels (see Chapters 14–16).

Simplicity

Nature-based assignments can be characterized by simplicity. Both clients in therapy and colleagues in training often comment how simple, yet effective, ecotherapy can be. If nature itself is seen as an integral therapeutic agent, a complexity of therapeutic activities need not be part of the treatment plan.

Past Positive Experiences

Nature-based activities can rapidly reactivate past positive experiences. A trip to a particular beach may re-create the carefree enjoyment of a lazy summer holiday. The sight of snow might reactivate the challenge, the exhilaration, the laughter of earlier attempts to toboggan down a gentle ski slope. Recollections of such positive experiences are intrinsic reciprocal inhibitors to feelings of anxiety and depression.

New Learning Opportunities

As well as reactivating past experiences of a solution-oriented nature, nature-based assignments may create new opportunities for new experiences. These new experiences may, in turn, develop further therapeutically relevant resources and strengths.

Change

The learning developed out of nature-based assignments can be constructed to achieve appropriate cognitive, affective, and behavioral change.

PROCEDURAL STEPS FOR ADMINISTERING NATURE-BASED ASSIGNMENTS

Assess Client Commitment

Assess the client's cooperativeness and level of adventurousness in terms of participating in strategic assignment work. The initial interview should provide an indication of the client's motivation and willingness to bring about change. The nature-based task needs to be geared to the client's level of adventurousness so that it can be determined whether the task is not so risky that it unduly raises anxiety levels, and yet, on the other hand, is not so unchallenging as to be unrewarding.

Completion of the Sensual Awareness Inventory is likely to offer the therapist information about this latter dimension. If a client lists passive nature-oriented experiences such as a picnic in a national park or gardening in the backyard, it may not be appropriate to initially establish an assignment that involves rock climbing or whitewater rafting. Conversely, for somebody who participates in active sport areas, a passive nature assignment might not be very appropriate if the goal is one of challenge and new learnings. On the other hand, it may be appropriate if the therapeutic goal is aimed at the achievement of relaxation and tranquillity.

In this first step, it is important to assess factors such as the client's commitment to change and level of adventurousness so that these factors can be appropriately incorporated into achievement of the therapeutic goal.

Define the Goal

The therapeutic goal and the assignment goal may differ. The assignment goal might be just one of the steps necessary to achieve the overall therapeutic goal. Hence, the therapist needs to ask questions about such issues as what the client wants to achieve from therapy, what tasks might help the achievement of that goal, and what are appropriate steps for the client to take in that direction.

Identify the Client's Resources

The therapist here is exploring questions such as what skills the client has to reach the therapeutic goal, what abilities can be drawn on, what strengths can be ratified, and how the nature-based assignment might identify, strengthen, and ratify these resources. The Sensual Awareness Inventory may give cues to the client's resources. It is possible to assess, from the inventory, the stronger areas of sensual awareness. A person may, for example, readily list 20 items of pleasure under the heading of sight but struggle to find 5 in the area of smell. If we wish to use a readily available sensual resource in a nature-based assignment, it may be more appropriate to focus on that client's visual strength rather than the area of smell.

As well as quantity of responses, the qualitative nature of responses on the inventory provides an indication of resources. A person might not necessarily list a high number of items in the smell area, but those reported might be particularly intense and powerful sensations that can thus be used as resources. The Activity section of the SAI further provides indications of abilities and interests that might be mobilized toward achievement of the therapeutic goal.

Explore the Missing Experiences

To reach the specified therapeutic goal, clients may need new experiences and new learnings that they have not yet gained in their journey through life. At this point, the therapist is likely to be asking questions designed to determine what the client needs to reach the goal, what new experiences will be helpful, what will help to resolve the problem, and what new learnings are needed to find the solution. Here again the Sensual Awareness Inventory may give some cues in regard to missing sensual experiences or activities that need to be satisfied for progress toward the solution.

Create the Assignment

Several factors need to be incorporated in the creation of a nature-based task. The assignment will need to (a) be goal directed, (b) enhance contact with nature in a therapeutic manner, (c) provide an opportunity to strengthen the client's resources, and (d) create new experiences or learnings to fill in the missing gaps.

Create Intrinsic Values

Once these core therapeutic requirements have been established, it is appropriate to consider creating an assignment that is also intrinsically fun, rewarding, and/or challenging. Contact with nature ought to be a pleasurable experience or at least have a pleasurable outcome. With regard to this latter point, Milton Erickson's frequently prescribed assignment for clients to climb Squaw Peak may have been a demanding task. The resultant contact with nature, however, is likely to be intrinsically pleasurable, as is the sense of achievement in reaching the summit. Once again the Sensual Awareness Inventory will provide information on the sensations and activities that are likely to meet this objective.

Ambiguity of the Goal

As discussed later in the taxonomy of nature-based assignments, assignments may be offered with specific or ambiguous instructions. But regardless of how the instructions are phrased, it is considered appropriate to maintain some ambiguity about the true objective of the task. If it is specified, the client may experience a sense of failure if the experience does not live up to what the client perceives are the expectations of the therapist. Conversely, if the assignment goal is not specified, it allows the client greater potential to discover her or his own experiences and own learnings.

It should be kept in mind that the client's discovery from a nature-based assignment may not be what the therapist had in mind in designing the assignment. If the client's discovery is relevant to the therapeutic goal and a step in his or her own process of discovery, then this outcome ought to be ratified.

Ratify the Experience

Nature-based assignments tend to be self-ratifying. Because the natural context is as solid as a tree or a waterfall, it can automatically ratify the client's experience. Any time that natural experience is re-created, it is likely to reactivate the learning and the memory of the goal achievement. The therapist nonetheless may facilitate the ratification with questions such as the following: "What is it about this experience that will remind you of what you have learned?" "How can you recapture that experience to maintain your new discoveries?" "Or what is it that will serve as a reminder of what you have achieved?"

Build Future Learnings

Because nature-based assignments tend to be intrinsically rewarding, clients are frequently motivated to re-create such learning experiences to resolve future problems. It is helpful to encourage clients in this continuing direction.

A PRACTICAL TAXONOMY
FOR NATURE-BASED ASSIGNMENTS

As a therapist I find it pragmatic to look at the creation of nature-based assignments in three ways. The first is using natural objects for therapeutic assignments, the second is the creation of activities based in nature, and the third is a combination of natural objects and nature-based activities. In doing this I am not proposing that objects and activities are mutually exclusive categories, because this is not consistent with the interactional concept already proposed about a person's relationship with nature. An activity in nature is interactive, and the use of a natural object similarly has interactive qualities. To touch, to watch, to listen, to smell, means that one is in a relationship with that object. The division made here is more a pragmatic one, simply to provide a structure for the way the therapist may perceive and administer nature-based assignments.

Natural Objects

Traditional healers use natural objects, such as a tree or a thermal pool, as ritual objects for appeasing the gods, healing the body, and creating a state of well-being. Environmental psychology has shown us that looking at natural objects such as a garden from a hospital window can speed our recovery, reduce the amount of medication we require, and bring about a more rapid discharge from the hospital. The function of natural objects in nature-based assignments is to similarly bring about therapeutic benefit.

Natural objects are defined as a part of the natural ecology rather than a human-constructed object such as a sculpture, a religious icon, or a mechanical object. Natural objects, as used in nature-based assignments, may be simple, such as a bird's nest, a leaf, or a rock. Alternatively, a natural object may also be a more expansive complex of multiple sensual stimuli, such as a seascape or a mountain panorama.

Natural objects can be used in three different ways (see Figure 7.1). First, an object may be *given* to the client during the therapy session or to take home

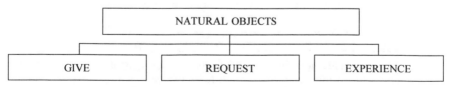

Figure 7.1 Using natural objects.

between sessions. To this end, I have several such objects in my consulting rooms: a delicate bird's nest; a hard, angular crystal; a pair of united, distorted oyster shells; a very red, fragile starfish.

Second, natural objects may be *requested.* A client may be asked to bring to the next appointment a shell from the beach, a flower from the garden, something from a forest, or a "natural object that has special meaning for you." To obtain a requested object, a client must engage in an experience with nature.

Third, a client may be directed to *experience* a natural object, such as a tree, a moon rise, a bird in flight, or beach sand on bare feet. Such assignments create a potential therapeutic opportunity by exposing the client to the object and the milieu in which that object is located.

Nature-Based Activities

Traditional healers assigned nature-based activities by sending patients to climb a mountain in search of a particular spirit place, to make sacrifices by a thermal pool, or to ritually bathe in a certain river.

A nature-based activity is a therapeutic task with certain unique characteristics. First, it is set in a natural context. As such, it exposes a person to the surrounding ecology and the variety of sensual stimuli in that milieu. Second, it involves the process of being or doing. The client is an active agent in a process that should be both rewarding and empowering. Third, a nature-based activity is one that will involve the client in an interaction or relationship with nature. A prescribed nature-based activity may thus be as simple as sitting and looking at the early morning dew on a spider's web, or it may be a multilevel task involving a variety of activities such as those discussed in Chapter 9.

As illustrated in Figure 7.2, the prescribed activity may be either specific or ambiguous. A specific task, for example, may be to sit under a certain tree and engage in sensate focusing using a particular sense modality. A more

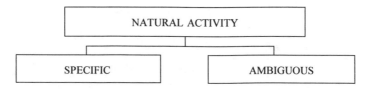

Figure 7.2   Using nature-based objects.

ambiguous suggestion would be to walk through a forest and simply "experience." Specifically, a client may be asked to take a hike to a certain area and focus on a certain response. More ambiguously, a client may be asked to go camping in a nonspecified forested area and wonder what he or she can discover. Ambiguous activities thus cast a much wider net and allow for greater client interpretation. They can subsequently be followed up by the therapist and used in guiding the client toward the specified goal.

Natural Objects and Activities

Nature-based assignments may also combine both objects and activity in strategic therapeutic tasks. A diagram for the use of such combined assignments is presented in Figure 7.3. For example, a natural object such as a seashell may be given to a client with the specifically required activity of returning it to a certain beach. Again the function of such an assignment is to facilitate the client's movement into nature, exposure to different sensual stimuli, and involvement in an interactive process with nature that will help facilitate his or her desired affective state.

As another illustration of the use of objects and activities, a client may be given an ambiguous activity such as taking a walk in an unspecified woodland area. The ambiguity can be extended with a suggestion along the following lines: "In that context you may find some naturally occurring object that has a relationship to what you are wanting to achieve here in therapy." In discovering an object and/or bringing it to the next therapy session, the client has exposed her- or himself to a therapeutically natural environment, undergone a process of searching to discover an object associated with problem resolution, and ratified that process with the particular object.

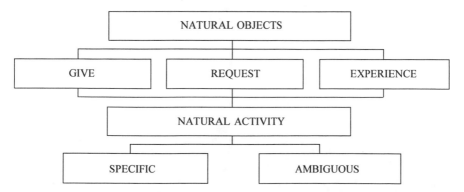

Figure 7.3   Using natural objects and activities.

Responses to the first five categories on the Sensual Awareness Inventory (Sight, Sound, Smell, Taste, and Touch) may provide client-preferred natural objects that can be used in nature-based assignments. The sixth category (Activity) can provide direct information on desirable nature-based activities. Case examples are provided in subsequent chapters on the applications of ecopsychotherapy.

Chapter 8

NATURAL ORDEALS

Sometimes we need to go out in nature and find some difficulty and say, 'Wake up!' to our internal energy.—Sergei Ushakov (cited in McRae, 1997)

Haley, in his book *Ordeal Therapy,* includes a brief four-page chapter titled "Using the Great Outdoors" (1984, pp. 121–124). In that chapter he, Milton H. Erickson, and John Weakland discuss two cases in which Erickson used natural ordeals. Apart from these brief examples, the idea of using the great outdoors as a nature-based ordeal was not developed any further in the book. Each of the cases mentioned by Haley had two significant features. First, the activity that the client is required to perform, though potentially beneficial for the client, is seen as an ordeal, as a difficult task. This differentiates natural ordeals from nature-based assignments, for in the latter the interaction with nature is seen as intrinsically rewarding.

Second, in Erickson's use of the great outdoors, it is the environment in which the activity is performed, perhaps as much as or more than the activity itself, that creates the opportunities for new experiences, new discoveries, and new learnings.

Ordeal therapy is described by Haley as both a strategic intervention and a theory of change. The basic premise of this approach is that if the therapist can make a problem behavior more difficult to maintain than to relinquish, the behavior is likely to be relinquished. In outlining the characteristics of the ordeal technique, Haley says, "It should not harm a person or anyone else" (1984, p. 7). He later develops this concept from not being harmful into the more positive idea of actually being good for the person. He says, "The ordeal must be severe enough to overcome the symptom, it must be good for the person so that he benefits by doing it, it must be something he can do and will accept in terms of its propriety, and the action must be clear and not ambiguous" (1984, p. 15). Using nature-based ordeals is a way of helping to ensure that the client is able to benefit in a positive manner from the therapeutic task.

Haley defines four types of ordeals. First, there is the straightforward task in which the client is required to perform a specific ordeal each time a problem occurs. Second, there may be paradoxical ordeals in which the client is specifically encouraged to have the problem he or she no longer desires. Third, it is possible for the therapist to become the ordeal such as when using confrontational techniques. Finally, ordeals may involve two or more persons (for example, with couples, in parent-child relationships, or in family structures).

There are several potential contexts in which an ordeal may be presented. If an ordeal is required to be undertaken indoors, such as at home or at work, the emphasis tends to be solely on the task accomplishment rather than on any additional learning from the environment (Burns, 1997). Here the task may be for an insomniac to polish the floor if he is still awake 20 minutes after going to bed. Such an indoor task may be appropriate because it may not be desirable for a person to participate in an outdoor activity during the night.

If the therapist chooses to offer the ordeal in the outdoors, there are two broad areas: a human-constructed environment and a natural environment. When the natural environment is used as the context, it not only allows for task accomplishment but also creates opportunities for new experiences that may, in turn, stimulate new healthy activities for the client and provide positive alternatives to the problem.

An overweight 50-year-old client requested assistance in losing weight. She still lived at home with her mother, who did most of the cooking. Her problems were snacking between meals, eating whatever her mother put on the plate, and failing to exercise adequately. She had recently bought an exercise bike at a department store sale, but she had made only one or two halfhearted attempts to use it and had rapidly lost motivation. She was assigned the task of keeping a record of everything she ate, which, in itself, is a task-oriented ordeal in an indoor context. She was required to note every time she ate between meals, and each time she did she was to take a brisk 20-minute walk alongside the river that was only a few minutes from her home. She immediately replied, "Can't I use my exercise bike?" My response was "No." When she insisted I conceded, "Only every second day, and then you can choose whether you use the bike for twenty minutes or walk along the river for twenty minutes."

My rationale for insisting that she walk along the river at least every second day was that, first, her previous attempts to use the bike had already failed. Second, walking created a different contextual environment. She was being removed from the context in which her eating problems were occurring. She would be experiencing new sensations that were likely to shift her focus from her problems onto the external stimuli of the river, the trees, and the birds. Third, the natural ordeal would provide physical exercise almost incidental to the pleasure that she gained from the milieu. This would help enhance her motivation to modify her eating patterns and increase her exercise.

Let me offer another case to help illustrate the features and steps for natural ordeals. Anita was a 19-year-old secretarial student who, in her penultimate year of secondary school, had developed the problem of nocturnal bruxism. The problem arose as she was approaching her end-of-the-year examinations and was feeling stressed. Her orthodontist had prescribed an oral splint to wear at night, but she found this uncomfortable and said that it made her more aware of sensations of mandibular joint tension that were not only present at night but also becoming more apparent during the day. As a result, she often chose not to use the splint and was finding that her symptoms were becoming worse. She was a fairly shy, retiring, and easily embarrassed young woman. She still lived with her parents, had a small circle of female friends, and spent much of her time in solitary pursuits such as horse riding.

She came from a family in which she was the last of three daughters. Her two older siblings had degrees in engineering. Anita felt that she was a disappointment to the family because she had not gained admission to a university and was not able to live up to the high example set by her sisters. Despite the fact that she was completing a secretarial course, she was unhappy with the path she was following, saying that she didn't want to be "locked in an office job." Over the weekends she worked part time doing market surveys via the telephone.

She had a history of asthma, but otherwise she was in good health and did not show any symptoms to merit a clinical diagnosis of depression or anxiety.

In addition to the orthodontic splint, she had tried yoga to help alleviate her bruxism and mandibular joint tension. For a couple of days after each weekly class, she noticed a reduction in her symptoms. She also had a course of hypnotherapy that initially helped alleviate her symptoms, but the symptoms began to reemerge with nocturnal grinding and mandibular joint tension occurring particularly in the morning. The tension increased to the point that she started to experience temporal and frontal headaches.

A detailed exploration of her symptoms revealed that if she awakened during the night and told herself not to grind her teeth for the rest of the night, she didn't. The same self-instruction didn't appear to work if she did it when she first went to bed. She usually went to bed about midnight and spent up to an hour reading before she fell asleep. She would arise at about 9 a.m.

In assessing factors that may have been relevant to setting a natural ordeal, I learned that she lived on a few acres in an outer suburban area where she was able to keep her horse. A forested block of land adjoined her family's property, and it was determined that this was a safe environment where she could go walking. Given the failure of other techniques and the fact that the problem was occurring during the night when she was asleep, we were faced with a behavior that was both difficult and resilient to conscious efforts at modification.

A natural ordeal was considered for several reasons. First, Anita already had established an ability to control the problem. If she awakened during the night, she was able to tell herself not to grind her teeth, and she maintained this commitment through the rest of the night. Second, it seemed appropriate to tap into this resource more regularly and more consciously. Third, an ordeal was seen as an appropriate strategy to make compliance with the therapeutic task less difficult than carrying out the ordeal. Finally, a nature-based ordeal was chosen because it was likely to offer the client several beneficial experiences. For example, it was likely to be relaxing, which in itself would be beneficial toward the client's therapeutic goal of being free of the bruxism. It was likely to offer pleasurable stimuli that would shift her attention away from her symptoms. If administered in the morning, it was also likely to counter the early morning mandibular joint tension that extended into her day.

She was therefore directed to set her alarm for 45 minutes after she had put her book down at night. When she awakened she was to tell herself, in the words she had previously found successful, "I won't grind my teeth for the rest of the night." Having done that, she was then to reset the alarm for 7:30 a.m. If, when she awakened at that time, she could feel that she had been grinding her teeth, she was to immediately arise, get dressed, and take a 30-minute walk through the neighboring forest area. If she felt relaxed in her jaws and had not been grinding her teeth, she was free to return to sleep if she wanted and arise at her usual time around 9 a.m.

She walked out of the consulting room with a smile on her face, saying, "This will definitely work." And for a week it did. She then started to omit setting her alarm and experienced a regression. It was insisted that she maintain the nature-based ordeal. When she did she again resumed control of the bruxism. This case illustrates the features of natural ordeals detailed subsequently.

FEATURES OF NATURAL ORDEALS

Natural Ordeals Are a Form of Indirection

Although the task itself may be offered in a firm and directive manner, the client is not being directly told to cease engaging in a particular behavior. Usually, by the time a client seeks therapy, such direct suggestions about the resolution of the problem have already failed. A client has most likely already been told: "You have to get rid of your drug habit," "You should stop overeating," "Stop feeling anxious," or "Make yourself relax." Anita had been told by her dentist, orthodontist, and parents how bad her bruxism was and that she ought to stop. That approach hadn't worked. Ordeals, though directive, are not direct suggestions.

Natural Ordeals Allow the Unwanted Behavior, Cognition, or Affect to Continue

Clients are not directly asked to give up a behavior that may be familiar, secure, or serving a particular function. They are permitted to engage in that behavior but, at the same time, required to experience a consequence contingent on that engagement. Anita was not told to stop grinding her teeth; rather, she was asked to go for an early morning walk.

Natural Ordeals Deal With Resistance to Change

Although a person may want to change a behavior, there is often some resistance to altering long-established patterns. Were this not so, the person would have already changed the behavior long before seeking therapeutic assistance. By allowing the problem to continue, natural ordeals bypass resistance to change.

Natural Ordeals Make the Unwanted Behavior, Cognition, or Affect More Difficult to Maintain

If the consequences or the complexity associated with a problem are increased, the problem becomes more difficult to retain. I became aware of this some 25 years ago while working for the Prison's Department. An inmate was referred with a problem of excessive micturition. He was urinating, according to the charts he kept, between 20 and 40 times per day. Average micturition rates are between about 5 and 6 times during the day and once or twice during the night. I worked with a behavior therapy approach (Yates, 1970) that brought no modification to his micturition rate.

After several weeks his charts showed a marked and unexpected drop from his excessive rate of micturition to a near-normal level. When I enquired what had happened during the intervening week, he told me that he had been shifted from his clerical duties in the prison to work in the garden. Puzzled by how this may have made the difference, I inquired what effect it had had on his behavior. He said that because he was working in the garden his hands got dirty. He therefore had to wash his hands before going to the urinal and to wash his hands again afterward. The increased complexity of the behavior had added sufficient difficulty to modify the rates of micturition. It alerted me to how a simple increment of complexity can bring about significant change.

Natural Ordeals Make the Desired Behavior, Cognition, or Affect Easier to Achieve

In attempting to rid herself of her bruxism, Anita felt she had come to a dead-end in a maze. All previous attempts had failed, so she felt powerless to stop grinding her teeth. Suppressing the symptom seemed impossible, but it was within her capabilities, and relatively easier, to set her alarm at night and take an early-morning walk. Natural ordeals thus make it easier to achieve the goal than to stop the symptom.

Natural Ordeals Create a Double Bind

Natural ordeals require that a person either give up the behavior or comply with the ordeal. Either course of action is goal directed toward the client's therapeutic objective.

Douglas was a fairly high-flying corporate lawyer. He worked long hours, had no recreational pursuits, and complained that he felt guilty about not giving time to his family, particularly his only son. His reason for presenting was that he suffered with recurrent frontalis tension headaches. Given the difficulty that he had in taking time out from either his work or family responsibilities, he was prescribed a natural ordeal in the nature of a double bind. The ordeal was that if he didn't take 20 minutes each day to practice his relaxation exercises, he was to take his son for a 2-hour walk through the woods on the weekend. He came to the next session, having failed to comply with the ordeal, saying that he hated walking and had decided not to do so. He had practiced relaxing with the exception of a day on which he was "too busy." Instead, he did something rather interesting. He bought his son a canoe, and they spent 2 hours canoeing together on a local river to comply with the prescribed natural ordeal.

Natural Ordeals Tend to Elicit Compliance

As in the case just described, if the compliance is not with the therapeutic suggestion itself, then it can be with the principles of the suggestion. Because there is likely to be pleasure in the relationship with nature, such tasks enhance motivation and compliance.

Natural Ordeals Tend to Create New Natural Learning Experiences

I have already explored how nature provides both a healing and a learning environment. Setting ordeals in this context creates new experiences for the client and new opportunities for learning and discovery.

Natural Ordeals Elicit Therapeutic Change

The task, within itself, requires a change in the ways in which a person is thinking, feeling, and acting. Creating a new environmental experience is likely to facilitate change.

Natural Ordeals Encourage New Choices

Choices may be in terms of a bind: One has the choice of relinquishing the problem or engaging in the consequences. As Douglas illustrated, one also has a choice to do something completely different, to create one's own ordeal.

Natural Ordeals Shift an Egocentric Focus to an Ecocentric Focus

On seeking treatment, the overweight 50-year-old woman described earlier was egocentrically focused on her obesity. Anita had become constantly aware of the tension in her jaws and of her powerlessness in terms of controlling her bruxism. Douglas, torn in a conflict between responsibilities to work and family, was failing to adequately fulfill either while his attention was directed toward the intensity of his headaches.

The natural ordeals of exercising beside the river, taking an early-morning walk, and canoeing created a more eternal focus on the pleasurable stimuli of a natural ecology.

Natural Ordeals Give the Control and Power to the Client

Because the client has a choice, the client also has control. Douglas took control of his situation by choosing to purchase a canoe and to begin regular outings with his son. He started to have fun, his relationship with his son improved, and he was relaxing, naturally.

Natural Ordeals Allow for Self-Generalization

Given the fact that natural ordeals are intrinsically rewarding and pleasurable, the client is likely to self-initiate continuing therapeutically oriented activities. The self-generalization effects of psychotherapeutic strategies are discussed further in Chapter 10.

Natural Ordeals Are Fun

Natural ordeals go beyond creating something that is good for the client; they tend to be intrinsically fun. They are fun in their prescription. Clients will often laugh and have a good chuckle about the prescribed task as they leave the consulting room. Engaging in the task is also fun because it tends to be a pleasurable experience simply to be in a natural environment.

STEPS FOR PRESCRIBING A NATURAL ORDEAL

Initially, it is important to establish a precise definition of the unwanted behavior, affect, or cognition. Defining the problem will required detailed examination of the context in which it occurs, the frequency of its occurrence, and the duration of each episode. A clear assessment of these variables will provide a baseline on which to measure the client's progress and will also give important clues as to the type of natural ordeal to be prescribed (Burns, 1997).

Step 1: Create a practical natural ordeal. For a behavior of excessive micturition with a rate of 20 to 40 times per day, one would not want to establish an ordeal lasting 30 minutes each time. The precise definition of the problem allows for establishment of a practical ordeal.

Step 2: Find a workable natural ordeal. The Sensual Awareness Inventory can provide information about a context that is likely to provide a client with pleasurable experiences. It may be appropriate to use a context that already provides pleasurable experiences or to assist the client to discover a milieu of potentially new sensations. The context needs to be accessible as frequently as the client is required to engage in the ordeal.

Step 3: Elicit client commitment. In offering the ordeal, it is essential to elicit the client's commitment to carry out the task. Here it is useful to ask questions such as "Are you willing to do anything to overcome this problem?" and thus establish a commitment before offering the task.

Step 4: Build anticipation. This may be done with a comment such as "I have something in mind that may help, but I don't know whether it is going to be too difficult for you." Such statements often have a client begging to know what the assigned task will be.

Step 5: Offer the ordeal with rationale. The ordeal needs to be presented in a manner that is plausible to the client. More details of this are given in subsequent chapters dealing with the 3 R's of ecotherapy.

Step 6: Offer the ordeal without question. It is important that the natural ordeal be offered in both a firm and affirmative way that acknowledges the client's commitment and implies compliance.

Step 7: Ratify the commitment. Here the therapist should confirm the client's commitment and the necessity of complying with the ordeal precisely as directed.

Step 8: Maintain the ordeal to success. Insist that the natural ordeal is a commitment to resolution and should therefore be continued until the goal has been achieved.

Step 9: Give the power to the client. Because changes often occur rapidly with natural ordeals, clients may tend to doubt their own ability to have achieved the change, particularly if the problem has been longstanding. The therapist ought to attribute the ability to the client and assist clients in exploring how they can use their discoveries to maintain their progress into the future.

Step 10: Ratify the problem resolution. The nature and types of ratification in ecotherapy are discussed further in Chapter 10.

Chapter 9

EXPERIENTIAL METAPHORS

Here in the peace and solitude of the mountain peaks, here where meditation leads me into a state of inner balance as I climb, I too am overcome with feelings of self-understanding, of belonging to the world, and of being alone with the cosmos.—Reinhold Messner, 1980

A client of mine, Wayne, taught me much about the development of experiential metaphors. It is now some 12 years since he first sought therapy. Three years prior to that, he was a 20-year-old with the whole world in front of him. He possessed a vital love of life. His father had been a league soccer player, and Wayne was proudly stepping into his father's shoes. He was training with a league club, and his sporting ambitions were high. He played squash, had accumulated many trophies, and was proud of his athletic prowess.

The other pride of his life was his uniform. He was a police officer devoted to the force and enthusiastic about his career. Unfortunately, it was probably his enthusiasm, concern, and public-mindedness that brought his whole world crashing around him.

One night as he and a fellow off-duty officer were returning home, they noticed two youths breaking into a gas station. They arrested one, but the second fled. After searching for a while and being unable to find this second individual, they placed the arrested youth in the front passenger seat of their private car. The other police officer drove, and Wayne sat in the back seat to watch over the apprehended youth. On the way to the police station, the youth attacked the driver, grabbed the steering wheel, and spun the car off the road, forcing it to collide with a steel lamppost. The car struck the post on the side on which Wayne was sitting. He sustained multiple head and body injuries. He was subsequently told that, on four different occasions during his transfer and admission to the hospital, he had died only to be resuscitated by the skills of the paramedic and hospital staff.

His hospital discharge file confirmed that he had suffered fractures to the left temporal skull and the right tympanic plate. He had a rotational brain stem injury, as well as right seventh nerve palsy and bilateral sixth nerve palsy. He also suffered a mild left hemiplegia. As he began to regain his ability to speak, it became evident that he was dysarthric. In addition, he had sustained knee and leg fractures. He was hospitalized for a period of 2 months, and after discharge he received neurological and orthopedic treatment as well as physiotherapy and speech therapy.

Some 20 months after the accident, his neurosurgeon recommended that he be seen by a psychologist, but a referral was not made for another 18 months. In the meantime he did consult a psychiatrist, complaining of problems in the area of sexual performance. The psychiatrist reported, "Since his accident, Wayne has had to accept a totally different lifestyle. He was previously a confident, extroverted and successful soccer and squash player, but he now has to be a spectator at sporting events. Before the accident he was giving his wife squash lessons. Now he suffers the ignominy of being beaten by her at squash.

"As a result of this change, Wayne has undergone gross loss of self-esteem, and he is in a state of chronic anxiety and depression. His seniors in the police force have not been able to find a niche in which he can play a useful role. Instead, he is given menial tasks that serve no purpose other than keeping him out of their hair. He feels, justifiably it seems, that he is an embarrassment to the force.

"Wayne is married and has been experiencing difficulties in his sexual relationship with his wife."

The psychiatrist concluded, "Because of the cosmetic and athletic disabilities that Wayne has suffered since the accident, I think it is likely that he will be struggling with problems of low self-esteem, depression, and anxiety for the rest of his life."

His prophecy remained valid when I saw Wayne a year later. He was still depressed, tearful, and uncertain. He was suffering with insomnia, felt a loss of control over his emotions, and had not regained full physical control. The mild hemiplegia remained present, as did the speech impediment. He felt embarrassed by these facts but more so by the fact that he suffered with encopresis and could not leave home for a short walk because of the fear related to his lack of bowel control. He complained that he had lost everything he ever wanted in life and was actively suicidal.

He wrote to me during the course of therapy, saying, "George, I really am in a bad way. I even had the thought of accelerating my car while stopped at a railway crossing today. Everyone keeps telling me that things will turn out fine in the end; I want to believe this, but everyone ain't me and everyone isn't going through what I'm going through right now."

Worrisome, ruminative thoughts kept him awake as he struggled through problem-focused nights. On a number of occasions I received letters that started "Good morning George." One such letter said, "It's now 3:50 a.m. Friday morning. I can't sleep, I'm upset, I'm always thinking, my mind won't wind down and let me relax even for a minute. I even went out and got drunk Wednesday night, but do you think that helped? No way."

In attempts to formulate Wayne's therapeutic plan, the complexity of this multiproblem case became apparent. First, Wayne had suffered severe physical and head injuries that were still significantly impairing his abilities. He was suffering with pain. In addition, being a person oriented toward physical activities, he had lost significant past resources for dealing with his feelings of frustration and anxiety.

Second, there were issues of litigation involved. Part of the reason for Wayne's referral to me had been the request for neuropsychological assessment. Despite the severity of his injuries, there was no evidence of significant organic deterioration in his higher cognitive functioning, although he did experience some difficulties with visual motor skills, visual encoding, and visual reproduction. These difficulties may, in part, have been related to the fact that the sixth nerve palsy in his right eye had caused gross diplopia, for which he had received some corrective surgery.

Third, he suffered with symptoms of a posttraumatic stress disorder and had significant feelings of grief about the loss of his career, the loss of his sporting ambitions, and a diminution of his libido. Consequently he also feared that he might lose his wife.

He was experiencing overwhelming feelings of anger and was at a critical point of having to decide about his career. He was no longer able to fulfill the physical duties of a police officer. He felt he was being pushed from menial task to menial task just to keep him in a job. The other alternative offered to him was to retire on a disability pension, which meant he would be relinquishing his lifelong ambition of being a police officer.

In another "good morning" letter he wrote, "It is going on 1:30 am. I have thought long and hard about what we talked about this morning: about my future, the fucking police force and the fact about making a decision, the all important decision about whether to take a gamble with everything at stake and get out or hang in there. I even tossed a coin to make the decision for me, but when the coin fell the wrong way, I made another big decision. I tried for best out of three and when I lost again, I came to the decision that tossing coins was no way to sort out your future."

It was apparent that the therapeutic program needed to deal with all of these factors. Initially we established nonsuicide contracts, because his state of depression and the nature of his ideation were indicative of a serious suicidal risk. These were followed through strictly and involved frequent phone contact with Wayne between consultations.

Hypnotherapy was introduced as a basis to help deal with the post-traumatic stress symptoms, to teach him skills in relaxing, and to help with his insomnia. He was offered counseling around the issues of his decision about his career, his adaptation to his physical disabilities, and his altered lifestyle.

The question also arose as to whether ecotherapy would be a helpful part of the overall therapeutic plan. It was considered that such therapy could be of benefit in assisting him to modify his undesirable affect, facilitate pain management, alter his worrisome thought processes, help promote his healing, and offer him options for discovering new directions or a new purpose in life. The strategies chosen included sensate focusing, nature-based assignments, natural metaphors, and experiential metaphors.

SENSATE FOCUSING

Because swimming was part of his rehabilitation program, he was offered sensate focusing tasks during this activity. He was invited to be aware of the sensation of the water on his skin and to note the tactile experiences. It was hoped that this focus on such tactile awareness would redirect his attention from his inner pain sensations. He was then asked to focus on the sounds he could hear through the water as a means of shifting away from the constant noise of the ruminative voices within his own head. He was further requested to be aware of the reflections and the light, shapes, and dancing motions of the visual experiences through the water.

NATURE-BASED ASSIGNMENTS

Nature-based assignments included the swimming tasks as well as walking and later jogging in nature settings such as local parks. Because of his bowel problems, we built in the safeguard of ensuring that the routes followed paths close to appropriately spaced public restrooms.

NATURAL METAPHORS

The rationale for using natural metaphors with Wayne was based on his specified therapeutic goals of wanting to be happy and wanting to sleep better. It seemed that use of nature-based metaphors could help Wayne relax, stimulate his level of arousal (as a means of overcoming depression), facilitate sleep, and promote healing.

Natural metaphors were developed to this end. The choice of metaphors was determined by several factors. First, it was considered that metaphors with a natural context would be conducive to achieving all of the desired goals.

Second, it was decided to use metaphors based on physical activity, because Wayne had demonstrated past physical prowess as well as the ability to learn and develop skills in such areas. His focus at the time was on physical issues because of the injuries that he had sustained in the accident, and he was faced with a physical challenge.

On several occasions he had said that he wanted to return to playing soccer and also that he wanted to be a marathon runner. My doubts about his abilities to achieve these goals are recorded in my case notes. On one occasion when I was going to be away from the practice for several weeks, he saw my associate. I left her some notes about Wayne's case, including a comment referring to his sporting ambitions: "Wayne still has unrealistic goals in this area." As it turned out, he was to teach me a lesson about underestimating a client's potential.

Third, it seemed that the metaphors should include a sudden, serious, un-expected, and unplanned problem to parallel Wayne's situation. Fourth, they should present a challenge to be overcome, even though it at first might seem impossible. There should also be a satisfactory outcome to the challenge, al-though it may not be the originally desired outcome. Finally, the challenge ought to provide the opportunity for new learnings, new discoveries, new skills, and new adaptive strategies for the future.

The metaphors, told within and outside of hypnosis, were based around some of my own recent (at that time) experiences in the Himalayas. Metaphors were offered over several sessions, often in the embedded metaphor model (Lankton & Lankton, 1983).

EXPERIENTIAL METAPHORS

In relating metaphors to Wayne based on my own experiences, I became aware of how powerful it had been to have the actual in vivo experience. Prior to traveling to the Himalayas, I had been going through a very difficult period in my own life, and it seemed that the mountain experience had replicated many of the issues involved in my day-to-day life. I had started out on my adult journey with plans and ambitions. Suddenly I had experienced separation, grief, depression, and loss. I was faced with a situation in which the old plans were no longer valid, one in which I needed to cope in a new situation on my own. The experience had been a metaphor of what was happening in my life at that time. And the processes that led to healing gains seemed to follow certain steps.

First, there was an *intent*. My goal had been to get away from some of the current experiences in my life, to have a holiday and seek new experiences. Second, there was a *journey*: a journey on foot in a new part of the world, a journey in a new natural context. There was a commitment of *time* allocated to the journey, to experiencing what that journey brought with it. The process also involved forming a new *relationship* with that particular natural environment. It meant learning the pattern of the weather, the terrain of the country. It meant learning to adjust my body to the conditions, my clothing to the elements, my gait to the terrain. It meant new discoveries, especially for someone coming from a region where snow is virtually unknown. There was a new relationship offered to me in the experience of feeling the gentleness of snowflakes falling on my skin, the harshness of being alone on a snow-covered mountain, the excitement of rolling snow into snowballs and having a mock fight with gig-gling local children behind the walls of a monastery.

Finally, the learnings from that experience brought about a *change*. I rediscovered my ability to laugh. I rediscovered my ability to experience peace of mind and calmness of body. I learned that things could be different. I discovered the power within myself, and the stimulation from nature, to be able to bring about those changes. And that awareness led me to explore how the process might be used in therapy with clients.

Wayne continued to work on his fitness. He swam and cycled regularly. He went through great anxiety over the decision of whether to remain with the police force. Finally, in another "good morning" letter he wrote, "Anyway, what this letter is about is I have come to a decision. I am going to leave. I am going to take the pension and quit."

But still he could not bear to put the decision into practice. Eventually the police department's medical board decided that he was no longer fit to continue his duties as a police officer. His career had ended. Around the same time, some 4 years after the accident, the aspects of litigation were settled, and Wayne received a financial settlement. He decided to use some of the funds to make his way around the world. While his announcement that he intended to visit the Himalayas may in part have been stimulated by the natural metaphors used in therapy, it created the opportunity to set up an experiential metaphor.

STEPS INVOLVED IN EXPERIENTIAL METAPHORS

Intent

The intent or goal may be set at several different levels. First, clients may already have established goals. If, for example, a client is intending to go to the Himalayas, it may be the expressed objective to achieve some physical goal such as trekking for several days, rafting the Himalayan rivers, or climbing a mountain. It could be that the object of the adventure is to discover something about the sights, sounds, and sensual experiences of a different natural environment. There may be the intent of discovering something about a new culture or spending time meditating in a monastery. For Wayne, the natural metaphors that he had been offered in therapy seemed to have afforded him the opportunity of setting his own goal to go to the Himalayas in anticipation of achieving further steps toward his recovery and well-being.

Second, the therapist may help clients develop specific therapeutic goals. With Wayne, this was done through a series of presuppositional questions such as the following: "What are you expecting to gain from your visit to the Himalayas?" "What would you like to experience while you are away?" and "How do you think your trek is likely to be helpful for you?" Such questions assist clients in focusing their attention toward the outcome and thus help them become more goal oriented.

Third, the therapist may set the goal for the client. While there should be a clear therapeutic rationale, this may not always be made obvious to the client. In fact, providing a rationale may limit the focus of attention and, hence, the benefits that the client achieves from the task. The setting needs to be potentially therapeutic, although it may not be that the therapist can actually predict the outcome. What is more important is that the therapist is able to use the outcome in a therapeutic manner to enhance the client's ongoing progress.

The Journey

The importance of a journey or pilgrimage has long been recognized by many societies. Writers, poets, philosophers, and travelers of many cultures across history have reiterated variations of the Japanese proverb that says "It is better to travel hopefully than to arrive." The well-traveled 17th-century poet Matsuo Basho said, "Every day is a journey, and the journey itself is home."

This sentiment is recognized by many who make their journey through the world, their pilgrimages through life. For Harvey (1983), a journey into Ladakh led him on a pilgrimage into his senses, a connectedness with nature, and a discovery of new inner reflections. In a land where his senses were heightened by the stimulation of nature around him, he described how "each gorge I walk through is so full of light that I wonder how the rocks sustain such an intensity of fire. A quiet breeze moves the leaves from green to gold. On the hills that surround me, snow has fallen, and it seems so good, that coldness, a reminder of the huge moon last night, flakes of moon on high hills. And something in this light too has been through an experience, 'moon' and 'cold': I have never seen such sunlight so sharp, so precisely delicate, as this. There are so many blues in this one cloudless blue, and each invokes a different memory" (pp. 65–66).

Gold (1988) notes that, since time immemorial, pilgrims have sought to follow various paths to the source of their beings. "Some," he said, "would travel long distances, often enduring severe physical hardships in the service of the spirit" (p. 13). He described Tibetan pilgrims making the journey to visit their beloved spiritual leader, the Dalai Lama. "Faith, perseverance, and devotion have led the people on a trek across dangerous, snow-packed mountain passes. An arduous journey this, and for one sublime purpose: to acquire a kind of energy and inner glow that burns well beyond that of the sun and smoky hearths back home" (pp. 17–18).

In many ways the journey through nature parallels our trek through life and can thus serve as a metaphor about life. Life is, itself, a journey. Being in a different context requires adaptivity. New challenges can lead to new learnings. Gold asks, "For aren't we all pilgrims in this life? . . . Wanderers in a wondrous world, without and within" (1988, p. 14).

Many poets and authors thus suggest that it is the experience of the journey, rather than the fact of arrival, that is important. Indeed, we have all learned that experience is one of the best teachers. Experiences can facilitate new learnings, broaden our understanding, and deepen our knowledge. The more we experience, the more we live and the richer becomes life's journey.

The therapist, in establishing an experiential metaphor, may thus assist a client in planning a journey that takes the client into natural situations in which her or his senses may be stimulated and new experiences elicited. The therapist may also start to assist in planning the wandering within, the journey of discovery, and the steps toward solution.

Wayne began to plan his journey with me. We began to talk about areas he could visit, routes he could take, scenery to be discovered. His anticipation began to heighten, his affect began to lift, and he was starting to look forward to new goals and new objectives. From being depressed and suicidal he set his sights on the very top of the world. His trek was to take him to Everest Base Camp.

Time

Time to experience, to sense, to perceive, is a crucial element in the formation of an experiential metaphor. Time itself is an abstract concept. Time has no power, and, despite what the old proverb may say, time does not heal. What is therapeutic and beneficial is what occurs in that time. What is healing relates more to what is done than to the passage of an abstract idea. The time allocated to an experiential metaphor may be long or may be brief. Sorrel Wilby and her husband became the first people ever to traverse the full arc of the Himalayas from west to east. Yet, despite the more than 4,000 miles they trekked, she was able to pause and speak of the experience of just one moment. "I do not know the meaning of existence; I do not know the answers; but here, here in these mountains, for just one moment there is no need to ask questions. Life is understood and that is why I return—we all return—to the abode of the snows" (1992, p. 59).

Relationship

Gold claimed that there was more to a pilgrimage than simply transporting one's body to a sacred site, a spectacular scene, or a revered teacher. He said, "A pilgrimage must also be made to one's expressive faculties, and with the powers of the imagination" (1988, p. 13). As Gold seems to imply, there is a relationship between the pilgrim and the environment of his or her pilgrimage. It would seem to be an interaction of the journeyer's receptive and expressive faculties and the land in which she or he journeys.

Aldo Leopold also captured the essential elements of time and person-nature interaction when he wrote: "To arrive too early in the marsh is an adventure in pure listening; the ear roams at will among the noises of the night, without let or hindrance from hand or eye. When you hear the mallard being audibly enthusiastic about his soup, you are free to picture a score guzzling among the duck weeds. When one widgeon squeals, you may postulate a squadron without fear of visual contradiction. And when a flock of blue bills, pitching pond-ward, tears the dark silk of heaven in one long rending nose dive, you catch your breath at the sound, but there is nothing to see except stars. This same performance, in daytime, would have to be looked at, shot at, missed, and then hurriedly fitted with an alibi" (Leopold, 1949, p. 61). In nature, we need time just to be. Within that time there is the permission to experience, to interact, to relate with nature through senses and imagery.

In encouraging therapeutic interactions with nature, it is desirable to encourage experiences such as arriving at the marsh too early, interacting with the purity of nature, and enjoying the wilderness unimpeded by the shackles of society.

Wayne was thus encouraged to relate with nature in his experiential metaphor. Rather than take buses to the significant architectural sites in the Kathmandu Valley, his assignment was to walk, to put his feet on the ground, to be in touch with nature, to take time to enjoy the vista, to experience his own adaptation of the elements.

The relationship between people and nature, between people and the universe, that was so integral to the philosophy and practice of traditional healers has also been recognized by Western scientists. It is probably inaccurate to even use the terms *people* and *universe*, because the words themselves seem to provide boundaries that limit our understanding of connectedness. Gregory Bateson, in *Mind and Nature*, talks of "the glue" that binds together "the starfishes and sea anemones and redwood forests and human committees" (1980, p. 4). He continues: "Mind became, for me, a reflection of large parts and many parts of the natural world outside the thinker" (1980, p. 5).

Bateson speaks of "the pattern which connects," referring to both a historic and current interrelatedness. From childhood we learn to look at animals and objects as autonomous entities. We are taught the name of a cow, a dog, and a tree. We learn the units of language, a noun, a verb. As our studies develop, we may move on to explore the psyche as though it were a separate entity of independent functioning. We may expand the parameters a little and look at the family unit or the social context. We are not usually taught the interrelationships, we are not encouraged to study or explore the connectedness. But, in truth, we are part of the interconnectedness of our ecology and our universe. Our minds, our emotions, our behavior are bound by the laws of the universe. We are intimately related with it. To assume anything different, to assume a higher level of intelligence that will enable us to transcend that connectedness, and to act in accord with those assumptions creates a state of dissonance.

Dissonance is a state of imbalance, and that imbalance has consequences in terms of our physical and emotional well-being. By encouraging clients to interact with nature, the therapist is facilitating a movement back into a state of consonance in which there is balance between the person and his or her natural ecology, thus facilitating maximum potential for well-being. This relationship is summed up in Bateson's words: "I surrender to the belief that my knowing is a small part of a wider integrated knowing that meets the entire biosphere or creation" (1980, p. 98).

It was in coming to understand the uniqueness of the Himalayan environment, and his interrelationship with it, that Wayne came to know things about himself. He was able to shift significantly from an inner focus on his symptoms to external stimuli that were able to provide him with new sensations, new stimulations, and new learnings.

When Wayne faced the physical challenge of his trek and the demands of surviving in a new environment, there no longer seemed room for the experiences of grief over the loss of his sport, his career, and his libido. On his return he reported that he had been free of suicidal ideation while away. Similarly, his anger had dissipated. Indeed, Wayne and I were able to agree that, given his progress, there was no need for any further consultations. He has, however, maintained contact over the last 12 years by occasionally visiting my office or by providing me with an update on his life in his annual Christmas cards.

Change

Aldous Huxley said, "Experience is not what happens to a man; it is what a man does with what happens to him." Converting a happening or an event into an experience that has immediate and ongoing benefits for a client is the very process of therapeutic change. An experiential metaphor is what Huxley would describe as "what happens." Its design is to establish a task, an event, or a series of events that will enable a client time to journey into an interactive process with nature that, it is hoped, will create new experiences of a metaphoric nature. The next step is to assist the client to process these experiences in ways that will provide ongoing adaptive strategies for future health and well-being.

One way to facilitate this process is with the use of presuppositional questions. What the client is being invited to do is to decide how to make use of the experiences for the present and future. In any decision-making process, there are basically three steps people need to take: (a) decide *what* it is they want to do, (b) decide *how* this might be achieved, and (c) decide *when* to put it into operation. This process is true of any decision we make. A client needs to go through the same decision-making processes to take the learnings from the experiential metaphor and adapt them into ongoing coping strategies. This may be facilitated by the therapist with questions such as the following:

- What have you learned from this experience?
- What have you gained from this assignment?
- What experiences do you want to be able to replicate?
- What things have you learned about yourself that will be helpful for the future?

Assisting with the application of these issues leads to the how questions.

- How can you now start to apply these learnings?
- How can you re-create the positive experiences?
- How are you going to make these learnings beneficial for your future?

No decision is complete without making a decision as to when it will be put into practice. The best intents in the world can be lost if we fail to come up with a time commitment. It is therefore useful to ask the client:

- When can you start to make use of these new learnings?
- When will be a convenient time for you to re-create this experience?
- If this was helpful, when could you do it again?
- When will be the next opportunity to do something similarly beneficial?

Such questions are likely not only to facilitate the immediate process of change but also to assist in the ongoing search for natural experiences that facilitate the cyclic pattern illustrated in Figure 9.1.

CASE FOLLOW-UP

On Wayne's return from the Himalayas, he was asked the preceding types of questions to help ratify his progress and facilitate continued well-being. That he began to seek out his own experiential metaphors on an ongoing basis was indicated in the fact that he returned to the Himalayas for a second visit, spent 5 months traveling through Africa with his wife, and then planned a jungle trek through the island of Borneo that was unfortunately canceled because of a family commitment.

As mentioned, Wayne kept me advised of his progress by making informal visits to my office and by sending Christmas cards. His case was more formally followed up 12 years after he first attended therapy. He had still not returned to the workforce. He remained in a stable marriage and had two young children. He had, despite my earlier predictions and those of his psychiatrist, returned to playing soccer. His team was at the top of the ladder, and he acknowledged

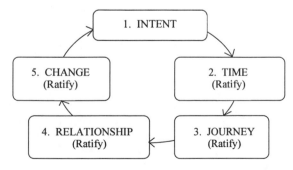

Figure 9.1 The steps in an experiential metaphor.

that, in the current season, he was playing fewer games. However, he put this down to the fact that his team was doing well and consequently attracting top-level players. He also commented that, at the age of 35, he was getting "too old" rather than attributing the situation to his still-present physical disabilities. He spent much of his time actively involved, at a social level, with the soccer club, organizing fund-raising activities such as quiz nights and raffles.

He had taken on triathlons as his summer sport, competing in gruelling events involving swimming, running, and cycling that would be off-putting to even some of the most physically able people. When I inquired about his affective state, there was no indication of significant ongoing feelings of grief, depression, or anger. He still suffered some feelings of hurt about his past losses, but he had let go of all suicidal ideation. In his own words, he was "cruising along nicely."

Chapter 10

THE THREE R'S
OF NATURE-GUIDED THERAPY

Psychology, so dedicated to awakening human consciousness,
needs to wake itself up to one of the most ancient human truths: we
cannot be studied or cured apart from the planet.—James Hillman
(1995)

Ecopsychotherapy may be used as a sole therapeutic intervention, employing any of the strategies described in the preceding chapters. Let me offer a case example. Fiona was a 52-year-old woman involved in the family business with her husband. Twelve months prior to being referred for therapy by her physician, she had been involved in a motor vehicle accident. She had been driving a large and relatively safe automobile when another vehicle failed to heed a stop sign at a major intersection and collided with the passenger side of her car. Her vehicle was pushed across the highway, luckily managing to avoid oncoming traffic.

She was fortunate not to suffer any significant physical injuries given that her car was totally demolished. Nonetheless, she went into a state of shock and experienced a sense of unreality. She became extremely fearful traveling in a car. Whether as a passenger or as a driver, she experienced palpitations, hyperventilation, and muscular tension. She was overcautious with her driving, and that in itself posed a potential danger. As her referring physician said, "She has been transformed from a relaxed, easygoing driver into a person who avoids driving at all costs. She was generally a well-balanced and able person, but the nature of the accident, the suddenness, and the impact speed have been something that she has not been able to come to terms with."

Given the fact that she had previously benefited from hypnotherapy for dental treatment, she was again introduced into hypnosis and taken on a sensual journey in imagery. She was simply invited to journey into each of her senses in turn and to experience the pleasures of the natural relaxing stimuli of each sense modality.

When Fiona came to the second consultation 1 week later, she was feeling "fantastic," "as though a fog or cloud had cleared" from her mind. She had taken herself out driving. While she previously had gone to all lengths to avoid the intersection where the motor vehicle accident had occurred, she now drove through the intersection without undue apprehension. She even traveled as a passenger in a car with a relative stranger as the driver. She said that the beneficial effects had spilled over into other areas of life in that she was feeling more optimistic and more positive in regard to her home life and her hobbies. In fact, she reported not having felt so good for many years. In a follow-up session 1 month later, she was maintaining her progress.

In most therapeutic situations, however, the problems are not as clear cut and the outcome not as responsive to a simple, single intervention. It may be that several ecotherapeutic strategies need to be employed or that ecotherapy needs to be combined with other psychotherapeutic interventions. Examples are provided in the subsequent chapters addressing the clinical applications of ecotherapy.

In the case of Fiona, ecotherapy was combined with hypnotherapy. It can equally well be incorporated into relaxation or meditation-based therapies to help facilitate sensate focusing at an imagery level. Ecotherapy is very closely aligned to strategic therapy and can readily be integrated into that model. Perhaps the main difference between strategic therapy and ecotherapy is that ecotherapy considers not just the strategy but the environment in which the strategic exercise takes place to be a potent element in the healing or change process. Because the orientation of ecotherapy is also toward the solution or therapeutic outcome, it is easily adapted into a solution-oriented model. As we shall see in Chapter 13, it can be incorporated into marital, family, or relationship counseling. Ecotherapeutic strategies fit comfortably with transactional analysis and inner child work as a result of the emphasis on pleasure and enjoyment. Developing effective cognitive, emotional, and behavioral change also means that ecotherapy is adaptable to cognitive-behavioral programs.

KEEPING IT SIMPLE

The basic premise behind ecotherapy is simple: Contact with the natural environment can and does bring about change at cognitive, behavioral, affective, and physical levels. Simple exposure to natural stimuli can result in rapid change. When possible, it is considered preferable to keep therapy at this simple level, as illustrated with the case of Fiona described earlier. It may, for example, be appropriate to assign a stressed businessperson the task of pulling over in his or her car to take a 10-minute walk around a park on the way home. It may not always be that such simple interventions work, and the complexity of the ecotherapeutic strategies will need to match the complexity of the client and the presenting problem. Therapists are encouraged to initially work with simple strategies such as sensate focusing and to observe the effects of these strategies on clients.

MATCHING THE TASK TO THE CHALLENGE

Ecotherapeutic applications are likely to be more effective when they are (a) relevant to the problem and (b) matched to the client, the client's resources, and the desired outcome.

In Fiona's case, the problem was that she was experiencing anxiety while traveling in a car and was engaging in a variety of behaviors to avoid riding in motor vehicles. She went out of her way to avoid the intersection where the accident had occurred and reduced both her business and pleasure travels to an absolute minimum. As shown previously, exposure to natural settings can produce a significant and immediate reduction in anxiety levels.

Fiona lived in a hilly outer suburban area known for its trees, wildflowers, and national parks. It was assumed that, by choosing to live in such an area, she already had a sense of affinity with nature and that an approach that put her in touch with her senses would be likely to match experiences familiar to her. This approach also allowed Fiona to tap into her own resources. Her expressed therapeutic outcome was to be without feelings of panic, without anticipatory fear, and without avoidance behaviors. Facilitating her awareness of natural, pleasurable stimuli created experiences consistent with the desired therapeutic outcome.

Fiona was not given the Sensual Awareness Inventory but may well have been offered the instrument on her second therapeutic session had she not made such a pleasing initial response. The Sensual Awareness Inventory allows the clinician the opportunity to look more specifically for ways of matching with the client, the client's resources, and the desired outcome.

THE THREE R'S OF ECOTHERAPY

The various interventions in ecotherapy explored in the preceding chapters are part of an overall framework I refer to as the three R's of therapy: rationale, restructuring, and ratification. Figure 10.1 provides a framework.

Rationale

The rationale is offered to elicit client involvement and motivation. It may be presented in several forms.

RATIONALE:

- no rationale
- therapeutic rationale
- client-acceptable rationale
- double-bind rationale

RESTRUCTURING:

- therapist-initiated directives
- client-sourced directives
- sensate focusing
- sensual journey
- sensual deprivation
- paradoxical focusing
- nature-based assignments
- natural ordeals
- experiential metaphors

RATIFICATION:

- objective ratification
- experiential ratification

Figure 10.1 The three R's of ecotherapy: A framework for applying nature-guided interventions.

No Rationale. First, there may be no rationale offered at all. A client might be simply invited or directed to engage in the task without any explanation of the task or why it is being offered. This has the advantage of being ambiguous and thus not setting any expectations about the possible therapeutic outcome.

Therapeutic Rationale. The therapist may offer a therapeutic rationale to the client along the following lines: "Research in environmental psychology has shown that exposure to a natural setting rapidly reduces the symptoms of anxiety, and as you wish to feel more relaxed, you may want to. . . ." This will be consistent with the therapist's therapeutic reasons for offering the appropriate exercise. It provides the client with a goal-oriented reason to engage in the therapeutic task.

Client-Acceptable Rationale. The rationale may be offered as a client-acceptable rationale that may not necessarily include the therapeutic rationale perceived by the clinician. The therapist may draw on the client's experiences, language, and interests in offering the intervention.

In the case of the teenage student who was suffering dissociative experiences (see Chapter 3), I asked the student whether he would like to improve his surfing skills. When he replied in the affirmative, it was suggested that to get the most out of his surfing, he really needed to know and understand the elements. As a means of helping him do this, he was initially required to concentrate on the tactile sensations of the water when he next went surfing.

Here the rationale that was likely to be accepted by the client was different from the therapeutic rationale. The client-acceptable rationale was in the context of improving his surfing ability, while the underlying therapeutic rationale was aimed at helping him focus his attention in a closely associated way on the environment with which he was in contact.

Double-Bind Rationale. The rationale may also appear to offer a choice but really provide a double bind in which both choices will be directed to the fulfilment of the therapeutic task. For example, with the young surfer, the rationale could have been presented in a double-binding manner in such terms as "I don't know whether it is going to be more helpful for you to do this task because the research shows that it is beneficial or because it is likely to improve your surfing."

Restructuring

The aim of restructuring is to bring about the desired therapeutic goal. In the preceding chapters, the ecotherapeutic strategies that can be utilized at this stage of therapy were described, including sensate focusing, sensual journey, nature-based assignments, natural ordeals, and experiential metaphors.

Ratification

The function of ratification is to validate that the therapeutic outcome has been achieved.

Objective Ratification. Ratification may involve a natural object within the client's milieu. Traditional legends frequently used this model. An example is the Biblical story of Lot's wife, who was turned into a pillar of salt for disobeying God's command.

In Kakadu National Park in northern Australia, a rock shaped like a bent feather sits atop a prominent cliff. According to local aboriginal folklore, the son of a tribal leader tried to have incest with his sister. They struggled on top of the cliff before he pushed her to her death. As she fell she grabbed a feather from his headdress that fluttered to the cliff top and was petrified. In attempting to flee the tribal elders, who sought to punish him for his crime, he ran through a bush fire and was badly burned. He plunged into a waterhole, instantly turning into a crocodile whose back still has scarred and crinkly skin from the burns of the fire.

Everyone who sees the pillar of salt, the petrified feather at the top of the cliff, or a crocodile in the waterhole knows that particular object validates the legend and consequently confirms the moral behind the legend. The object is verification of the process.

Using these principles, the therapist may invite the client to bring an object in as validation that the therapeutic change has been achieved. The therapist may even ask clients to engage in a process that will ratify this experience, such as taking a photograph of the waterfall they visited or the sunset they watched. The advantage in having a client produce an object is that it often serves as a concrete validation of therapeutic achievement.

Experiential Ratification. The ratification may be in the experience rather than in the production of an object. This may be suggested by the therapist by way of implication. Such an implication could imply cognitive, behavioral, or affective ratification. For example, one of the following may be suggested to a client: "When you have engaged in this nature-based assignment, you may notice a difference in the way that you feel" (affective ratification); "When you start to experience the comfort of sitting beside a stream you may observe your-self taking a deep breath and letting go" (behavioral ratification); or "When you have taken a walk through the park you may become aware of a difference in the way that you are thinking" (cognitive ratification).

Postintervention ratification can be facilitated by the types of questions described in the change stage of experiential metaphors in Chapter 9. The aim is to confirm the attainment—or steps toward the attainment—of the client's goal, thus aiding the empowerment of the client and the desire to continue goal-oriented activities.

SELF-GENERALIZATION EFFECT

It will be observed in ecotherapy that there is often a client-initiated gener-alization effect once positive experiences have been gained. Clients continue the process of seeking and achieving experiences of health and happiness. An example of this self-generalization process is illustrated in the case of James, a 49-year-old man who presented to therapy complaining that his life "was a disaster."

In the last 12 months, he had started to experience panic attacks, had diffi-culties in coping at work, and was suffering increased feelings of fatigue and irritability at home. He had sought psychiatric assistance and was placed on antidepressant medication, but he was reluctant to continue with this treatment because of its effects on both his cognition and libido.

He was employed as a senior university lecturer, a position consistent with his career plans. He had, however, assumed more and more administrative responsibilities, which distanced him from the classroom duties that he particu-larly enjoyed. In addition, structural reorganizations in his educational institu-tion meant that there was little chance for his career to continue progressing in the direction he desired. He felt angry and frustrated that bureaucratic changes had blocked his career options and long-planned career path. His distress was probably exacerbated by the fact that he considered himself a good and devot-ed employee who had applied himself to his occupation with pride and com-mitment. He had been working in excess of 60 hours per week but had reduced this workload to about 50 hours immediately prior to consulting me.

He had not been taking either designated or adequate holidays. He was 2 years overdue for his sabbatical leave. When asked about this, he attributed it in part to his commitment to work and in part to a fear that if he left his current position during the organizational restructuring, his job might not be available to him on his return.

His work-hard philosophy had spilled over into all avenues of his life. Although he had a number of recreational and personal interests, they failed to provide him with relaxation or enjoyment. Whenever he became involved in an activity, he quickly found himself on a committee, in some organizational capacity, or striving to be at the top level of competition. He had recently joined a swimming club, which he hoped would permit him to relax. Instead he found that two things occurred. First, he was driven by a strongly competitive need to train hard and win. Second, he took on the responsibility of coaching other members, rapidly becoming the club's senior coach. In addition, he was a part-time disc jockey on a regular radio program, was learning an oriental language, and occupied the roles of both president and safety officer in his professional union.

His own interpretation of these very driven activities was that he was "making up for a lost childhood." As an infant he had been diagnosed as having a congenital blood disease. Throughout his childhood he had suffered with bouts of anemia, and he had a low level of immunity and a low level of energy. He described his childhood as being sheltered and protected in that his parents did not want to expose him to risk factors for fear that he might become seriously ill or even die.

At the age of 21, he had his spleen removed, and the symptoms that had plagued him throughout his childhood and adolescence disappeared. He took to life with a new vigor, as though attempting to make up for lost time. He sought activities that had previously been denied to him, including what he described as "aggressive sports" such as rugby.

Approaching the age of 50, he had begun to wonder whether this compulsive drive had taken its toll but felt unable to change it. Physically, he certainly had his problems. He suffered with gout and arthritis, and he had kidney stones. He complained of renal colic, prostatitis, and feelings of fatigue. He experienced onset insomnia as well as a tendency to awaken during the night, and he said that he was existing on about 4 hours of sleep. He did not complain of any disturbances to his appetite but commented that he frequently missed lunch because he was too busy working. In the previous 18 months, he had noticed a diminution of his libido and was concerned that it had deteriorated even further since commencement of antidepressant medication.

Unfortunately, James lacked support and affection in his marriage. After 22 years of marriage to a woman 5 years his junior, he considered himself able to demonstrate more care and patience with his students than with his wife. Their communication was virtually nonexistent, they had experienced many arguments throughout their marriage, and he felt that his wife was thinking of separating. His only son, to whom he was quite attached, was in college, and James was already dreading the day when his son would graduate and start to make his own way in life, leaving James at home alone with his wife.

James was given the Sensual Awareness Inventory at his first therapeutic session (see Figure 10.2). His treatment plan followed the three R's of nature-guided therapy.

Rationale

A number of rationales were offered corresponding with each new intervention that was presented. At times when James was offered nature-based assignments, no rationale was given at all. At other times, client-acceptable rationales were presented (for example, "Given your love of the sea, I wonder how much more enjoyable and beneficial it would be to do some of your swimming training in the ocean"). Therapeutic rationale was phrased in statements such as "Other people have found it helpful to. . . ."

Restructuring

First, the restructuring included solution-oriented counseling in regard to the management of his work situation and marital relationship. Second, he was taught relaxation strategies to deal with anxiety. Third, he was assigned nature-based tasks designed to quickly achieve and maintain a state of relaxation. These tasks were also designed to increase his sense of stimulation and enjoyment. His responses to the Sensual Awareness Inventory were used as a basis for designing the nature-based assignments, because they provided resources that quickly tapped into a state of well-being. Because of the ocean theme on his SAI, these included tasks such as walking along the beach and swimming in the ocean. Finally, he was directed to engage in sensate focusing exercises during his nature-based assignments.

Ratification

His experiences of changes were ratified with presuppositional questions designed to help him validate the experience of the therapeutic task, confirm

Under each heading, please list 10–20 items or activities from which you get pleasure, enjoyment, or comfort.

SIGHT	SOUND	SMELL	TASTE	TOUCH	ACTIVITY
Unspoiled nature	Waves breaking	Good food	Fresh water	Smooth flesh,	Eating a good meal
Wide horizons—no	Music, many kinds	Exotic spices	Good food	sensuous and soft	Listening to music
signs of	well written and	Fine wines	Exotic spices	but firm, well	Travel—meeting new
civilization	performed,	Salt—the ocean	Salt and lemon	conditioned	people and places
Starry night	medieval winds,	Clean fresh air	Hot curries	Smooth stones: jade,	Surfing
Water, especially	baroque brass,	Mountain air, ice	Provencal cooking	marble, and	Swimming
ocean, unspoiled	all classical,	cold and	Italian food	granite	Walking on a beach
Beautiful women, all	contemporary,	refreshing	Oriental food	Sensuous fabrics:	and in the woods
ages, races	blues, rock, jazz,	Tropics, steamy and	Fish	silks	Driving in country
Well-formed,	if melodies	heavy	Fresh oysters	Cotton to wear	Reading a good
sensuous bodies	Children laughing	The beach, salt,	Crustaceans	Artifacts, gold,	book
Architecture in good	People happy	sweat, coconut oil	Tropical fruits	silver, porcelain,	Going to a concert,
position and	Silence	Sensual smells,	Fine wines, earthy	fine china, wood	theater, or movies
harmony	Sounds of	perfume, naked	reds, crisp whites	Nature, trees, rocks,	Lying in open air—
Arts, crafts,	wilderness, wind,	flesh, lovemaking	Sensuous flavors	sand, shells	doing nothing
jewelry, etc.	water			Water, warm and	
				relaxing	

Figure 10.2 James' Sensual Awareness Inventory.

142

the emotional changes he had made as a result, and develop strategies for generalizing the therapeutic benefits.

He was initially seen for 10 sessions of treatment. At a follow-up session 3 months later, he reported that he had taken an overseas trip without anxiety, had not had a panic attack for several months, and was sleeping well.

When additional stresses in the work situation subsequently arose, he returned for therapy, which then included counseling regarding the work situation and sensate focusing exercises. After three sessions he reported that he was feeling "a lot more peaceful, relaxed, and calm." He said that he was better able to cope with the world around him and that he was spending less time at work, had improved his efficiency, and had decided that he needed to look after himself first. He was relating better with his wife and son and felt that, as a byproduct, his health had improved. He had not been feeling as physically unwell. He was planning to take the next semester break to visit his family on the other side of the country and was also making plans to use his long-overdue sabbatical leave.

At the next follow-up, another 3 months later, he indicated that he had progressed a long way. He was continuing to relate well with his wife and attributed this to the change in his own personal attitude. The objective pressures at work had increased, but again he was maintaining a better attitude toward these pressures. He was going home at the scheduled completion of his duties rather than working late each night. He had also made the conscious decision not to take home a briefcase full of work every night; to replace the briefcase, he purchased a new wallet that was sufficient just to carry his personal essentials. He had, he said, "discovered the joy of life."

When I inquired what that meant for him he replied, "It is as simple as enjoying the sun." He had been seeking out more of the simple pleasures of nature. As an example of this self-initiated generalization effect, he had stopped taking the bumper-to-bumper freeway home from work because it caused him to arrive home feeling tense and irritable. Instead he had chosen to take a less frequented coastal road that took him about 10 minutes longer.

On the way he rolled down his car windows to enjoy the fresh smell of the sea breeze. He was able to appreciate the patterns of clouds in the sky and watch the light reflecting on the sea. He could hear the roar of the surf onto the shore and the call of seagulls in the air. He had self-initiated a change in his routine activities that brought about greater pleasure and tapped into a major theme recorded on his Sensual Awareness Inventory. He commented, "By taking the extra ten minutes I arrive home refreshed."

Therapists may follow several steps to facilitate this process of generalization.

1. Assess the natural sources of pleasure, well-being, relaxation, or healing for the individual client either using the Sensual Awareness Inventory or ascertaining these factors through conversation.
2. Facilitate the client's involvement in natural tasks of sensual pleasure by using the strategies described in the preceding chapters. The initiative to create these pleasures may need to come from the therapist, because it is most unlikely that clients seeking therapy will be affording themselves such sources of enjoyment.
3. Help the client appreciate such stimulation. Once the assignments or tasks have been set, follow-up questions may focus on what the client has gained from the experience, what pleasure was achieved, or what differences it made in the client's experiences and feelings.
4. Assist the client in seeking more such stimulation. Here it is helpful to explore with clients how they have gained from the assigned task and how they might be further able to develop or expand the experience.
5. Ratify and reinforce the client's self-initiated attempts to seek personal enjoyment.

SELF-HELP EXERCISE

The exercise in Figure 10.3 can be presented by the therapist during a consultation or can be given to the client as a self-help exercise. It may be preferential to work through it with the client on two or three occasions initially so that the client can experience what difference it may make. The client can then be offered the exercise in a printed form.

The first question to ask the client, or to have clients ask themselves, is "Do you want to change the way you are feeling, acting, or thinking?" If the answer is "No" or "I'm not sure," the next step is to encourage clients to fully experience their emotions, actions, and cognitions. Once they have experienced them adequately, they are asked to go back to the first question ("Do you want to change the way you are feeling, acting, or thinking"?).

If the answer is "Yes," either initially or subsequently, clients are then asked, or asked to ask themselves, "What would you rather be feeling, doing, or thinking?" When this answer about their desired state is attained, they can

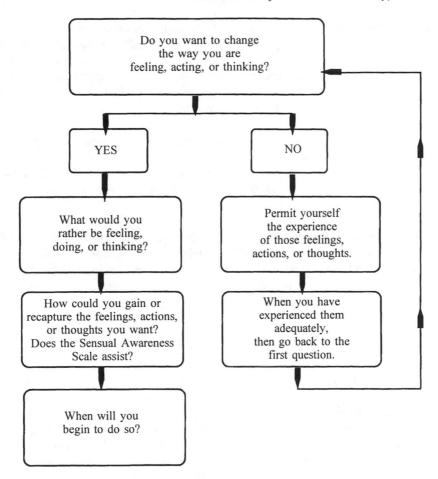

Figure 10.3   A self-help exercise for change.

then be asked "How can you gain or recapture those feelings, actions, or thoughts that you want?" Here it may be useful to refer clients back to their individual Sensual Awareness Inventory responses, particularly if they have trouble spontaneously finding things that would facilitate their desired state. Once the means have been defined, they may be asked "When can you begin to do those things that will help alter your emotional, cognitive, or behavioral state?" The answer to this question binds the client to a commitment to achieve the therapeutic goal.

It is this same process that James used when altering his route home from the congested freeway to the more relaxing coastal road. He asked himself the question "Do I want to change the way I am feeling and thinking as I drive and when I arrive home?" The answer was a clear "Yes." If it had been "No, I don't want to change that feeling" or "I'm not sure whether I want to alter it," then he would have been encouraged to experience his thoughts and feelings on the way home and when he arrived home. Having done so, he would then have been directed back to the initial question.

If clients again arrive at the same answer (that is, no desire to change anything about the behavior), then it would be the end of the exercise as there is no contract for change. Often, however, asking clients to allow themselves the experience can act like a paradoxical suggestion, inviting them to explore other alternatives.

For James the answer was "Yes," thus leading to the next question: "What would you rather be feeling or thinking?" His answer was that he would rather be arriving home feeling more relaxed, less stressed, and having had the opportunity to switch off some of the hassles of the work situation. To achieve this, he asked himself how he might gain those feelings.

His Sensual Awareness Inventory was of assistance in that there was an ocean and water theme running through his inventory at various sensual levels. He found enjoyment in looking at wide horizons without signs of civilization. He took pleasure in the sight of unspoilt nature, especially the ocean. Topping his list in the area of sound was breaking waves. The water sounds of nature—waterfalls, streams, oceans—were also mentioned. For smell he listed the salty air of the ocean, as well as the smells of the beach. Swimming, surfing, and beach walking were all listed among his pleasurable activities. Having defined what and how, his next task was to decide when to change the route that he had been taking home from work for the last 16 years. When he did he began to achieve the desired thoughts and feelings.

This self-help exercise may be given to clients as a handout similar to the format of Figure 10.3. Having a printed form makes it easier to follow the exercise at the required times.

This section of the book has examined and illustrated the strategies and procedures of ecotherapy. The next section explores the application of these interventions for the treatment of clinical problems and the attainment of therapeutic goals. Interspersed throughout the following chapters are examples of outcome-relevant, goal-oriented exercises to illustrate the type of therapeutic interventions that may be offered to clients.

PART IV
NATURAL HAPPINESS

Chapter **11**

ECOTHERAPY FOR RELAXATION AND COMFORT

From Nature doth emotion come, and moods
Of calmness equally are Nature's gift.—William Wordsworth
(from *Healing Nature*)

Pause for a moment. Imagine sitting on a smooth rock beside a gently bubbling stream on a clear, warm spring day. Maybe one or two soft cumulus clouds drift lazily across the pastel blue sky. Birds sing a chorus of joy to the new life of the season. It's almost as though you can hear the earth beginning to warm after the damp and cold of winter. The season is in a process of change as each day becomes a little longer, a little warmer, a little brighter. And you are part of this nature, part of this new season of life and vitality. You may watch the waters of the stream bubbling, dancing, cascading over the rocks, breaking into streaks of white, and gathering with sudsy bubbles at the bottom of the little cascade. The flow seems constant, but it is forever changing, in shapes, in colors, in patterns. As you gaze into its moving waters, you become totally absorbed. Listening to its repetitive gurgling song, you find yourself entranced in its motions.

At this point shift your attention for a moment and explore your own emotions. Right at that time of being absorbed in the waters of the stream, what were you feeling? Were you aware of any anxiety? If you were experiencing anxiety before you began to imagine that scene, did the anxiety dissipate? Has it helped facilitate a feeling of relaxing?

Subjectively, we may have known for a long time the benefits of stepping out of the office into a local park if we have been experiencing a stressful morning. We may know how, if caught up in an argument at home, taking a stroll along the beach can dissipate the thoughts and energies of those conflicts. These things we have always been aware of, but maybe not always practiced, have been validated in research. Ulrich, Dimberg, and Driver (1991) have shown that even very passive leisure encounters with natural environments have marked stress-reducing influences, both emotionally and physically. In contrast, many urban environments will often hamper recovery from stress.

To assess the psychophysiological variables involved in this process, Ulrich and colleagues showed stressful movies to 120 subjects who were then required to watch a 10-minute color-and-sound videotape of varying natural and urban settings. They were monitored on four bodily functions: heart rate, skin conductance, muscle tension, and pulse transit time (which correlates with systolic blood pressure). The subjects also provided self-ratings of their emotional states. The results confirmed, through verbal and physiological measures, that recovery from stress was both faster and more complete when the subjects were exposed to natural rather than urban environments. At the emotional level, natural milieus produced significantly greater reductions in feelings of anxiety, fear, anger, and aggression. Interestingly, the responses were not only associated with the lowering of what we might consider undesired feelings but were associated with an elevation of more desirable feelings such as elation and pleasure.

> *Exercise 11.1:* Use the Sensual Awareness Inventory to find situations, activities, or objects that are intrinsically relaxing and comforting.
>
> It may be that there are soothing themes that flow through several sense modalities, such as the sights, sounds, smells, tastes, and tactile sensations of a particular setting like a seascape.
>
> Choose one of these particular settings. Create that setting in your imagination, in much the same way we did sitting beside the stream at the beginning of this chapter.

Nature also brought about greater stress recovery, as indicated by lower levels of skin conductance, lower blood pressure, and greater reductions in muscle tension. Videotapes of traffic scenes 9 minutes after exposure showed that blood pressure had elevated even more than during the initial stressful stimuli. Over a similar period, videos of pedestrian malls held blood pressure at the same poststress levels, whereas viewing a natural scene attained maximum reduction of stress within 6 minutes. Heart rates decelerated following the onset of the natural presentations, whereas an acceleration occurred with exposure to the urban settings. In the areas of skin conductance and muscle tension, nature was once again the winner in terms of more rapid recovery, more significant recovery, and better retention of stress reduction. All of these results were obtained within a 4–6-minute exposure to the natural environments.

Responses on the physiological measures led Ulrich and colleagues to suggest "the possibility that the natural settings elicit responses that include a parasympathetic nervous system component" (1991, p. 83). It is important to note that, in this experiment, the contact with nature was a very passive one. The subject was simply asked to sit and watch a video for a period of 10 minutes. Nature itself was represented through a technological image that offered stimulation of only two senses: sight and sound. No personal, dynamic, or interactive processes were taking place with that fixed image.

Other researchers such as Hartig, Mang, and Evans (1990) have sought to explore more active participatory encounters with natural environments. Hartig et al. were interested in discovering whether enhanced task performance was one of the benefits that could be expected from interactive leisure experiences with natural environments. They compared a group who had participated in a backpacking trip with a control group. The former performed better on a proofreading test, suggesting higher levels of relaxation, concentration, and cognitive processing as a result of their involvement in a natural setting. Consistent with other studies, there was also an elevation in their positive affect as well as lower scores on indices of stress and anxiety.

Hartig and colleagues then assigned subjects into three groups. One group took a 40-minute walk in a natural setting. A second group was required to take a walk of equivalent time in an urban area, while the third was directed to relax while reading magazines or listening to music. Again, those interacting with nature returned reporting more positive feelings and greater levels of relaxation.

> *Exercise 11.2:* Some of the research examined here shows that focusing on a single sense modality can help change feelings in a more positive direction, alleviate stress, and enhance sensations of pleasure.
>
> You might like to examine how you can use a single sense modality to do this. It is recommended that you do this in a real, natural environment. If this isn't always possible, there are other options.
>
> One way might be to tune in to a particularly relaxing sound. There are, for example, many compact discs available with natural sounds, bird calls, rolling ocean waves, forest sounds, whale songs, and so forth.

Another use of a single sense modality might be to take a photograph of a favorite holiday scene and then enlarge it. Put it in a viewable place and look at the photograph when you wish to recapture the pleasantness of the experiences that you had in that particular setting.

We know that stress affects us in a variety of ways. Physiologically, it increases our sympathetic activity, our cardiovascular activity, and our skin conductance and muscle tension. It can cause the blocking of alpha activity, lead to higher levels of stress hormones (for example, epinephrine), and reduce our immune functioning. These factors can, in turn, quite directly affect our health, causing disruptions in our basic drives and having an impact on our sleep, appetite, and libido. We may begin to feel agitated, apprehensive, fearful, frustrated, and angry. There may be alterations in our behavior that are also detrimental to our health and well-being. If we are ill, stress can affect our attitude and behavior so that we are less likely to care for ourselves, and consequently we recover less promptly. It may cause us to engage in unhealthy behaviors such as cigarette smoking, binge eating, drinking, and drug use.

Ulrich and colleagues' research shows clearly that in stressed individuals, the greater number of natural encounters they have, the greater the stress-reducing influences. In contrast, urban environments may impair and delay stress recuperation. Not only is the speed and quality of recovery enhanced via natural contacts, but there is the suggestion that natural views modify in beneficial ways the parasympathetic nervous system, which might not be the case with exposure to urban scenes.

The work of Mehrabian and Russell (1974) has shown that viewing pleasant scenes can reduce the desire to engage in unhealthy stress-related behaviors such as smoking and drinking. All this leads Baum (1991) to muse on a very interesting hypothesis. According to Baum, "Some believe that stress affects the speed at which we age, so one could argue that the reduction of stress via leisure activity could make us live longer. It certainly makes sense that it could make us stay healthier" (p. 407).

Baum, while aware of the benefits, raises the very pragmatic question that it may not always be practical for people to put themselves in the physical environment of nature. We can't all live in the country with green undulating paddocks and quietly grazing animals, and we can't always enjoy a park or look out over the continually changing moods of the sea. Necessity may dictate that we reside close to work and social activities. Yet our need to have contact with nature may occur more frequently than does our annual vacation.

Rosen, a New York psychiatrist with an urban-dwelling clientele, found the same problems with the environmentally based stories and exercises of Milton H. Erickson. At a teaching seminar he asked Erickson, "Do you find that city people can also get something from stories about flowers and gardens and such, even though they might not have had much experience with those things?" Erickson replied, "I have sent more than one depressed man to go and dig and plant a flower garden for someone." Rosen pressed the issue: "I am trying to find the New York equivalent of climbing Squaw Peak." Erickson's response was "Find a nice crooked tree in Central Park with a squirrel in it" (Zeig, 1980, pp. 250–252).

Even in urban areas, there are situations in which therapists will be able to develop nature-based therapeutic assignments. It is always possible to find a neighborhood park, a place to watch a sunset, or an ocean to visit. It is possible to feed birds in the backyard, to grow a flower in a window box, or watch the clouds overhead. As we have seen, the research on the benefits of these activities is clear. What Hartig, Mang and Evans (1990) have shown us is that some of the therapeutic tasks we may have previously assigned to clients in an urban setting are not as effective for creating relaxation as exposure to nature. Offering clients therapeutic directives such as relaxation exercises, reading, or listening to music may not be the best creators of relaxation. Similarly, taking a walk through an urban environment may not be as effective in changing emotional states as spending the same amount of time in a natural setting.

> *Exercise 11.3:* Research suggests that passively being in a natural environment can quickly and effectively modify feelings of anxiety, allow a return to normal physiological functioning, and enhance both positive affect and thoughts.
>
> Use your Sensual Awareness Inventory to choose a natural setting that you find peaceful and tranquil.
>
> Access that setting in reality. If it is a particular beach, for example, go visit that beach.
>
> This exercise requires no more than passively being there. Nothing needs to be done or accomplished. The task is simply to be and experience.

A CASE OF TRAUMA AND ANXIETY

The first time I met Vanessa was at the request of the police. They requested that forensic hypnosis be used to help her recall information about an assault. Her nose was bandaged following surgical repair to a fracture. Her face was badly bruised, her eyes extremely bloodshot. Sixteen days after the assault, her injuries were still very visible.

Vanessa was the 33-year-old single mother of three young children. Four years before, she had suffered a violent and traumatic breakup of her marriage. She had gradually started to get her life back on track, had been undergoing psychotherapy, and was reestablishing her sense of self-esteem. She sought and attained entrance to a university at which she commenced studying social work.

One night after having put her children to sleep, she was preparing to study when she felt the presence of somebody behind her. As she turned around and saw a man, she was struck over the head with a heavy instrument. Her head was battered repeatedly against her desk, causing loss of consciousness. Her skull was fractured. Bones were broken in her nose, jaw, and cheek, requiring a metal plate in her jaw. Some of her teeth were knocked out and others fractured. While unconscious, she was violently raped and suffered severe vaginal injuries. Her attacker fled, leaving her injured, bleeding, and unconscious on the floor.

The police, with her consent, were seeking to find out whether she could recall more about her attacker. Unbeknownst to Vanessa, they already had a suspect, and her recollections were consistent with other information they had. The suspect was arrested and confessed to the attack.

The arrest, while relieving Vanessa's fear that he might attack again, did nothing to change the trauma that she had experienced or the symptoms that remained. She was experiencing overwhelming panic attacks that she described as "huge" and "shattering." She was continuing to experience the pain and discomfort of her physical injuries. She was frequently fearful, saying that she had lost self-confidence and self-esteem. She couldn't concentrate on her studies and wasn't coping successfully with her responsibilities as a mother. She was seeing a female counselor at a sexual assault referral center but also asked to see me after the forensic hypnosis, feeling it would be helpful in her adjustment to have a male therapist.

In our first therapy session, she was offered posttraumatic debriefing. She was also given the Sensual Awareness Inventory. During the second consultation she reported continuing—and intense—panic attacks. We did not explore the dynamics of the sudden attack by a total stranger or the similarities she said she experienced in the feelings between her attack and the breakup of her marriage. We did, however, discuss items of sensual awareness that were likely to bring about modification of her current feelings. She commented that she just needed to get away from everything so that she could spend some time meditating in a peaceful environment to help become "centered." Her express goals were to be free of the feelings of panic, to cease being scared, and to lose her intense feelings of self-doubt.

We explored the practicalities of "getting away." Her parents were willing to look after the children. She booked herself into a coastal inn where she spent 5 days. She was prescribed nature-based assignments to undertake on her retreat. She was, for example, directed to take a long beach walk with ambiguous instructions such as simply experiencing what there was to experience. She was given metaphors relating how other clients had benefited from such experiences. In this way, the groundwork was laid for creating an experiential metaphor.

When she returned for her third therapeutic session, there was a marked improvement not only in her physical healing but also in her emotional and mental state. She told how she had spent time walking along the beach, beside the banks of the river, and through neighboring woodlands. Two experiences in particular stood out.

First, she had found a beautiful spot on a riverbank where she sat on a rock. She described in detail the trees, the scene around the river, and even a moss-covered log that stretched into the flow of the water. As she sat she become aware of the reflections in the water and started to contemplate how one image was real and one was an illusion. She thought about how reality and illusion could look so alike and at times be hard to differentiate. She picked up a stone, threw it in the water, and watched the illusion shatter. Tears filled her eyes. Rather than chastise herself for her tears, she simply let them flow. She said it was like her "past blocks" were shattered with the illusion in the water. She began to experience a sense of peacefulness, reporting that at that moment things again "came together."

Her second natural experiential metaphor occurred when she took a hike through 500 acres of woods. Walking, absorbed in her own thoughts, she became lost. At first she started to feel panicky. It was getting late in the day, and she was fearful of being lost in the woods at night. She saw the situation as similar to her attack. Something unplanned, unexpected was posing a threat to her well-being. She thought about what she needed to do and came to the conclusion that she had to rely on her own intuition. She reminded herself of the need to trust her sense of direction to make the right choices. She found her way back to the farmhouse just as the last rays of sunlight were disappearing below the horizon. The metaphoric parallel she saw between this experience and her previous trauma led her to reestablish a sense of confidence in her intuition that she reported having lost following the attack.

> *Exercise 11.4:* Use the Sensual Awareness Inventory to define a tranquil environmental context in the same way as in Exercise 11.3.
>
> In this exercise, however, the client is asked to engage in the activity of relaxing. This might involve a previously acquired relaxation skill or possibly one taught in the therapeutic context through progressively muscular relaxation, meditation, yoga, or self-hypnosis.

Given her response, I encouraged her to use her SAI to create a positive and pleasurable interaction with nature each day. As she noticed new experiences, new feelings of comfort, or new ways of managing trauma and panic, she was asked to add them to her inventory to maintain her ongoing progress.

Vanessa's treatment followed the three R's of nature-guided therapy described in Chapter 10.

The Rationale

Because Vanessa had been studying social work and completing units in psychology, she was offered a therapeutic rationale for engaging in nature-based assignments that included quoting studies that demonstrated the affect-altering impacts of exposure to nature. She was also presented with metaphors that matched her problem, as well as her desired outcome of being "centered."

The Restructuring

Vanessa was given nature-based assignments to be undertaken during her retreat to a coastal farm. These assignments were crafted to include the characteristics of experiential metaphors (see Chapter 9).

The Intent. Vanessa had expressed goals in going away. She wanted to resume her sense of self. She wanted to feel more relaxed and to regain the state of well-being that she had fought so hard to achieve in the preceding 4 years.

The Journey. Her journey into the country was like a pilgrimage. She was on a mission to regain an important part of herself. She had the journey of driving several hundred miles through agricultural, forest, and coastal terrain. Her assignments directed her to journey along the seashore and into woodlands.

Through these directives, the opportunity was created for her to take an inner journey as well.

The Time. She had allocated 5 days to be away in which she had nothing else to do but experience nature in ways that might be helpful for the attainment of her goals. Each assignment required the commitment of time.

The Relationship. In being in nature, she was in a situation in which she had the opportunity to relate with a healthy, recuperative environment. She described this relationship well in her account of sitting on the riverbank and becoming involved in the experience of the reflections in the water.

The Change. Vanessa spoke of the changes she experienced when she described the shattering of "past blocks" and how life again "came together." Through her assignments she began to learn to trust herself and her own intuition, and she began to reestablish her feelings of confidence.

The Ratification

First, there was the ratification of the experience. Vanessa brought back memories of her experiences by the river and in the forest that confirmed the processes of change she had experienced. These were discussed in therapy to further validate both the process and the progress of her goal achievement.

Second, encouraging her to continue using her Sensual Awareness Inventory lent further objectivity to the validation of how she could quickly tap into natural resources for the modification of her feelings when desired.

Third, she was presented with the self-help exercise for change (see Chapter 10) and encouraged to be mindful of the experiences she'd had while she was away. These experiences provided a means of validating her ability to alter unwanted cognitions, feelings, and actions.

Finally, as described later, in subsequent therapy she was presented with a photograph of a tree. This had the twofold objective of further ratifying the progress she had made and of providing her with a means to continue to be in touch with states of well-being.

The Follow-Up

She continued to improve in self-confidence, experienced a reduction in her feelings of panic, and was actively seeking natural experiences. This suddenly changed, however, with the trial of her assailant about 4 months later. For breaking into her home, making an unprovoked attack, causing her serious head injuries, sexually assaulting her, and leaving her unconscious, the man was sentenced by the judge to a minimum of 2 years imprisonment. With parole he could be released in a matter of months.

Vanessa had previously made little mention of her attacker. She seemed to be more concerned for him than angry at him. Her energies had primarily been directed toward getting her own life back on track and caring for her children. She had faith in the system that justice would be done and that her assailant would in time face the consequences of his actions. The leniency of his sentence was, as she put it, "like being abused all over again."

Her feelings of panic returned. She lost her sense of direction and self-control. Additional stress factors emerged as journalists, radio talk shows, and television crews invaded her privacy, demanding that she relive the experiences of her attack and comment on the lenient sentence.

When she again presented for therapy, there had been a marked deterioration in her emotional and cognitive state. I started to explore how we could reinstate the previous nature-guided interventions that had been so helpful. Unfortunately, she was not able to get away again for several days. Her weekends were occupied with her children's recreational pursuits and other commitments. She lived in an urban area and was fearful of taking walks where there might be the possibility of a further attack.

She commented, "I need to spend time with some trees again. I find trees healing." When this possibility seemed unlikely, I reached for my briefcase. I had just collected my photographs from a recent hiking vacation through an area of beautiful river gorges. I pulled out a photo and handed it to her. In the foreground was the pure white trunk of a ghost gum. It sat on a floor of fresh, verdant winter grass. The backdrop was the red-and-ochre face of the river gorge. The lines and colors were both stark and contrasting. For a few moments she sat absorbed in the photo. Not a word was spoken. When she did lift her eyes, she said, "Isn't it silly. Just looking at a photograph helps me to feel so much better." I asked her to take the photograph and put it somewhere prominent. If she couldn't experience a real tree, she was to spend some time each day looking at the photo.

The next week she described the photographic image of the tree as a "life saver." She had placed it beside her bed and each morning spent time looking at it before she arose. As a result she had approached each day feeling more relaxed and with a greater sense of inner strength. She was encouraged to continue using the photograph and, when both possible and safe, to spend time with trees in vivo.

> *Exercise 11.5:* After engaging in each of the preceding exercises, pause and ask yourself the following questions: How might I be able to re-create that feeling again? When would be a convenient or regular time to do so? What was most relaxing or comforting about that experience? How did that relaxation feel? What was most helpful in achieving that tranquillity?

Chapter 12

ECOTHERAPY FOR HAPPINESS AND PLEASURE

We must reenter natural evolution again . . . to recover our own fecundity in the world of life.—Murray Bookchin (1988)

St. David's head is at the westernmost tip of Wales. Nestled in the bay beneath it, on the coast of Penbrokeshire, is the seaside town of Solva. It was to this spot that dolphin researcher Horace Dobbs was attracted by reports of a friendly, wild dolphin. What he encountered was an adolescent male bottle-nosed dolphin. What he was about to experience was something he had not quite anticipated.

For some time Dobbs had been interested in what he saw as the beneficial emotional effects of dolphins on people. After talking about his thoughts in a film lecture, he was approached by a hotel owner concerned about a personal friend who was residing at the hotel. He was being treated along traditional lines for depression. Dobbs agreed to take the middle-aged man on his next voyage to meet a dolphin they had called Simo.

On the way Dobbs's research assistant, Tricia, enthusiastically talked with Bill, their middle-aged guest, about her encounters with Simo and other dolphins. She spoke positively about her experiences and emotions. Dobbs explained, "She also told him how she had experienced a great feeling of what she described as 'pure love' coming from Simo when she was with him. Furthermore, she explained how the dolphin reacted to what people felt inside. It didn't matter in physical terms whether they were fat or thin, rich or poor—if they were gentle and sensitive inside, the dolphin would respond accordingly. The dolphin would not judge them by human standards but the standards of an intelligent being without possessiveness but in harmony with its environment" (Dobbs, 1987). In ecopsychotherapeutic terms, Tricia had provided a rationale for the exercise and set expectations about the outcome.

Dobbs and his assistant had set up a nature-based assignment that also had the elements of an experiential metaphor. Anticipation was created on Bill's part about the intent and about what he might expect to gain from the encounter with Simo. There was probably some change in his frame of reference while communicating with someone like Tricia, who was so excited and positive.

A commitment had also been elicited. Bill agreed to meet the dolphin, boarded the boat, and submerged himself in the ocean with a wild creature. He took a pilgrimage into Simo's world. Metaphorically, and in reality, he journeyed out of his own world into a realm of new sensations. He took the step of experientially interacting with nature.

Dobbs recorded: "The dolphin loved him. And we watched the man change from being apprehensive, scared, and withdrawn to a smiling joyous person, who became totally involved with the dolphin and forgot everyone and everything around him." In that process of interacting with total absorption in the experiences of the moment, Bill experienced an emotional transformation that led to alterations in his behavior. He let go of his depressive behaviors and began to exhibit the behavior of someone enjoying himself. As Tricia put it, "He blossomed—just like a sunflower." When they returned to shore, Bill was almost tearful in describing his experience and his feelings to his family. His tears, however, were no longer those of depression; rather, they were tears of joy.

From the restructuring of his emotions through a nature-guided activity, there was a spontaneous ratification of the experience, first, in his knowledge that it could happen and, second, in relating it so enthusiastically to his family.

Dobbs (1987), following this experience of introducing Bill to Simo, wanted to help others in similar situations. He realized, however, the problems involved in taking large numbers of depressed people into the ocean with a wild creature. He didn't even know whether the dolphin would be there at the desired times. He therefore proposed resolving the problem by showing people videotapes of close interactions with cetaceans instead.

Exercise 12.1: Invite clients to videotape a favorite natural setting, whether a forest scene, a seascape, or a singing bird.

When the person is not able to access that pleasant environment in reality, he or she can be directed to take 10 or 15 minutes to watch the video sights and sounds of that personally familiar, tranquilizing scene.

A GOAL OF NEUTRALITY

Over the last century, most forms of therapy have aimed at removing a symptom. In the area of depression, they have sought to make a person not depressed. In the area of anxiety, the goal has been to eliminate anxiety. The object has been a state of neutrality. The literature of the past has talked very little about how to feel happy, enjoy pleasure, be optimistic, or blossom "like a sunflower."

Therapy, by setting a goal of neutrality, has aimed at something that is virtually impossible. The human state is not one of neutrality. Our feelings are constantly varying in terms of both the nature of the emotion and the intensity with which we might be experiencing it. For a client, the goal of neutrality must indeed be extremely confusing. How do you aim at nothing? What is nothing? In nothing there is nothing to look forward to. It can't be seen, you can't know when you have achieved it, and so the therapeutic goal itself is likely to be fraught with further frustration and disappointment.

As I sat writing this chapter, the telephone rang. It was a colleague wanting to refer a 29-year-old depressed and phobic patient who had rarely left home since his father died 10 years ago. It had been proposed that he be placed in a government institution under the care of a psychiatric team to "get rid of" his phobia and depression. Treatment emphasis had been on taking away what had been his means of coping and survival for the last decade without offering him anything in return. I explained to my colleague the thoughts I was just putting down in writing, and she replied, "Yes. I can see him being in an institution for the rest of his days. It would be far better for him, and far more economical, if we were to buy an airline ticket to send him to hike in the Himalayas."

When depressed people come to therapy, they do not want to learn more about depression. They are really saying, "Please tell me about happiness. Please teach me about feeling well. Please show me ways to experience joy. Please help me to discover feelings of pleasure."

Fortunately, more and more therapists are beginning to realize that happiness is a legitimate therapeutic outcome. Paul Watzlawick (1983), in a tongue-in-cheek way, wrote about this in a book titled *The Situation Is Hopeless, But Not Serious: The Pursuit of Unhappiness*. Seligman (1990) saw depression as the ultimate form of pessimism. Conversely, he viewed optimism as a clear indicator of one's freedom from symptomatology, as well as an index of one's coping skills and well-being. He wrote of learned optimism as an attainable state. Walters and Havens (1993) have developed, within a hypnotic framework, scripts to elicit natural pleasures in the areas of our individual senses and focus on the development of optimism.

Neither here nor in subsequent chapters do I intend to move into a debate about the theoretical basis of depression. The arguments for biochemical theories versus psychosocial influences may be explored by reading authors such as Beck (1967), Sartorius and Ban (1986), Seligman (1975, 1990), and Yapko (1989, 1992, 1997). However, I offer an example of how a nature-based program has been used to ameliorate the symptoms of depression.

Seligman (1975) described learned helplessness as a condition in which people come to learn they cannot control outcomes. Depression, defective problem-solving skills, difficulties in facing failure, and low self-esteem may be among the associated cognitive, emotional, motivational, and self-concept impairments. These problems arise from a person's attributional style. People with learned helplessness are more likely to attribute failure to stable, global, and internal causes (for example, their lack of ability) and to attribute success to more fickle causes (for example, good luck).

To modify this attributional style, Newman (1980) looked for a structured wilderness program to assist the development of more realistic causal attributions. Several advantages were seen in wilderness contact. First, there are less demands on information processing in the wilderness and hence more opportunity to reflect on one's own attributional style. Second, as many environmental psychologists argue, the stresses of day-to-day, human-constructed environments are diminished in nature, thus allowing a greater sense of calm and control. Third, the variety, unexpectedness, and challenge of natural stimuli can require skills of coping. Finally, because survival in wilderness areas may demand a different attributional style, old patterns of functioning can be modified.

Newman claimed that structured programs, based in wilderness areas, could thus result in a number of benefits to ameliorate learned helplessness and depression. They could facilitate the progress of new coping skills and lead to a sense of mastery. They could assist in the development of control and competency, thus enhancing the client's self-concept and self-esteem.

The exercises in this chapter and the treatment plan for the following case study are not the same as Newman's structured wilderness-survival programs. They are based on the nature-guided strategies described previously and are designed for depressed clients seeking clinical assistance. They do hold in common the therapeutic characteristics Newman attributes to nature and the therapeutic objectives of enhancing realistic attributions, skill development, competence, control, and self-esteem.

> *Exercise 12.2:* You have listed 10 to 20 items under each heading of your SAI; thus, you now have a choice of between 60 and 120 items that bring you pleasure.
>
> Choose one item each day that provides some sense of satisfaction or happiness. It need not be difficult or time consuming. It may simply be to stop and smell a rose, listen to a favorite sound, get up earlier than usual and experience a sunrise, or treat yourself to a favorite meal.
>
> In doing so, give yourself the opportunity to do something different from what would be your normal practice.

A CASE OF DEPRESSION

Let us take a look at a case of depression and how engaging in simple interactions with nature can bring about a significant change.

Mary, age 50, was referred by her neurologist, who described how she was having trouble with short-term memory, forgetting what she was saying in the middle of a conversation and forgetting what she was about to do. She might make a cup of coffee, forget she'd done it, and immediately afterward make a second. She failed to recall things she'd been told, forgot appointments, and was unable to remember dressmaking patterns that previously she had been able to do quite well. She had put on weight, was overeating, and was indulging too heavily in alcohol. She had become unduly clumsy, suffered nagging frontal headaches, and was quickly triggered to aggression. Her neurologist requested a neuropsychological assessment to assist in a differential diagnosis of a pseudo-dementia or early dementia.

The assessment indicated that she was a woman of above-average intellectual capabilities whose memory skills, right across the board, were even higher than expected given her intellectual capacity. However, her Beck Depression Inventory results suggested a "potentially serious" level of depression, with significantly depressed affect and high levels of both self-denigration and self-criticism. She reported feelings of indecisiveness, introversion, and irritability, along with fatigue and psychomotor retardation. There was a high level of guilt and some passive suicidal ideation.

Her history confirmed she had some good reasons to feel depressed. As a young child, she reported being sexually abused by both her father and a close family friend, the latter forcing her into acts of fellatio. She married in her late teens and had three sons, two with congenital growth disorders who were treated with pituitary hormones. She remains in fear for their well-being, because there is a risk of them developing the fatal Creutzfeldt-Jakob's disease.

In the 4 years prior to seeking psychological assistance, Mary experienced a disproportionate number of traumas and losses. She was greatly disturbed by being a witness to an assault. One son announced that he was going to have a surgical sex change. As a consequence his marriage fell apart, and Mary worried about the effects on her grandchildren. Around the same time the son of a close friend died of AIDS. The infant child of another friend was killed in a motor vehicle accident, and a teenage relative died of leukemia.

Mary had been dislocated from her own home, going to live with her father to nurse him through a terminal illness. She felt it her duty despite the fact that she disliked him intensely. Contrary to her religious beliefs, she wished him dead. When he did die, her guilt was further escalated. Needless to say, this had significant repercussions on her marriage, which balanced as precariously as a high-wire acrobat strung between a pair of city skyscrapers.

She had been giving so much to others that she had neglected not only her marriage but also the satisfaction of her own needs. Consequently, she had virtually no personal interests, hobbies, or recreational pursuits.

> *Exercise 12.3:* Study your SAI and find what themes may exist. You may find that there are a number of thematically related items and that engaging in such activities can provide much sensual satisfaction.
>
> Such a thematic example could include the following: the sight of a heavily timbered forest, the rustling sound of leaves in the breeze, or the songs of birds. Maybe you like the smell of damp soil or the feeling of rain pattering on your jacket. If you enjoy walking, it may be a source of multimodal pleasure to take a walk through the woods on a rainy spring day.
>
> Plan your time so that you can engage in such a multimodal sensual pleasure at least once a week.

Sensate Focusing

From Mary's SAI, there was an indication that she enjoyed the sight and smell of roses. We spoke about roses during one therapy session and explored ways in which she could engage in this pleasurable experience for herself each day. She failed to follow the precise sensate focusing directives offered to her but self-initiated other activities. She wrote to me the day after our consultation. "I thought I would write to you. I bet that it is a surprise to tell what I have decided to do. I am very uncomfortable focusing on doing something nice for myself each day, so I have decided since my memories have given me most pain I would grant myself one good memory a day and write it down.

"Yesterday I was so embarrassed. I got such a shock that I wished myself anywhere but there [a reference to her suicidal ideation]. But it was so funny when I was on the train later I was sitting there visualizing making my husband rose petal sandwiches, marinating his meat in rose perfume, rose petals in the stew, lighting rose candles, sprinkling rose petals all around the room, some other ideas that I won't write down. I started to giggle, people next to and opposite me moved and put a lot of space between us, all were giving me funny glances. By the time I got off the train I was laughing out loud while walking down the street. I found a freedom of spirit that hasn't been there for a long time. Thanks for letting me find my own way through it. The rose petals are a great idea."

During her consultation the day before she wrote this letter, she had expressed the suicidal thoughts referred to in her letter. She wasn't shocked by the thoughts, which had been present for some time; she was shocked more by the fact that she had openly discussed them with someone else. She was committed to a no-suicide contract, and we then began to explore ways in which she could create more pleasurable experiences. It was in this context that the subject of roses emerged and the exercise of sensate focusing was prescribed.

As she wrote, she rejected the assignment of doing something nice for herself each day. On the train on the way home from the consultation, she adapted the assignment to think about ways she could use roses to pleasure her husband. Within a brief time she had been able to shift her thoughts and feelings from issues of suicide to ones of pleasure, enjoyment, and laughter. Her sense of empowerment in doing this was reflected in her expression of gratitude of being permitted to find her own way through the issues.

A Nature-Based Assignment

Under the Activity heading of the SAI, Mary indicated that she enjoyed walking. Nature-based assignments were established with the hope of satisfying two therapeutic goals: to provide stimulation that would continue to lift her depressed affect and to provide exercise to help achieve one of her other therapeutic goals of losing weight. In assessing the availability of potentially usable natural environments near her home, it was ascertained that she lived near a river with treed embankments along which ran a pathway. This presented the opportunity to prescribe her a specific nature-based activity of walking along the riverbank for 45 minutes each day and to observe what she experienced in each sense modality. On the first day she was to focus on her sense of sight, on the second it was to be her sense of sound, and so on, through each modality.

Again she wrote about her experience. She said that she took time out of her walking to sit and quietly watch the sunset. "It was good. The clouds were so many different colors, white, dark gray, golden, the sky a lovely blue. And right in the middle of the dark gray cloud a rainbow—the color of some of the clouds were peach and gray. The fluffy white clouds also turned a peach color. It was not pink, not apricot. Somewhere in between there was lightning and the color was going from the clouds. I am glad I took the time out."

> *Exercise 12.4:* Explore the variety of things listed under your Activity heading.
>   Find an activity that offers you a pleasure you don't often experience.
>   Grant yourself the permission to do it.
>   Start to anticipate the activity and make a commitment to enjoy the experience of doing it in a favorable environmental setting.

An Experiential Metaphor

During treatment Mary announced that she and her husband were planning to take a vacation to Central Australia to visit Ayer's Rock. Vacations away from home when people are in a different environment and prone to different experiences present a good opportunity to set about creating an experiential metaphor for the client.

Mary expressed disappointment that her cardiologist had already advised her against climbing Ayer's Rock. The assent is rather steep and challenging, requiring a certain level of fitness. Mary was overweight and unfit. I doubt she would have been able to make the climb, but I also saw that it was important for her to have the choice. I therefore put the responsibility back in her court, saying that I thought that she ought to go to the rock, take a look at the climb, and consider whether it was in her own best interests. She was asked what she thought she might gain by visiting the rock so as to develop a goal and a sense of anticipation. Simply getting there would provide the journey, and whether she climbed it or not, visiting the world's largest single monolith is a pilgrimage in itself. To help facilitate the relationship with the local ecology, she was asked to simply spend some time experiencing the environment. Having set up the intent, the journey, the relationship, and the time characteristics of an experiential metaphor, it was anticipated this would bring about change. It was also suggested to her, as a means of ratifying her experience, that she bring back a photograph of Ayer's Rock as she saw it.

Again, in her rather prolific writing style, she put pen to paper about her experience. She described how her husband and others had started to climb at 5:30 a.m. to be at the summit at sunrise, three quarters of an hour later. She chose not to make the climb. She wrote, "Instead, I walked around the base. I was on my own. I could neither see nor hear anyone else and in the expectant stillness of the dawn, it was like the beginning of time. The rock seemed to be alive, and it was as if it was whispering the secrets of the past, promising much for the future. I felt blessed to have had that time just there alone in such a spiritual place. Time stood still. Later I learned the traditional owners [the Aborigines] prefer visitors not to climb Uluru [the aboriginal name for Ayer's Rock]. I am glad I chose not to climb. The experience of standing alone in the vastness was truly a spiritual experience. The healing is complete."

Her account clearly illustrates the process of her journey as she walked around the base, along with the relationship that she established with the rock, as intimate as if it were whispering secrets to her. The element of time was represented in the appreciation of the time she had alone and the fact that time seemed to stand still. These factors led to a change. She was able to look forward to a promise of the future and sense that her own healing was complete. With her letter she enclosed a photograph of a golden sunrise emerging behind the dark silhouette of Uluru.

*   *   *

Nature holds a multitude of stimuli and is therefore an invaluable resource in increasing pleasurable input for a person suffering stimulus deprivation. The stimuli in natural environments are softer, are more pleasing, and, as already discussed, have a better "biological fit" than stimuli in human-made environments. Interacting with the magnitude and quality of natural stimuli makes it difficult to be depressed at the same time. In fact, it is proposed that natural environments can act as a reciprocal inhibitor of depression. Try to imagine how difficult it must be to feel depressed as you watch a school of dolphins frolicking in the surf, or as you hold your own baby for the first time, or as you cross-country ski over cotton-wool snow that decorates mountains and towering Ponderosa pines. Could Bill have maintained his depression in the water as he related with Simo the dolphin? Or Mary her suicidal ideation as she experimented with thoughts of roses or watched the sunrise over Ayer's Rock? Perhaps, but the stimuli provided by nature are generally inconsistent with depression and thus likely to create a natural shift toward more positive, optimistic states.

Mary still has problems. Some of them won't go away. What has changed is the way she thinks and feels about them. She has discovered a vast reserve of natural stimuli that can readily assist her in creating greater feelings of happiness and pleasure. Thinking of roses instantly brings a smile to her face. The poster-sized photograph of an Ayer's Rock sunrise hanging on her kitchen wall puts her in touch with a sense of healing and spirituality. She knows the advantages of taking a walk by the river and is empowered in the knowledge that she can choose to be in touch with these facilitators of nature-guided healing when necessary.

> *Exercise 12.5:* After engaging in each of the preceding exercises, pause and ask yourself the following questions: What was the pleasure that I derived from that experience? How did I feel different for having engaged in it? If the feeling was good and the process beneficial, what might I do to provide myself further such opportunities in the future? When can I put that into practice?

Chapter 13

ECOTHERAPY FOR ENHANCED RELATIONSHIPS

Natural wonders keep human life wonder full when humans keep a world full of such wonders.—Holmes Rolston (1991)

For many couples, the origins of their relationships are closely associated with the wonders of nature. Courting couples may stroll hand in hand along the beach, picnic by a stream, or park their car in a romantic spot under a full moon. They may make love in a forest, on an isolated beach—or at least have a fantasy of doing so.

There is little question that such natural contexts are considered conducive for courtship. Constructed environments such as an underground parking lot or a city shopping mall generally have less romantic appeal. This, however, is not a hard and fast rule. Some human-made environments, such as restaurants, may be specifically designed to create a romantic ambience. The natural environment, nonetheless, does afford us certain factors that perhaps make it more conducive to the rituals of courtship.

First, nature may heighten the state of a person's sensual awareness. We have already seen the research evidence for this, as well as the fact that most people record predominantly natural stimuli on the Sensual Awareness Inventory.

Second, nature affords a sense of privacy. In nature we can be free to be ourselves. It is where we belong.

Third, the natural environment can allow us a sense of evolutionary, biological, and emotional "fit." And that sense of oneness with our milieu is more likely to facilitate a sense of oneness with each other.

Finally, if the environment itself is conducive to facilitating pleasurable and sensual experiences, then it is likely to facilitate the pleasuring of each other.

As couples "settle down" into a relationship, the activities of courtship and contact with nature tend to diminish. Couples tend to become involved in the day-to-day management of the household, the commitments of work, the issues of raising children, and the concerns of balancing the budget so that courtship tends to take a secondary place, and the stimulating, rejuvenating elements of interacting with the natural environment also tend to be lost.

The case of Ben and Cathy illustrates both the detachment from nature, and each other, that can occur in a relationship and the rediscovery of the things that hold a couple together. Ben and Cathy had been married for 26 years when they consulted me about their marital problems. Cathy told how, over the course of their marriage, they had increasingly been growing apart. Ben had been involved in his work. Cathy had been involved in raising the children. Now that her three sons had left home, she found herself feeling somewhat isolated, lonely, and without a real purpose. She complained of being at home all day with nobody to talk to. When Ben arrived home, she wanted to sit down and talk.

Over the years Ben had climbed the hierarchy in his job, from tradesman to senior administrator. He found it both challenging and demanding, requiring long hours at work. When he got home at the end of the day, he had had enough problems. He simply wanted to flop down, crack open a can of beer, and turn on the television. The last thing he needed was to hear the problems of Cathy's day. He was ready to relax and enjoy the comfort of his home, while she, having been involved in household activities all day, was ready to go out, visit a restaurant, take in a movie, or do something more exciting.

Each had a genuine concern for the other, but they had begun to get involved in constant petty arguments over minor issues. Ben, for example, began to complain about meals. He hated eating large pieces of undercooked onions because they gave him indigestion. Cathy complained that she hated preparing onions because the odors irritated her eyes. Discussing issues for which they never seemed to find a solution focused them more and more on the problems of the relationship and thus increased their feelings of dissatisfaction. They were not creating what they needed to make the situation work, nor were they initiating situations of mutual positive experience.

I requested that, rather than complaining about the onions, they engage in an assignment aimed at finding a solution before our next consultation. They discovered that frozen diced onions are available in supermarkets. Ben smiled insightfully and said, "Life is made up of a lot of little onions."

I asked about what brought them together in the first place. They began to describe the pleasures and joys that they had in first meeting and courting. There was a noticeable shift in affect. They began to smile. They started to make more eye contact as they reminisced about experiences such as sitting with fish and chips and a bottle of wine on the beach to watch a sunset. They were each presented with the Sensual Awareness Inventory and asked to complete it independently. Having done so, they were then asked to place the two completed forms side by side on the refrigerator door. Each day they were to examine their partner's inventory to find one thing they could do to pleasure the partner.

The therapeutic rationale behind this task was to help re-create pleasurable activities such as those that had brought them together in the first place and to establish new pleasurable activities relevant to their present. It was also hypothesized that using the Sensual Awareness Inventory to create positive sensations was a way of breaking the negative-focused, nonresolutional pattern in which they had become stuck.

> *Exercise 13.1:*   Discuss the things you and your partner enjoyed doing together in your courtship, especially where they involved contact with nature, such as walking hand in hand at the beach, parking at a scenic spot, or picnicking in a national park.
> Together, select a time to recapture one such experience.
> Then do it.

When they returned for the next session, they brought news that I had not anticipated. In our initial consultation they had not advised me that they had put their house on the market. Although their sons had left home, they were planning to buy a bigger and better house. Within a few days of being on the market, the property sold, and equally as quickly they decided to take half of the money each and go their separate ways. They had not completed the Sensual Awareness Inventory and not engaged in mutually pleasuring activities. Nonetheless, they each chose to see me separately to help their adjustment to the separation.

Cathy did something she had not done in 26 years. She got a job in the real estate industry and started to prove to herself that she was a very competent and successful sales representative. She bought her own house and began dating other men. She was beginning to discover things about herself that she had lost over the last quarter of a century.

Ben began to make similar discoveries. One of the first things he did was purchase a sports car. He had wanted one all his life but never felt free to do so given his financial commitments to his family. At first he doubted his own ability to relate with the opposite sex, but he soon found himself the attention of other women and was never short of a date.

It was therefore a surprise when they consulted me together about 18 months later. Ben initiated the conversation by saying, "A few months ago I was walking down the street and bumped into Cathy. I thought to myself, 'Gee, I like the way she walks.'" She looked at him and said, "I thought to myself, 'He is not a bad-looking guy.'" Then the interesting thing began to happen. They began to do what they had lost over the decades. They began to date each other. Ben would go to her house with a bunch of flowers. She would cook his favorite meal (presumably with frozen diced onions!). He invited her away for a weekend in a little log cabin in the woods. They walked amongst the trees, paddled on the seashore, and sipped wine under a clear starry sky. They even told me they had taken fish and chips and a bottle of wine to the beach to watch a sunset, just as they did during their courtship.

For several years afterward, I received a Christmas card updating me on their relationship. It seemed they had rediscovered the formula that facilitated their pleasuring of each other. By interacting with nature with heightened sensual awareness, they heightened their appreciation of each other. Although they initially failed to complete their Sensual Awareness Inventory, they had quite spontaneously put into practice the therapeutic recommendations originally suggested.

THE SENSUAL AWARENESS INVENTORY
AND RELATIONSHIP ENHANCEMENT

In the case of Belinda and Malcolm, the couple completed their Sensual Awareness Inventories, thus allowing the opportunity to look at how the SAI may be used in nature-guided therapy for the enhancement of couple relationships. One would think that being on a holiday, particularly a long-dreamed-of holiday, might be a time to relax and leave behind the problems of home. For Belinda and Malcolm that, unfortunately, wasn't the case.

In their late 40s and their second marriage, they had, for the 10 years they had been together, dreamed of, discussed, and planned a caravanning holiday around Australia. Along with their underwear and toothbrushes, however, they had also packed their worries. As they traveled, with the scenery of a magnificent country passing them on either side, they were talking about their problems back home. When they pulled into a caravan park, the conversation again centered on stressful issues half a continent away. During their journey Belinda began feeling extremely anxious, suffered muscular tension, was highly agitated, and felt as though her head were about to explode. Despite being on medication for hypertension, she was aware that her blood pressure was out of control.

Malcolm was reacting with irritability and verbal aggression. He readily acknowledged that, for most of his life, he had struggled with a rather violent temper. He had been verbally abusive in the early years of their marriage but had mellowed during the latter years, feeling he had brought his temper under control. It was being retriggered.

Belinda saw a physician who adjusted her medication and recommended that they both receive psychotherapy. Because they were traveling their time in Perth was limited, and I was able to see them only for two appointments.

Belinda reported that she came from a very maternally dominant family, describing her mother as a critical and down-putting person who constantly made Belinda feel guilty. She perceived that she had replicated this pattern in her first marriage in that her husband was always denigrating of her, even after they had divorced. Her son from that marriage was a drug addict, and her daughter accused Belinda of sexually abusing her as a child. Belinda denied any such abuse, but the daughter severed their relationship and had refused to speak to her mother for the previous 2 years.

In addition to this, she had a brother who was both alcoholic and epileptic. He suffered with frequent seizures and had remained a bachelor all his life. She felt a great sense of responsibility toward him and was harboring much guilt that she had left him to fend for himself while she and Malcolm were taking their vacation.

Neither was Malcolm devoid of problems. He had three children from his first marriage. He said that his former wife had "poisoned their minds" with fictitious and malicious stories about him and Belinda. They had been led to believe that Belinda was the ogre who had caused the breakup of their parents' relationship, and as a result they had totally rejected their father for more than a decade.

He had been raised on the family farm and spent his adult life working the property with his father in the hope that one day it would be his inheritance.

His brother, who had not liked farming life, moved to the city to take up an office job. When the father died suddenly of a heart attack, the mother asked Malcolm's brother back to the farm. It was like the return of the prodigal son. Malcolm believed that he was the one who had done all of the work and that his brother had returned only to get a share of the inheritance. In the end Malcolm proposed subdividing the property and selling off their equal portions, but his mother and brother objected, leaving Malcolm with few other options for employment and no capital to buy into his own property.

These were the issues that were accompanying Belinda and Malcolm, despite the fact that the holiday had been designed to escape them. Nonetheless, the couple seemed to share a genuinely warm and affectionate relationship. They were caring of each other during the consultation and quickly tapped into each other's humor.

The question I faced was what I could offer in just two consultations that would be meaningful and helpful in the management of their problems. Many of their problems, such as their familial relationship difficulties and rejection by their children, were either issues of the past or ones over which they had little control. That they were spending so much of their valuable vacation time ruminating over these matters had contributed largely to their current feelings of anxiety and irritability.

On the basis that it would be therapeutically desirable for them to create more time in positive experiences and less time focusing on unsolvable problems, they were each given a copy of the Sensual Awareness Inventory and asked to complete them independently. The completed forms (see Figures 13.1 and 13.2), while recording the usual and anticipated items of predominantly natural experiences, also held some surprises. Malcolm's list, for example, included Belinda as the first item under each heading. Malcolm also rated highly on Belinda's list. Given their familial histories of poor relationship models and the number of hassles they were experiencing, it was pleasing to see that, after 10 years of marriage, they still valued each other so highly. This, along with the richness of the natural experiences that they enjoyed, provided the opportunity for instructing them in ways to use the SAI to enhance the positive experiences of their travel and relationship while minimizing the focus on their problems. This case illustrates how the SAI can be used to create several nature-based strategies.

The Self-Help Formula for Change

Belinda and Malcolm were given the self-help formula for change (see Chapter 10). They were asked to use this formula both in the singular and in the

Under each heading, please list 10–20 items or activities from which you get pleasure, enjoyment, or comfort.

SIGHT	SOUND	SMELL	TASTE	TOUCH	ACTIVITY
Malcolm	Malcolm laughing	Hay	Roast meat	Lambswool covers	Fishing
Baby animals	A bird in the	Leather	Cooked onions	Malcolm	Vacationing
Sunsets	national park	Fresh-mown lawn	Aniseed	Malcolm's face after	Walking
Waves at beach	Magpies	Horses	Salmon	a shave	Oil painting
Reflections on	Water trickling in	Roast meat	Caramel milkshakes	Baby ducks	Walking in rain
water	stream	Onion cooling	Chinese food	Day-old chickens	Talking to Malcolm
City lights over	Water lapping	Carnations	Chicken	Horse's nose	Barbecue with
water	Breeze in trees	Babies after bath	Garlic bread	A shower	friends
Baby ducks	Thunder	Lemon-scented gum	Peanuts	Warm shower after	Knitting
A painting after I	Kids giggling	trees	Casseroles	being caught in	Gardening
have finished it	Sprinklers in	Malcolm	Savory foods	the rain	Xmas
(a good one)	caravan park	Pipe tobacco	Iced coffee	Waterbed	Massage from
Kids playing	Rain on roof	Fresh sawdust	Shrimp	Lying, talking in	Malcolm
Sleeping babies	Crows	Rain	Crabs	front of heater	Cuddling Malcolm
Shetland ponies	Steam train	Wood fire		in winter	Buying things for
Red roses		Eucalyptus leaves		Cold showers in	other people—not
Xmas lights		Fish cooking		summer	just Xmas presents
		Prawns cooking		Clean sheets	Shrimping

Figure 13.1   The wife's Sensual Awareness Inventory.

177

Under each heading, please list 10–20 items or activities from which you get pleasure, enjoyment, or comfort.

SIGHT	SOUND	SMELL	TASTE	TOUCH	ACTIVITY
Belinda	Belinda	Belinda	Belinda	Belinda	Belinda
Ocean on a calm day	Birds in a national park	Newly sawed timber	Grapes	Patting Rottweiler	Walking
A river with trees overhanging it	Bell birds	Newly turned soil	Watermelon	Patting cats	Talking
Gorges	Waves breaking	Water on dry soil	Chocolate-coated ice creams	Patting horses	Walking barefoot in the rain
Great Ocean Road	Water on the side of a boat	Mown laws	Rockmelon	Belinda's hair, etc.	Gardening
Ferns in a bush	Steam trains	Baked dinner	Mango		Mowing
City lights	Outboard motors	Onion cooking	Leg of lamb		Giving Belinda massage
Waterfalls	Fishing in an aluminum boat	Leather	T-bone		Looking at our country
Mist after a storm	Music	Hay	Lamb chops		Fishing
Sunrises	Silence	Rainforests	Chicken		Shrimping
Sunsets		Lemon-scented gum trees	Shrimp		
		Babies' hair after their bath	Peaches		
			Peanuts		

Figure 13.2   The husband's Sensual Awareness Inventory.

178

plural. For example, if, as an individual, Belinda found that she was thinking or worrying about either her adult children or her brother, she was to stop and ask "Do *I* want to be thinking these thoughts?" or "Do *I* want to be feeling this way?"

On the other hand, if they found themselves in ruminative conversation over the hassles of the farm back home while driving along a scenic coastal road, they were to ask "Do *we* want to be conversing about these matters right now?" If the answer, either as an individual or as a couple, was in the negative, they were directed to use their Sensual Awareness Inventory as a means of selecting experiences to help them attain the thoughts, feelings, or behaviors in which they would prefer to be engaged.

Creating Pleasure for Oneself

The SAI can be used as the basis to direct the client to seek a pleasurable experience for him- or herself. If Malcolm found that he was getting irritable or that his temper was welling up, he was to look at the SAI for an appropriate and attainable experience that would help him focus his attention on something more pleasurable. This, for example, might be the sound of waves breaking, the smell of a fresh-mown lawn, or the tactile experience of patting an animal. Belinda might achieve the same objective by watching reflections in water, listening to the sounds of a trickling stream, or enjoying the fragrance of eucalyptus trees.

Creating Pleasure for One's Partner

A person may also use the SAI to pleasure his or her partner. If we subscribe to the world of advertising, a man might be led to believe that the way to please a woman is to buy her chocolates, a diamond ring, or a fur coat. If she is watching her weight, prefers to spend money on her home rather than herself, or is opposed to the slaughter of animals, he might be way off the mark. The SAI allows one to take a very individual look at the sort of things that bring a partner pleasure.

If Malcolm wanted to do something that would pleasure Belinda, he would be much better advised to cook her a meal on a wintry night when they could listen to rain on the roof, dine at a table decked with carnations, and perhaps look out over a sunset or waves on the beach. In Belinda's case, she could invite Malcolm to take a walk along a gorge up to a waterfall where they could sit in silence and enjoy the experience.

Pleasuring Each Other

Belinda and Malcolm were asked to take time each night after their meal in the caravan to plan an activity they would enjoy doing the next day. To do this it was suggested they might want to exchange SAIs so that they could sit with their partner's form in front of them, look at the things their partner would enjoy, and come up with suggestions that might be mutually pleasurable. The discussion, planning, and anticipation of such events can at times be as therapeutically beneficial as the enactment of the mutually pleasant task. For Belinda and Malcolm, it was hypothesized that engaging in such a conversation would diminish their likelihood of engaging in the other conversations that had led them into feelings of anger and frustration.

Remembering Past, Mutual, Nature-Based Pleasures

Either at the end of the day over a meal or while driving, Belinda and Malcolm were directed to spend some time recalling pleasurable experiences they'd had together, particularly in a natural environment. Such an exercise may help clients become more aware of the pleasurable experiences that brought them together in the first place and shift attention away from stress issues that cannot be modified.

Questions for Extending Mutual Pleasure

Couples may be taught to ask each other questions similar to those included in Exercise 13.5 (see later in this chapter).

Nature-Based Assignments

Clients can be encouraged to use the SAI to develop conjoint nature-based assignments. Also, they may be coached in following the procedural steps for such assignments set out in Chapter 7. Clients can be guided through the process of defining their goal and using their own and their partner's SAIs to discover what may help them achieve that goal. They may also wish to explore, identify, and develop any missing sensual experiences. For example, a couple wanting to develop greater intimacy in their relationship but perhaps reporting few items of tactile awareness in the SAI may be encouraged to participate in activities that concentrate on the development of natural tactile pleasures. The therapeutic object is to create mutual experiences that are naturally fun, rewarding, pleasurable, or challenging.

Shared Experiential Metaphors

Couples can also be instructed in how to develop shared experiential metaphors. This type of assignment is designed not simply to create an experience but to have metaphoric intent with regard to matching the client's problem, developing the client's resources, and providing a metaphoric resolution. Clients are guided through the steps of experiential metaphors set out in Chapter 9.

They may be taught how to define the intent or goal they wish to attain. They are assisted in taking a pilgrimage or journey that is likely to lead them into new experiences relevant to those they want to resolve. The experiential metaphor needs time to integrate as well as time to relate with the environment and each other. A joint interactive process with the natural world is encouraged. Couples are then assisted in steps that may facilitate the desired changes in their relationship and taught ways to use these feelings in a manner that will help in the ongoing search for future experiential metaphors as a couple.

Extending Sensual Pleasure

To help maintain and generalize the benefits for Belinda and Malcolm, they were encouraged to continue to add to their SAI as they made discoveries of further natural pleasures. This activity not only has the benefit of increasing the number of stimuli that may be therapeutically used by a client but also creates an expectancy that the client will become aware of more pleasurable sensations to add to the list.

> *Exercise 13.2:* Study your partner's Sensual Awareness Inventory and note the things that bring him or her pleasure.
> From your observations, select an experience that will pleasure your partner.

Helping couples to work jointly together to create and put into practice nature-based activities offers several rewards. First, there is likely to be the therapeutic reward experienced in achieving the set objective of the task. For Belinda and Malcolm, sitting together while watching reflections in a river lined with overhanging trees not only would be intrinsically satisfying but would also help achieve the goal of moving away from a problem-focused vacation.

Second, discussing, planning, and putting into practice such assignments involves clients in positive, anticipatory communication. This helps break the vicious symptom cycle from the previous focus on problems rather than resolutions. Belinda and Malcolm's entire vacation had become problem focused. For the sake of their health and happiness, it needed a reorientation.

Third, communicating jointly about a task helps clients to access the type of experiences they may have been spontaneously creating during the early stages of their relationship.

Finally, developing nature-based exercises together offers the couple a model for creating continuing positive, shared experiences.

The case of Belinda and Malcolm is not presented to illustrate an outcome. They were seen for two consultations before resuming their journey around the continent. The case is used more as an example of how the SAI can be employed for brief and integrative therapeutic interventions in couples work.

> *Exercise 13.3:* Study, along with your partner, each other's Sensual Awareness Inventory.
> Explore your common themes of enjoyment. Discuss how you could engage in an experience of mutual pleasure.
> Form a plan of how to practically do so.
> Put the plan into practice.

ENHANCING FAMILY RELATIONSHIPS

Researchers and therapists in the area of family relationships have defined in various ways the essential characteristics of meaningful interactions within the family structure. These characteristics can be summarized in four categories:

1. The ability to communicate meaningfully
2. Effectiveness in resolving family and personal problems
3. The means for creating pleasant shared family experiences
4. The ability to create positive bonding in family relationships

Ecotherapy is aimed at enhancing and developing these characteristics of effective interaction within both couple and family relationships.

Chuck was extremely dependent for a 20-year-old. He chose not to consult me by himself and brought his mother to the appointment. Every question I put to him he redirected to his mother. He would either just look at her until she replied or turn to her and ask, "Well?" In this way she spoke for him and he avoided conversation almost completely. After I asked to speak with him alone, he communicated a little more freely but nonetheless remained somewhat reserved. His speech was slow, he carried his body into the room as if it were a dead weight, and his face expressed a great sense of sadness.

He dated his problems back to when there had been a significant change in the family structure 6 months ago. His father was a businessman who had gained a senior appointment in another city about 2 hours away. There his parents had built a new home that they anticipated would see them through to their retirement.

They retained their original home so that Chuck and his sister could continue residing there with minimal disruptions to their life. Chuck took the separation from his parents very harshly. He became depressed, developed a variety of physical symptoms that his physician diagnosed as psychosomatic, and experienced suicidal ideation. On two occasions he had sat drinking alcohol and looking at a bottle of tablets while he pondered the thought of killing himself. He had been disturbed only by the arrival of his sister. On a couple of other occasions he said that he had driven his car at high speed while occupying thoughts about crashing it into a tree or light pole. Although he had not been the most joyful of people before his parents moved away, both he and his mother denied there had been any earlier history of depression.

Chuck was thus facing a number of problems, all involving relationships. First, in the family he seemed to be very dependent on his mother, feeling both scared and incapable of attempting to survive on his own. His relationship with his father was very distant. They hardly spoke to each other, and Chuck attributed this to the fact that his father had always been occupied in business, while at home he was described as "gutless" and unable to stand up for himself.

Second, Chuck's relationship with his sister was extremely ambivalent. Although she was older than Chuck, he felt very responsible for her given the fact that she suffered from Tourette's syndrome. He found himself annoyed and embarrassed by her compulsive grunting sounds, particularly in social situations. He was in conflict between his feelings to care for her and, at the same time, anger that she didn't cease her embarrassing behaviors.

Third, he was experiencing relationship problems at work. He had never related well with his immediate superior, but the situation had deteriorated after his parents moved. He lost interest in his job as a greens keeper at a sports field, and he lost motivation about a course of occupational studies. When he first consulted me, he had just taken 2 days leave from work because of an argument he'd had with his boss.

His social life was not free of relationship problems either. Prior to his parents moving away, he had been an active member of a surf lifesaving club. Following their departure he felt fatigued, lacked motivation, and was physically unwell. But this was only part of the reason for his resignation from the club. Around the same time his parents left, he found a new female friend. They started to date, but as she was previously involved with one of the other surf club members, the matter was obviously talked about by the members. Her previous boyfriend had been more popular than Chuck and apparently roused ill feelings toward Chuck on the part of other club members. Not knowing how to manage these situations, Chuck found himself in several physical fights. As a result he gave up his only recreational love, surfing.

> *Exercise 13.4:* As a family, complete individual Sensual Awareness Inventories.
>
> Allocate a mutually convenient time to discuss the scales. Focus on the family's common themes of pleasure, ensuring that each member's needs are addressed.
>
> Plan the time and means to create a mutually pleasurable activity or activities.

Ecotherapeutic interventions were introduced to assist Chuck in developing more effective ways of relating. The first area of intervention was seen as his relationship with his father. The rationale was that in helping him to build the relationship with his father he would be developing several new skills. First, he would be overcoming a longstanding relationship problem. Second, he would be learning to initiate effective relationship skills. Finally, it was thought that this process might help to reduce his dependency on his mother.

When he was first seen, it was not believed that he would be motivated sufficiently to complete the Sensual Awareness Inventory, and so his sources of sensual pleasure were discussed. There was a distinct ocean theme running through all areas of his sensual enjoyment. This was related to his surfing background and the fact that he used to row surf boats for the lifesaving club. When we began to discuss things that brought his father pleasure, an ocean theme was again present. His father had a small boat and was an avid angler. Chuck was given assignments such as arranging to go fishing with his father. He soon began to enjoy these visits and was looking forward to spending time with his father.

In the next treatment stage, it was believed that developing similar positive strategies of interacting with his girlfriend would produce benefits. First, he would be learning ways of relating meaningfully with his partner, and, second, he would be reducing the time he spent with—and the responsibility he felt for—his sister. He was assigned the task of talking with his girlfriend about the things that they both enjoyed in the areas of their senses. This was a variation of Exercise 13.4 in that the SAI was not actually administered.

Having been in the surf club, Chuck's girlfriend also enjoyed water sports and activities. Together they joined a different surf club. Chuck took her on some of his weekend visits to his family. He described these times as good, saying that, as a family, they were starting to have fun together rather than fighting.

As well as enhancing his relationships, the pleasurable nature of the prescribed ecotherapeutic interactions helped Chuck to alter his affect. His suicidal ideation disappeared, he returned to work, and, after six consultations, he believed that he had life back on track and needed no further appointments.

In this case, only one member of the family was seen. This was in part due to the distance and physical problems of arranging consultations with the whole family, but it may not have been necessary to directly involve the other members in helping Chuck reach his goal. Of course, ecotherapy can be administered when consulting entire families and when working in parent-child relationships to help ensure the facilitation of communication, the effective solution of problems, the creation of pleasant shared experiences, and the development of positive familial relationships.

> *Exercise 15:* At the completion of each exercise, ask your partner or other family members the following questions:
>
> 1. What did you/we gain from that experience?
> 2. How do you/we think we could benefit from doing more of that sort of thing?
> 3. How can we do something similar, or different, for fun again?
> 4. When is it going to be convenient to create such an experience?
>
> In exploring these questions, remember to:
>
> 1. Discuss your own feelings and experience.
> 2. Listen carefully to the feelings expressed by your partner or family members.
> 3. Search for mutually pleasurable experiences rather than problems.

PART V
NATURAL WELLNESS

Chapter 14

THE NATURE-MIND-BODY CONNECTION

To insure health, a man's relation to Nature must come very near to a personal one.—Henry Thoreau (1987)

As we have seen, Ulrich et al. (1991) used psychophysiological methods to investigate the role of natural environments in helping people cope with stress. Stress reactions, in contrast to relaxation, are associated with an increment in physiological activities such as heart rate, blood pressure, skin conductance, muscular tension, blockage of alpha, electroencephalographic activity, and stress hormones. In measuring some of these physiological responses, in their relationship to attention, cognition, emotions, and stress responses, Ulrich and colleagues found that stressed individuals experienced rapid stress reduction in natural settings, whereas recovery could be hampered by urban environments. They went on to observe that views of natural scenery, unlike views of an urban milieu, involve an autonomic nervous system response through parasympathetic channels.

The work did not postulate any explanation and leaves us with a question: If there is a direct link between nature and autonomic nervous responses, what is this connection, and how can it be used in a therapeutic context? How can brief interactions with nature bring about changes in psychophysiological symptoms, and what are the means available for replicating the process for the benefit of our clients? We have already seen, in the wisdom of traditional healers, the process of creating states of well-being through interactions with the natural ecology. The methodological approach of research psychology is confirming this knowledge. Let us explore this information and the nature-mind-body connection.

HEALING FEELINGS

First, we have seen how, given the choice of different environments, people almost invariable opt for nature. Purcell, Lamb, Perin, and Falchero (1994) explored landscape preferences in culturally different subjects half a globe apart. Australian and Italian university students were asked to rate scenes as natural or human constructed and to indicate their preference for each scene, first, as an overall preference; second, as a place to live and work; and, third, as a site at which they would like to vacation. Nature rated as the preferred choice in all three categories. An interesting observation in this study is that cases in which nature and human construction came together, such as in a rural scene with farm buildings, tended to be rated as human constructed, suggesting that there was a tendency to observe nature in a rather pure manner.

Second, there is evidence to show that our preferred milieu brings about shifts toward positive affective states. Russell and Mehrabian conclude that the physical environment can strongly "elicit emotions" (1976, p. 17); the preferred environment features positive feeling states, while undesirable environments can elicit both negative feelings and unhealthy behaviors. There seems to be a conclusive opinion among researchers that "we find ourselves more relaxed and at ease in natural surroundings" (McAndrew, 1993, p. 254) and that these preferred natural settings are "intrinsically satisfying" (p. 251). Others, such as Baum (1991), conclude that there is a measurable link between natural contexts and well-being.

Third, feelings have direct psychophysiological associates. Siegel takes this beyond the modification that occurs in our heart rate, our respiration, or even our muscle tone to say that "feelings are chemicals and can kill or cure" (1986, p. 16). He goes on to explain that "there are approximately 60 known peptide molecules in the body, . . . like endorphins, interleukins, and interferon. They make feelings chemical and affect the link between psyche and soma" (1986, p. 20). These peptides are the messenger molecules or chemical transmitters of information that communicate between mind and body in an endless loop. The limbic-hypothalamic area of the brain is like a signal box that not only communicates messages but controls the system. Talking of the peptides, Siegel says, "They make possible the move from perception or thought or feeling in the mind, to messages transmitted by the brain, to the hormonal secretions and on down to cellular action in the body" (1986, p. 36).

Here Siegel defines the formula of the nature-mind-body connection. Given the choice of environmental contexts, we seem to have a preference for nature. Nature provides us with sensory stimulation, varied, changing, and multi-faceted. These stimuli are input by our various senses and communicated through the relevant neural pathways to the brain. Here the perception is converted, via the limbic-hypothalamic system, to a hormonal secretion that communicates with our body. This communication is not necessarily selective of any one system and indeed can relay healing messages through not only the neural peptide network but, as mentioned earlier, the autonomic nervous system, the endocrine system, and the immune system.

The work of Ulrich et al. (1991) provides a clear example of this model in operation for two polar-opposite dimensions. By showing an anxiety-arousing movie, Ulrich et al. displayed how an unpleasant context presents visual and aural stimuli that elicit sympathetic activity, elevating heart rate, blood pressure, muscle tone, and skin conductance. A therapeutically desirable model is seen in the outcome of his stressed subjects watching videos of nature. These natural scenes offered visual and aural stimuli that were pleasurable to the subjects. Eyes and ears absorbed these stimuli and communicated them through neural pathways, leading to an altered cerebral state and the release of neurotransmitters that sent messages to the parasympathetic nervous system, which brought about healthy changes in the psychophysiological modes being measured. In fact, if other systems had been observed, we might have noticed a wider range of bodily shifts toward a state of health and well-being.

This is a process known as transduction, in which one form of energy or information is transformed into another form altogether. The inert substance of coal can be transformed by fire into heat. That energy can transduce water into steam, which in turn may be converted into mechanical energy to rotate the wheels of a steam engine. This mechanical energy can be transduced into motion by which a train can move heavy objects over a long distance. It is this process of transduction that takes place in nature-mind-body healing. The vibrating vocal chords of a bird in song are transduced into air waves that fall on a listener's eardrum and are converted, through vibrations of skin and bone, into a message transduced through a neural pathway to the brain. That information is transformed into messenger molecules that, in turn, transduce changes in physiological and affective states.

The transduction process from preferred or positively perceived stimuli results in healthy and harmonious physiological states. The aim of psychotherapy is, in itself, a process of transduction. The therapeutic contract with a client is to shift energy from symptoms and problems into solutions and wellness, whether at an emotional, physical, or spiritual level.

Recently I sat with a client who commenced her conversation by saying "Life is awful." Certainly things had been difficult. She had been granted stress leave from her job as a teacher and was on workers' compensation for an indefinite period. She complained of how "horrible" her job had been because of the "terrible" students she'd had to teach. They had no respect and were completely unruly. She'd had to sit through summer afternoons in unconditioned classrooms. The administration had been continually making changes, and the situation was now "hopeless." She described a feeling of helplessness. She'd had a "revolting" marriage, and her husband had left her for another woman. Life was "unfair."

Within a few minutes of listening to her story, I found myself feeling almost equally powerless as I realized the intensity of the energy that she had invested in her symptoms. To even contemplate transforming her well-established negative situation seemed a monumental task. In contrast, work at the creation of positives is relatively simpler. If we teach joy and happiness, we are altering the experience of depression. If we help facilitate healthy immune function, we are enhancing well-being. To transduce the song of a bird into an emotion of joy or a positive alteration in our parasympathetic nervous system in itself modifies feelings of tension or activates a sympathetic nervous response.

NATURE AS A SOURCE
OF STATE-DEPENDENT RESOURCES

In addition to the stimulus-response-transduction process examined here, some researchers claim that state dependence, or state-bound memories, learnings, and behaviors, is also involved in the information transduction in mind-body healing. Researchers such as Murray and Mishkin (1985) have been seeking to follow the pathways through which our perceptual input is transduced to the limbic-hypothalamic system, where it is integrated with memory and learning. Here it is stored, as if in a library, for future reference and transduction into psychophysiological responses. This reference system is referred to as state-dependent memory or learning because "what is learned and remembered is dependent on one's psychophysiological state at the time of the experience" (Rossi, 1986, p. 36).

Rossi continues, by way of an example: "Memories acquired during the state of hypnosis are forgotten in the awake state but available once more when hypnosis is reinduced. Since memory is dependent upon and limited to the state in which it is acquired, we say it is 'state-bound information'" (p. 36). It is not the scope of this work to trace the communication pathways by which the sound of a bird falling on the auditory cortex is communicated to the limbic-hypothalamic system. Instead let us focus on the way natural experiences are incorporated into state-dependent memories, learnings, and behaviors; the resources available in this area; and the therapeutic ways in which they can be used.

State-Dependent Memories

Robert is an accountant. He presented for therapy, on referral from his physician, complaining that life seemed pointless, that he had been drinking excessively and was plagued with suicidal ideation. He said, "This shouldn't be so." He had recently passed postgraduate examinations in his profession. He had a stable and well-paid job, being employed by a personal friend for the last 18 years. His wife held a challenging job as personal secretary to a university professor. He had some worries that he would not be able to save sufficiently for his retirement, and, in scrimping and saving for this event that was still a couple of decades away, he had almost ceased living in the present. He belonged to a sporting club but didn't participate in the sporting activities. He was on the club's committee, serving as an honorary treasurer.

His mother had recently died, and he reported intense feelings of guilt that seemed to be the trigger for him seeking therapy. The hospital caring for his mother, in her advanced state of cancer, had telephoned one day to say that she didn't have much longer to live. On his way to the hospital he stopped at the hotel to fortify himself for the experience. As a result of this delay in his journey, by the time he got to the hospital, she had already died, leaving him with feelings of guilt and a sense of failure as a son.

After respectfully listening to his story and permitting him the experience of his grief, I presented him with the Sensual Awareness Inventory. For the first time his face lit up in a smile and he said, "In looking at this the first thing I experienced was the smell of rain on dry ground." When I asked how it felt he said, "Great! The best time of my life was my childhood." He went on to describe, with delight, the enjoyable times he had being raised as a child on a farm.

When he came back the next week with the inventory completed, he began discussing numerous other pleasurable experiences. These were all in the nature of state-bound memories that the exercise had afforded him the opportunity of accessing. To my surprise he told me that, in the week since our last appointment, he had consulted a professional employment service that had arranged an interview for him with a major accounting firm. He left the small private practice without any career prospects and took up a senior position with the large firm. He rented out his old home "as an investment" and bought an oceanfront block of land on which to build a new one.

State-dependent memories of happiness and wellness, such as those Robert accessed so quickly, are often acquired in childhood explorations, while on vacation, or at family picnics. These are times when the environment is pleasant and conducive to positive experiences and when family relationships are relaxed, free, and fun-filled.

It seems that natural settings are stored in our memory as significant and enjoyable experiences. In an Israeli study of almost 200 subjects, including architecture students as well as schoolteachers and principals, Sebba (1991) sought to explore the most significant places in individuals' childhood memories. She found that 97% of her subjects reported that a natural outdoor setting, such as a park or the seashore, held the greatest significance for them.

In Chapter 1 I examined how natural sacred sites developed state-dependent memories and healing properties not only for individuals (Mazumdar & Mazumdar, 1993) but also for entire societies (Swan, 1988; Eliade, 1989; Roseman, 1991). Relph (1976) used an ecologically based metaphor to describe these natural places and experiences of our emotional attachment as "fields of care," which he defined as "settings in which we have a multiplicity of experiences and which call forth an entire complex of affections and responses" (p. 38).

State-Dependent Learnings

In the natural milieu, we are able to make, early in our life, some of the most significant discoveries that will take us through our journey of being. These are learnings about ourselves, our relationship with others, and our relationship with ecology. According to Relph (1976, p. 43), "There is for virtually everyone a deep association with and consciousness of the places where we are born and grow up, where we live now or where we had particularly moving experiences. This association seems to constitute a vital source of both individual and cultural identity and security." And, because Sebba (1991) points out that the significant places for almost everyone are natural outdoor settings, it would seem that these are one of the major sources for developing our individual and contextual concept of self. Cooper-Marcus takes this concept further to include the interactive processes already discussed here as characteristic of traditional healing. She says that "emotions and place are inexplicably connected, not in a causal relationship but in a transactional exchange unique to each person" (1992, p. 111).

The importance of the environment in creating these learnings is evidenced in cultural folktales. Folk stories for century upon century have been means of communicating the values, morals, and traditions of a society, as well as helping to prepare its members for the events that life is likely to bring their way. Thus, folktales, as well as relating spiritual and mythological aspects, are frequently based in natural settings, involve a person's interaction with nature, or include animals and their relationship with humans. Sakya and Griffith claim that "the use of real settings in folktales is important as people are always prepared to accept and enjoy themes and situations with which they are familiar" (1980, p. 13). Placing tales in natural settings allows for a person to identify and indeed to even access state-dependent memories. From this identification, a person can be led and guided to the learnings communicated through the story. The learnings elicited in this manner are often produced in natural contexts (for example, sitting around a campfire at night under a starry sky).

Are Nature Memories Inherited?

Specific natural stimulation may elicit specific emotional and psychophysiological changes. The mind modulation of bodily processes can be influenced by state-bound resources. The rapidity and effectiveness of natural stimuli in eliciting these responses may lead us to question whether there is some earlier inherited or genetic predisposition to prefer natural environments and derive psychobiological responses from them.

Throughout history humankind has depended on nature as a means of survival. Great civilizations as diverse as the Mesopotamians and the Mayans collapsed not through wars or exotic diseases but, rather, through the failure of the environment to continue to support the growing population. Ancient people relied on nature as a source of entertainment as well as a means of survival. It is only since the development of electricity that we have been able to technologically reproduce sounds or moving images within our own homes. Evolutionary theorists describe the physical development of our species in terms of similarities such as those between the bone structure of the human hand and the pectoral fins of the whale. Is it not equally likely that our evolution has maintained in us the necessary psychological resources to cope with what has traditionally been our environment? That, in terms of evolution, we are more adapted to the natural ecology than high-density inner suburban constructions?

We have, through the millennia, survived as a result of our attachment to, and interaction with, our natural landscape. Low (1992) sees this place attachment as not only creating emotional and cognitive experiences but forging a relationship between people and the land. It is a relationship that has developed through a variety of linking factors, including genealogy, cosmology, pilgrimage, narrative, and economics. The genealogy, the evolution over generation after generation perhaps has similarities to what Meares (1960, 1970, 1978) spoke about in his concept of atavistic regression. He defined this as "a regression from a normal adult mental function at an intellectual, logical level, to an archaic level of mental function in which the process of suggestion determines the acceptance of ideas" (1960, p. 59). He saw us regressing, in deep stages of meditation, to an earlier state in our evolutionary history. He also considered this regression the basic mechanism in the induction of hypnosis, in much the same way as Rossi sees state-dependent memories as integrally related with hypnosis and healing.

Maybe this inherited memory is what Pert and Ruff (1987) are referring to when they claim that extremely deep, unconscious processes are expressed at all physical levels, down to individual organs such as the heart, lungs, and pancreas. Their work, they say, demonstrates that all of the cells of the nervous system and endocrine system are functionally integrated by networks of peptides and their receptors.

The depth of unconscious processing in these areas and the similarities of such processes across cultures seem to suggest a genetic inheritance rather than an acquisition in just one human life span. It would certainly be more economic for our species to pass on these universally required skills. Consequently, we may postulate that nature-mind-body connections in the areas of health, happiness, and well-being are well established resources uniquely available to our species and are thus both readily and easily accessible.

Accessing State-Dependent Resources

State-dependent natural memories are rich in resources that can be accessed for therapeutic gain. The eliciting of such memories can quickly bring emotional responses of peace, calm, or tranquillity. They can quickly produce emotions of happiness, joy, and love or create arousal through fun, excitement, and stimulation. The state-dependent learnings based in nature may be ones of decision making, confidence enhancement, and esteem building, while the state-bound natural psychophysiological consequences may be health, wellness, energy, and vitality. Rossi (1993) speaks of accessing and transducing state-dependent memory, learning, and behavior systems through hypnosis and the language of suggestion. State-dependent memories can also be accessed and transduced through the re-creation of positive individualized experiences of our world of nature. Just as by returning to hypnosis one may access material of which a client has been amnesic, so by returning to natural stimuli we can quickly access positive resources for wellness and recovery. In many ways, nature itself serves as a metaphor. Nature is alive and living. It is constantly going through a process of change, rejuvenating and regenerating. Our experience with nature is indeed an experience with this ongoing life force.

The stimuli provided by natural phenomena initiate the process of transduction. They may also elicit an independent response, drawing on state-dependent memories and learnings, or even tap into deeper genetic memory. By accessing these rich and vast resources, we can—effectively, quickly, and practically—alter states of mind, affect, and body. Means of accessing these for dealing with specific problems are dealt with in subsequent chapters.

Cheek illustrated the practical use of sensory perceptual input in the healing process with preoperative training (Rossi & Cheek, 1988, p. 146). The model he proposed involved three steps: (a) initial training in anesthesia and well-being, (b) accessing and use of inner resources, and (c) ratification of postoperative healing. The resource that he accessed in the second stage was to invite clients to select a time when on vacation. They were directed to be aware of sensory perceptual input in terms of the things that they were seeing, the people they were relating with, and the foods they were enjoying. Here Cheek assumed a direct sensory connection to our healing processes. His hypnotic suggestion to his client was as follows: "As you do this [that is, imagine the sensations found stimulating and pleasurable during that holiday] you will be using all the normal biological processes for healing for your body" (p. 146).

ECOTHERAPY: THE FORGOTTEN DIMENSION IN MIND-BODY HEALING

Ecotherapy is an antecedent step that seems to be acknowledged but not used in the psychobiological model in any systematized manner. Although Rossi's (1993) model of mind-body healing tends to bridge the longstanding dichotomy that segregated these aspects of our being, it still does so in the reductionistic model of Western medical science. Exploring the cortico-limbic system (which processes planning and integration), the hypothalamic nuclei (which transduce through the autonomic, endocrine, immune, and peptide systems), the amygdala (with its cross-modal associations), and the thalamus (which serves a relay function), he examines how the processes transduce information to the level of our genes. Such a reductionistic approach is itself dichotomous because it is segregating the internal functions of the human being from the totality with its relationship with the world.

Rossi's model treats people as autonomously functioning units separated from their natural system, ecological milieu, or biodiversity. In this way the model tends to follow the criticism raised by Roszak. "In the Western world the bio-medical model of the psyche was patterned upon the pre-existing bio-medical model of the body. The body to which the mind was assimilated was already a disenchanted object. Stripped down to its psychophysiological components, it was understood to be 'nothing but' a machine. Anatomical sketches of the 17th and 18th century reveal a fascination with the idea that the limbs and organs of the body can be analyzed into springs, levers, pumps, pistons. This is the distant origin of our conviction that the body can be improved upon by spare-part surgery. The psyche came to be seen as nothing sacred as the body to which it was attached was nothing sacred. The connection between the two was the nervous system, seen as an electro-chemical apparatus. Along these reductive physical lines, one treats the psyche by way of drugs, electro-shock, or surgical intervention" (1992, p. 78).

Such an inner focus furthers the schism that separates humans from the total community of animals, insects, and plants that occupy the planet. It limits the focus, according to Roszak, to specific therapeutic interventions that are most likely to be based on a solely physical emphasis.

Admittedly Rossi goes beyond the concerns of Roszak but is still limited with the types of strategies that he proposes for mind-body healing. He says, "All processes of meditation (Smith, McKenzie, Marmer, & Steele, 1985), hypnosis (Bowers, 1977), imagery (Achterberg, 1985), active imagination (Jung, 1960), the systems approach to therapeutic communication (Watzlawick, 1978, 1984), and even the placebo response (White, Tursky, & Schwartz, 1985) can be understood as means of exploring, accessing and utilizing the many modalities and languages of mind-body communication" (Rossi & Cheek, 1988, p. 163). However, despite awareness of the sensory perceptual source and its importance in the transduction processes, this source, which can be the initiator of the entire process, is not explored as a resource or for its potencies in therapeutic process.

Ecotherapy focuses on accessing natural state-dependent resources that alter affect, cognitions, behavior, and psychophysiology in the direction of problem resolution. The more one accesses these positive, creative, and healthy resources, the less the problem is likely to be experienced and the more naturally a person is likely to feel well.

For Kiefer and Cowan, state dependency is intrinsically linked to its context: "The state-context dependency theory . . . creates a bridge between a growing body of laboratory work on neurophysiology and psychopharmacology on the one hand and ethnological field studies on the other" (1979, p. 55). An understanding of this nature-mind-body link, the ecopsychobiological relationship, opens the opportunity for ecotherapy to be used not only in affective, cognitive, or behaviorally directed therapies, as described in the preceding chapters, but also in the healing of the body.

Chapter 15

NATURE-GUIDED MIND-BODY HEALING

If the basis for a treatment which has saved countless human lives exists in something as apparently insignificant and innocuous as a piece of mouldy cheese (penicillin) then I suggest we should open our minds very wide when looking to Nature for help to cure our ills.—Horace Dobbs (1988)

Before beginning to explore at the nature-mind-body healing processes and their clinical applications, it will be helpful to examine some of the theoretical and experimental rationale underlying the application of ecotherapeutic healing.

THE DIRECT ECOBIOLOGICAL RELATIONSHIP

Researchers who have directed their attention to person-environment issues generally agree that there is a causal relationship between the environment and emotional experiences. For Strongman (1987), the importance of the environment in emotional experiences was clear cut. "It is indisputable," he concluded, "that the environment has an emotional impact on the individual" (p. 225). Earlier Ittelson, Rivlin, Proshansky, and Winkel (1974) had claimed that "spaces and places, no less than people, can evoke intense emotional responses." Going on to comment about this in regard to human-built environments, they said, "Rooms, neighborhoods, and cities may be 'friendly,' 'threatening,' 'frustrating' or 'loathsome,' they can induce hate, love, fear, desire, and other affective states" (p. 88). With this variety of affective associations to a constructed person-environment context we can also assume a similar "indisputable" link between a natural environment and our emotional state. Mehrabian and Russell (1974) refer to this link as being "direct," almost seeming to exclude any intermediate perceptual-cognitive linking between the stimuli of the environment and the state of a person's emotional response, although they do accept that emotional reactions may be influenced by the internal emotional condition of the person in contact with nature. These internal emotional conditions seem to bear some relationship to what Rossi (1993) refers to as state-dependent memory, learnings, and behavior.

If (a) natural environmental stimuli are those most preferred (Sebba, 1991), (b) such natural environmental stimuli directly affect our emotional state (Strongman, 1987), and (c) states of mental and emotional pleasure are transduced into pleasurable healthy states of physical well-being (Rossi, 1993), then we may conclude that exposure to preferred natural stimuli has a direct causal effect on our state of physical health.

THE HISTORIC ECOBIOLOGICAL CONNECTION

Physiological changes associated with environmental stimuli seem to be an archaic part of our evolutionary history and biological makeup. According to Amedeo (1993), physiological changes such as adrenalin flow, blood circulation, respiration, muscular tension, gastrointestinal activities, temperature, and secretions that occur with changes in emotional states are "set off by nerve cell activity in the limbic system, which is said to be, in an evolutionary sense, an older part of the brain—one not involved in intellectual functions but in life sustaining ones" (p. 86). The limbic system, developed over a million generations, associated with physical and emotional changes, and serving a life-sustaining function, is directly linked to our natural environment. As such, the environment itself has a historic influence in affecting and modifying our emotional system, our physical well-being, and our survival.

Coming from a somewhat different angle, Hartig and Evans (1993) claim that, after millennia of evolution and adaptation to surviving and reproducing in savanna-like natural settings, early humanoids genetically became part of those particular environments. We are the direct genetic inheritants of those physiological and psychological adaptive systems necessary for such environmental survival. Thus, according to Hartig and Evans, "Our basic capabilities for apprehending, interpreting, evaluating, and acting upon information from the environment are best suited to environments from which humans emerged" (1993, p. 437).

Historically the most adaptive individuals were those most likely to survive. Our ancestors were thus able to avoid unpleasant or threatening environments while showing preference for those conducive to their well-being. Hartig and Evans state that "although preference responses may now have less significance for biological survival, they retain benefit value in that they signal positive states (e.g., aesthetic satisfaction, lack of anxiety). These states imply the operation of the various psychological and physiological systems involved in knowing and acting" (1993, p. 437). They conclude that such evolutionary theories consider our ability to realize the benefits of natural experiences as "in-built."

In other words, we have a cerebral, genetic, and evolutionary capacity to relate with the natural ecology for our survival and the wellness of each member of our species. During the lengthy emergence of our species, an ecobiological relationship has evolved enabling us to learn and incorporate adaptive mechanisms to ensure a healthy relationship with the natural environment.

URLICH'S PSYCHOEVOLUTIONARY MODEL

Urlich's (1981) research has demonstrated that there is a rapid emotional response to certain environmental configurations. On the basis of this he developed the psychoevolutionary model (1983; Ulrich et al., 1991), which attributes rapid and direct responses to evolutionary-based adaptive processes. The rapidity and directness of these responses seem to be due to the fact that cognitive processes are bypassed both in a person's initial emotional response and in the consequent level of arousal. In other words, there are specific, conducive natural stimuli that will elicit a feeling state long before we stop to think about them.

For example, a dark cave that could possibly harbor animals of prey or hordes of screeching bats may fill us with a feeling of fear and elicit an avoidance response before we consciously process the reasons. Similarly, the sight of a rainbow, seen through many cultures as an auspicious sign, may initiate a sense of wonderment and a desire to pause in observation, without conscious rationale. Urlich's psychoevolutionary model proposes that perceptual attention is selective and that this selection will be determined by an observer's current affective-arousal state. This state will, of course, be influenced by both immediate and previous experiences of one's interaction with nature. What is preferentially selected for attention elicits an initial affective reaction, bypassing cognitive processes and influencing cognition and motivation as well as the individual's psychophysiological arousal.

In 1981 Henry and Meehan, who carried out a review of the literature examining psychosocial stimuli, physiological specificity, and cardiovascular disease, found a relationship between processes and human immune functioning. This opened up the opportunity for others, such as Parsons (1991), to specifically explore the potential influences of environmental perception on human health.

Because the amygdala and hippocampus are involved in the integration of emotions, motivation, memory, and learning (Lewis et al., 1981; Kesner, 1984; Pert, 1985, 1987), these two components of the limbic system are associated with attentional tuning and are thus actively involved in the selection of environmental preferences. With evolutionary-developed and genetically stored preferences for ecologically aesthetic stimuli already programmed in that older part of our brain, the accessing of such familiar stimuli is likely to ensure a physiological state of well-being.

Parsons proposes that environments we perceive as uninhabitable, unaesthetic, or incompatible "may be uniquely stressful" (1991, p. 16). A person living in an urban environment is exposed to a low-grade, subconscious stress level that may be detrimental to physical well-being. Exposure to preferred natural stimuli, on the other hand, disrupts this stress response and, depending on the quality and duration, can provide health benefits. Hartig and Evans express it this way: "Nature experiences may inoculate people against stress" (1993, p. 451).

IS THE ECOPSYCHOBIOLOGICAL RESPONSE INTERACTIVE?

As we saw in Chapter 1, healing has traditionally been viewed as an interactive process with the environment. Researchers in the field of environmental psychology find themselves concurring with this traditional wisdom. Investigators such as Ittelson et al. (1976) recognize individuals as agents who act upon their environment and are in turn influenced by it. It is not a passive process in which the person is an unresponsive receptor of perceptual stimuli or one in which the environment does not respond or become influenced by the presence of the person. It is indeed a two-way street.

Meaning is attributed to the environmental stimuli by a person. The way in which these stimuli are then transduced into a psychobiological response is determined interactively by cues from the environment and the internal emotions, knowledge, and memories a person brings to that context. Rapoport (1982) describes it as a nonverbal communication between the environment and those who interact with it.

THE RESTORATIVE FUNCTION
OF THE ECOBIOLOGICAL RELATIONSHIP

The concept of the restorative power of nonverbal communication with nature is widely acknowledged (Pigrim, 1993). Kaplan and Kaplan (1989) see nature as being conducive to what they refer to as "effective functioning." They defined nature as vegetated landscapes regardless of whether they involved a rural or urban context. This definition includes country meadows, city parks, and backyard gardens as well as wilder and more pristine environments such as national parks. The preference that people show for such natural contexts not only reinforces the concept of inherited attractiveness to nature but also validates the body of research confirming that nature rapidly invokes positive emotional and physical responses.

With a 14-day outdoor challenge program studied over several years, Kaplan (1974, 1984) demonstrated a variety of self-reported improvements, including enhanced positive affect, ability to concentrate, outlook on life, and self-concept. Briefer exposures to nature were also discovered to have restorative value (Kaplan, 1983, 1985). Even nature contact, such as in backyard gardening, was found to be a source of psychological gain and tranquillity (Kaplan, 1973). Kaplan and Kaplan (1989) thus see a wide range of natural contexts as being a restorative environment in which human functioning can be replenished. Others, such as Hartig, Mang, and Evans (1990), have further experimentally assessed and confirmed the Kaplans' notion of the restorative effects of natural environment experiences.

VARIABLES IN THE RESTORATION PROCESS

Four interactive variables are seen by the Kaplans as the crucial attributes in this concept of restoration, and it is argued that these factors are most likely to occur in the natural ecology.

Being Away

First, in nature there is a sense of "being away." By this it is meant that there is a feeling of being removed from one's day-to-day environment and experiences that are likely to create certain levels of stress or place demands on voluntary attention. The distancing may be geographical, it may be psychological, or it may be a combination of both. It is the sort of experience that people will readily report as associated with natural environments, such as while vacationing at the beach, backpacking through a national park, working in a domestic garden, or scuba diving on a tropical reef.

Extent

Second, in nature there is a feeling of extent. This is the type of experience a person may have while lying back at a campsite looking up at an uninterrupted nocturnal sky of twinkling stars. One might have a simultaneous feeling of connectedness with the totality of the universe and a sense of being but a small part of an overall larger context. In the clinical setting, people who have had such an experience often report that it brings what was previously seen as an overwhelming problem into a more realistic context.

Fascination

Third, nature is a rich resource of fascination. Its contents and processes provide our senses with a multiplicity of varying, intriguing, and pleasurable stimuli. It captures our involuntary attention, such as in the universal fascination we experience with the infinitely variable light show of a sunset.

Oneness

Finally, there is an experience of compatibility, a sense of oneness, a sense of the "biological fit" that engenders a psychological and physiological feeling of belonging within a supportive and harmonious environment. "It is as if there is a special resonance between the natural environment and human inclinations" (Kaplan & Kaplan, 1989, p. 93).

As we continue to look at the restorative power of natural environments, it is useful too to look at the literature review carried out by Knopf (1987). Knopf's overview led to the conclusion that behavior is differentially affected by natural environments in five ways. First, accustomed patterns of functioning, feeling, and problem solving may be challenged by a natural context. This may become increasingly so with the greater unfamiliarity of nature, such as experienced in a wilderness milieu. Second, nature is neither critical nor negative. It maintains an impartiality and an indifference to us, our problems and our self-concepts. Third, because there is a certain amount of relative predictability about nature, and also some sense of control, we are able to be more relaxed and thus less in need of suspicious, defensive, or protective behaviors. Fourth, nature allows greater freedom of expression. One may be more at ease with oneself, thus having greater freedom for self-expression. Finally, there is a greater sense of personal control in natural than in human-determined contexts.

ECOBIOLOGY IN THE TREATMENT OF LIFE-THREATENING ILLNESS

In the psychological and psychobiological approaches to the facilitation of cancer therapy, there have been a wide variety of interventions as diverse as the aggressive, attack-the-cancer-cells approach of the Simontons (Simonton, Simonton, & Creighton, 1978) and the very passive meditational approach of Meares (1982–1983). While there remains little doubt that anxiety, depression, and low ego strength are correlated with suppression of the immune system, attempts to define the significant factors that enhance the immune system and thereby prevent the onset of serious illness have not met with the same consensus.

Locke et al. (1984), along with many others, define the major enhancement factor in terms of a person's coping ability. For Spiegel (1993), however, the variables cannot be defined in such a singular concept. He describes a number of factors that are facilitative and restorative for people facing life-threatening illness. Interestingly, these factors closely parallel those defined by the Kaplans (1989) and Knopf (1987) as the restorative elements involved in the natural environment. When Spiegel speaks of "taking time" and "transforming time," for example, he seems to be talking in language similar to that used by the Kaplans in defining the variable of "being away."

The supportive and restorational characteristics that Spiegel sees as crucial in cancer therapy are important variables available in nature. Naturally, they provide the desirable context for prevention of, recovery from, and management of serious illness.

AN ECOPSYCHOBIOLOGICAL MODEL FOR
FACILITATING HEALTH AND HEALING

The natural environment has a primary, direct, and immediate effect on our emotional state. This effect is one that has developed over the millennia of evolutionary history as our species has acquired the necessary mechanisms for survival and well-being. These inherent adaptive mechanisms incorporate our neurophysiology and psychobiology. We are indeed part of our world, and we communicate with our biosphere in a nonverbal manner. Such communications serve a restorative function, and there are features of this process of restoration that parallel what researchers and clinicians are finding to be the core elements necessary in the treatment of significant illnesses such as cancer. The nature-mind-body link is more than just another means by which to achieve relaxation, facilitate stimulation, or offer distraction; it is a unique, archaically evolved, rapid, and beneficial means of creating a state of well-being and facilitating the process of healing.

The ecopsychobiological model for facilitating healing is presented in Figure 15.1. The term *ecopsychobiology* is used to illustrate the interactive elements of the relationship between mind and nature, nature and body. This is not designed to suggest that there are three autonomous entities that choose to interact like three individuals on separate telephone extensions. It is probably more useful to see the oneness or connectedness as a total communication system than to look at it as separate parts connected by defined wiring. Figure 15.1 is based on the work of Achterberg and Lawlis (1984), Rossi (1993), and Ulrich (1983). The model seeks to offer a guide through the pathways of nature-guided healing and to provide a format that might be used by the therapist.

1. The Individual's Initial State

The internal state of the individual will initially determine (a) whether that person seeks a preferred natural environment and (b) what stimuli are attended to within that context. This may be influenced by the person's state of affect, the history of his or her past contact with nature, and the benefits provided in previous natural experiences. If a person, for example, is feeling depressed, he or she may not be motivated to seek out natural stimuli. Even in a pleasant environment, one's focus of attention may be so internally based that little notice is taken of the external environment. Conversely, if a person is feeling excited about a seaside vacation and perhaps has childhood memories of happy summer holidays on the coast, then that person is more likely to seek out the maximum stimuli, anticipate the maximum benefits, and, consequently, experi-

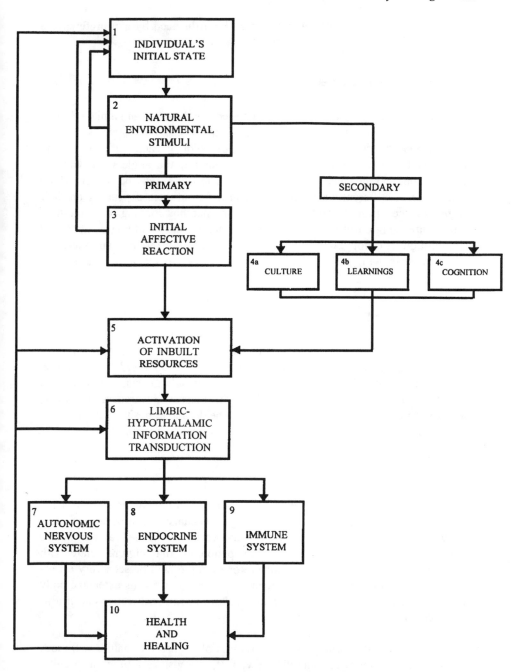

Figure 15.1 A psychoecobiological model for facilitating health and healing.

ence the maximum gain. Attention will also be influenced by any preference a person may have for a particular sense modality.

2. Natural Environmental Stimuli

The stimuli that nature provides are multimodal and contain an infinite variation within each sense modality. For example, in the visual field there is not one leaf of a tree that is identical to the next. The color of each leaf will vary in proportion to the amount of chlorophyll it contains, the angle with which it faces the sun, and the shade that falls upon it. The leaves may be still or rustled by the breeze. Different leaves may move at different rates depending on their weight and their position on the tree. If we are standing looking up at the tree, or if we are lying on our backs at its base watching the twinkling of nocturnal stars through its canopy, our senses will be stimulated differently, and therefore our experiences will be different. In nature, we never perceive the same thing twice.

3. Initial Affective Reaction

The stimuli from natural contexts provide a direct or primary affective re-action. This might be one of dislike that could initiate an avoidance response; however, if the stimuli are in accord with the person's chosen environmental preference, as selected, for example, from the Sensual Awareness Inventory, then this primary affective response is likely to be desirable, positive, and healthy. If so, it may in turn lead to activation of inbuilt healing responses.

4. Secondary Responses

Natural stimuli, as well as primarily activating emotional states, may have secondary influences that are filtered through mechanisms that screen or inter-pret the sensory input. First, there are cultural variations in the way that nature is perceived and, consequently, the way people of that culture relate with nature. A mountain in West New Guinea, for example, will be seen very differ-ently by Western miners who are contented to excavate it for its extensive body of copper ore and by tribal natives whose culture has for generations seen it as both home and a source of survival.

Second, our past learnings and experiences of exposure to nature will mod-ify our interpretation of the stimuli received. If, at a visit to a beach as a child, we were severely dumped by a wave or suffered a near-drowning incident, our responses to viewing a seascape may be different from those of a person with happy memories of seaside holidays.

Third, our current attitudes or cognitions about nature will be another influential factor. Whether we see nature as a pleasant, friendly, and beneficial environment or whether we see it as threatening, unfamiliar, and scary will determine nature's effects on our ecobiological processes.

5. Activation of In-Built Resources

As I have noted, there is a consensus among researchers in the field of environmental psychology suggesting that natural stimuli bypass cognitive assessment in activating adaptive mechanisms that have long been established as part of our psychological and biological makeup.

6. Limbic-Hypothalamic Transduction

The mechanism at the core of the nature-mind-body process of interaction is the limbic-hypothalamic system. As the provider of life-giving functions to our being, the limbic-hypothalamic system transduces information from natural stimuli to the autonomic nervous system, the endocrine system, and the immune system.

7. The Autonomic Nervous System

The autonomic nervous system can perhaps be seen as working somewhat like the thermostat in a refrigerator or oven, seeking to maintain an optimal balance between the sympathetic and parasympathetic systems. An optimal balance leads to a state of wellness and is, in itself, likely to be preventative in terms of the onset of illness. Correcting the balance, such as by reducing stress, may thus reduce the factors that stimulate the development of cancer cells or other illnesses.

8. The Endocrine System

Stress may lead to the production of adrenocorticoid hormones, which in turn suppress the immune system. By reducing these adrenal stress hormones, the endocrine system can help reduce the amount of abnormal cell development.

9. The Immune System

Healthy levels of immunity serve both a preventative and curative function. When the immune system is functioning healthily, it guards against the contraction of disease. When illness is present, an increment in immune activity can facilitate destruction and removal of viruses, toxins, and cancerous cells.

10. Health and Healing

Natural stimuli that activate inner adaptive resources, facilitate healthy information transduction, and stimulate the autonomic nervous system, the endocrine system, and the immune system in both preventative and restorative modes may thus facilitate, for example, the reduction of oncogene activity and lead to a regression in cancer.

This ecopsychobiological model for health and healing is dynamic. It is not a one-way street; rather, it provides feedback loops that can both ratify and reinforce an ongoing state of health and well-being. This process of feedback is considered a crucial element in the self-generalization phenomenon of ecotherapy discussed previously in Chapter 10.

Chapter 16

BEING WELL, NATURALLY: THERAPEUTIC USE OF THE ECOPSYCHOBIOLOGICAL MODEL

Trees, clouds, rivers, rocks
people, seeds, fish
mould, slime, gas
animals, birds, insects—
are all separate forms of life.

But
together
we are also
a single living thing.—Katherine Scholes (1995)

THE ECOPSYCHOBIOLOGICAL MODEL
IN A CASE OF CANCER

As the ecopsychobiological model (see Chapter 15) illustrates, nature is more than just another object of distraction or stimulation. On the contrary, it is a unique therapeutic agent that, in itself, holds preventative and treatment potential. The link between nature and health is as ancient as our species. We have, from the beginning of our evolutionary history, been one with our natural environment. Nature continues to afford direct and rapid access to physical health as well as psychological well-being. With nature on our side, the art of ecotherapy is basically to facilitate the client's accessing of these already-present, natural pathways to health.

Using the three R's of ecotherapy (see Chapter 10), there are several levels in the ecopsychobiological model at which the therapist can intervene to aid the accessing and potency of this approach. At Stage 1, the individual's initial state, the offering of a therapeutic rationale is likely to influence the way a client perceives and interacts with nature. At this level, too, therapeutic restructuring may begin if it is appropriate to assist clients in making cognitive, affective, or behavioral shifts that will enable them to gain more from natural environmental stimuli.

At Stage 2, a variety of ecotherapeutic strategies, including sensate focusing, nature-based assignments and experiential metaphors, might be used (see Chapters 6–10) to facilitate clients seeking of natural stimuli and also the direction of both primary and secondary responses to that stimuli. Once the process has been initiated, the therapist can seek to ratify both the initial therapeutic reaction at Stage 3 and the therapeutic modification of the symptom or disease (Stage 10).

> *Exercise 16.1:* Remember a time, in nature, when you felt really healthy, alive, and well. Recall the important sights, sounds, smells, and other sensations of that experience.
>
> Re-create the same or similar experience.
>
> An example: At the western end of Rottnest Island, off the coast of Western Australia, is Cape Vlamingh. It is one of my favorite places. I can sit on the rocky promontory safely above the surging waters, meditatively focusing on each sense. Waves roll in from two directions, colliding with each other before crashing on the coast. Balls of foam are thrown into the blue summer sky, whitewashing the black reef rocks. The roar of the sea drowns out other sounds and thoughts. It crashes thunderously at the base of the promontory, trickling in rivulets from the rocks as it retreats to build up yet another roaring surge. The smell of salt and seaweed fills the air. My skin is simultaneously warmed by the sun and cooled by the spray, whose saltiness I can taste on my lips.
>
> Invariably I leave that spot with not only a sense of joy but a feeling of energy as though my whole body and soul have been rejuvenated. Although it is not always possible to visit, whenever the opportunity is available I engage in this pilgrimage.

Let me offer a case illustration. Selina consulted me more than 20 years back. She was the first cancer patient with whom I ever worked. She was referred by her physician with the diagnosis of depression, and when I took her history I was not at all surprised that she felt depressed. Selina herself was quick to point out that she saw her depression as secondary to her cancer and asked whether I would work with her cancer with hypnosis or other psychological techniques. I let her know clearly that I had never worked in those areas before but that I had a friend, a psychiatrist, who had experience in the area and if she wanted I would refer her to him. When I called and told him the diagnosis, his reply was, uncharacteristically, "There is no point. She will be dead within three months."

I didn't have the heart to tell her this. The reasons for my feelings will become obvious shortly. Fortunately, I was saved the anguish of putting it to her. I hedged around it by saying that I had spoken to my colleague and that he wouldn't be able to see her for a while. She replied, "I am glad. I felt comfortable talking with you last time and would like to keep working with you."

Again I pointed out that I had no experience in these areas but would be willing to study the literature and communicate with colleagues who were working in the field. I then offered that if she was prepared to accept that condition and see me on an experimental basis, I would be happy to work with her.

Selina's history indicated that she was born in 1915 to a Jewish family in Germany. She married into her own faith a few years before the Second World War commenced and had two young children at the start of the war. She and her husband were able to flee their homeland, making their way in very difficult circumstances around the globe to China, where they suffered out the remainder of the war years in Shanghai. Following the war they migrated to Australia. They were German-speaking people in a postwar Allied country and consequently felt unaccepted. Soon after their arrival, Selina had a third child. Her husband, who was an artist, had extreme difficulty in finding employment both because of the nature of his occupation and because of his national background.

When he finally gained employment, they sought to purchase their own home. It seemed to Selina like life, for the first time in their marriage, was settling down. Her husband, however, was soon to leave her for a younger woman. At a time when social welfare services were not what they are today, she struggled to maintain a full-time job and support her three children. On top of this, she completed her own secondary education, gained university admission, and studied at night to achieve a degree in education. She loved teaching and became very committed to her profession.

Her real devotion, though, was to her children, and she felt hurt when the elder of her two daughters broke away from Judaism, married a Christian clergyman, and moved to London. Her second daughter took up a job on the eastern seaboard of Australia, also leaving home. But the greatest hurt of all came when her son joined an Eastern religion and moved to the United States. He totally rejected his Jewish mother, hung up whenever she tried to phone him, and returned her mail unopened.

She began to live more and more for her profession. She felt valued and wanted by her school pupils. And her commitment to teaching was frequently recognized by the students' parents. Despite the fact that she still had much to contribute, she reached the age at which, by law, she had to retire. Within 6 months of retirement, she was diagnosed as having cancer.

She sought out the best local specialists. She traveled across the country to a well-known cancer institute, consulted one of the country's senior oncologists, and underwent surgery. She said that her surgeon opened her up, took one look, sewed her back up, and said, "You'll be dead in three months." I was not surprised she felt depressed. With her history, I certainly didn't have the heart to reiterate the comments of my colleague with whom I had discussed her case.

> *Exercise 16.2:* Study your Sensual Awareness Inventory. Choose
> seven items that, for you, are associated with health and well-being.
> Experience one of those items each day for the next week.

I introduced Selina to hypnotherapy, as she requested, and taught her a technique of self-hypnosis. In this state she was invited to go back in her experiences to a place of well-being, a place where she'd experienced both happiness and health. It so happened that she had lived in a rural town in Germany. Sometimes with her sister, sometimes alone, she would make her way across the fields to a wooded creek. She described her images of how the trees linked, almost in an embrace, above the babbling waters of the stream. Sometimes she and her sister would play make-believe games. Sometimes she would simply lie back, watching the patterns of the leaves and the shapes in the branches, fascinated with the colors, the light, and the shade. Here she felt a sense of being at peace with herself. Although at the time of seeing her, I had not yet formulated the ecopsychobiological model in my own thinking, I did follow the steps of the three R's of ecotherapy.

First, she was offered the rationale that because such experiences had facilitated feelings of happiness and well-being in the past, it was likely that they would initiate similar feelings in the present. Using the materials that Selina brought forward, she was invited to engage in sensate focusing into the experiences of that childhood place. There were noticeable alterations in her ideomotor responses as she did. The muscles of her face began to relax. A smile, the first that I had seen since we met, began to subtly creep onto her face.

Second, she was offered nature-based assignments to help her discover situations in which she might be able to capture similar, but also different, sensations from what she had as a child. She took the task very seriously, beginning to search out urban parks and outlying national parks that would offer stimulation similar to that she had achieved in her childhood. The activity created a shift in her inner focus. Whereas previously she had been sitting at home dwelling on her illness, she now began to look outward for pleasurable sensations. She had begun to reestablish a sense of purpose.

She found a national park where, if she sat quietly by a stream at dusk, kangaroos came down to drink. She described how she felt a part of the universal sense of being, where there were no questions, no analysis, no past or future: just simply the feeling of belonging.

She came back to a session saying, "Now that I know I am going to die, I am freer to live than I ever have been in my life." And indeed she got on with living in a way that she never had done before. She joined a woodlands walking club. Not able to keep pace with a full day's trekking, she would organize with the leaders to take a short cut or would simply sit in the woods and enjoy nature until the group came back to pick her up some hours later. She went to visit her daughter in Melbourne, as well as her daughter in London. Her affect had improved dramatically. She was free of pain and reported feeling much healthier. A review by her oncologist showed that there had been a regression in the size of her tumor. Her self-initiated therapeutic efforts were ratified by her progress. Given the fact that she seemed to be successfully generalizing the therapeutic interventions into a variety of areas of her life, we suspended therapy.

Some 8 months later she returned again, appearing somewhat depressed. She told me that the oncological review had shown an increment in the cancer and that she had "fallen in a bit of a hole." We reinstituted the hypnotherapy, sensate focusing, and nature-based assignments. She again responded readily and enthusiastically. She took a longstanding female companion on an ocean cruise of the Pacific islands. When she returned, her oncologist once again reported a diminution of the tumor. She decided that she needed to resolve the situation with her son, who had joined the Hare Krishna movement. He wasn't communicating with her or responding to her communications, so she simply took a flight to America, landed on his doorstep, and came back feeling that she had worked through a number of their differences. Again, given her progress, we ceased regular consultations.

> *Exercise 16.3:* Study your Sensual Awareness Inventory. Imagine that you have just been released from the hospital after a major illness or injury.
>
> Choose from the Sensual Awareness Inventory those ingredients that would create the ideal situation or experience for your recuperation. Re-create that situation as if you are actually in a period of recuperation.
>
> Re-create the situation at chosen intervals for your continuing well-being.

One morning when I arrived at work, my receptionist drew my attention to the morning paper. She opened it to the death notices and pointed to Selina's name. It was two and a half years after she had first attended me. In that time there had twice been a regression in the size of her tumor, there had been significant easing of her symptoms, and she had lived life with a freedom she had never known before.

I do not in any way want to claim that ecotherapy altered the course of her disease or extended her life. There are too many variables to define exactly what factors or combination of factors may have been influential. I am inclined to agree with Spiegel (1993) when he says that therapy is about making the most of whatever time is left, about living better rather than longer. Nature-guided therapy is directed toward the betterment of life, which could, in turn, mean longer.

I offer the case of Selina to illustrate how the steps of ecotherapy may be applied in working with patients who have serious or terminal illnesses. These steps may be helpful in facilitating affective modification as well as in potentiating the healing process.

While the ecopsychobiological model has been presented in the context of facilitating cancer therapy, it is not limited to this area. These steps may be helpful in working with people with cancer, AIDS, or other terminal disorders as well as nonterminal diseases. It is considered that the model is also beneficial in recovery from serious accidents, such as with the case of Wayne in Chapter 9. The features of the ecopsychobiological model apply equally in that case, and the steps followed were along lines one would use in working with other illnesses.

As noted previously, researchers have clearly demonstrated that contact with nature, such as looking out a hospital window into a garden, can facilitate recovery, accelerate discharge from the hospital, and reduce the amount of medication required. This research is endorsed by clinical case studies and also anecdotal accounts, as shown in the following illustration.

THE ECOPSYCHOBIOLOGICAL MODEL
IN PAIN MANAGEMENT

I can find no better way to illustrate how nature can be of benefit in pain management and curative processes than in the very eloquently written personal account of Lin Jensen. Professor Jensen retired after 30 years of teaching at Monterey Peninsula College in California. As a professor emeritus of writing and literature, he is very capable of presenting his account of his experiences, the reproduction of which he has kindly granted permission. In his essay, we see the processes of rationale shaping the individual's initial state of awareness brought to the particular environment. We see restructuring processes that influence how those natural environmental stimuli have their impact, and we also observe the primary effect of these stimuli on his symptomatology. In addition, there is a self-initiated process of ratification and generalization.

Jensen comes to his observation already with positive attitudes about nature and the environment. He lived on a 20-acre property where he divided his time among gardening, birdwatching, and writing. He still serves as a subregional editor for *American Birds* magazine, observing and reporting for that publication on the distribution of bird species within Plumas and Sierra counties. For Jensen, there is already a rationale for watching birds. There is already an awareness of the effects of this activity on his well-being. He comes to the observation with a certain set of expectations of what nature might provide but not necessarily with the expectation of exactly what it does provide. As well as these primary effects, his knowledge and interest in the area are filters for the secondary stimuli that, in his case, produce positive expectations and are thus likely to activate positive in-built resources.

The restructuring followed a process of sensate focusing as he became acutely aware of a small flock of sparrows. With this, there was a shift in his affective experiences, moving quickly from a state of depression and pain to a primary experience of joy so rapid and immediate that it bypassed the process of conscious recognition. With this came a reassessment of his own position and a change of experience.

The ratification was not the sight of the birds, which were soon a memory. Instead it was a view of the garden, a metaphor that closely paralleled his own position in a way that was both concrete and reassuring. Sometimes it is easy to analyze this process in retrospect, to interpret it or to squeeze it into a certain framework. I don't, in any way, want my comments to be limiting and would prefer that you allow yourself to share Jensen's experience in his own words.

Window Birds

In early October, I crawled down off a ladder where I was caulking some siding on the house, doubled up with pain that emanated from my lower back and traveled down my leg. I went into the house and lay down on this very bed where I am now composing this writing.

Today is November 16th, and, with the exception of the most necessary movement within the house and a few outings such as being driven to therapy or to the Reno Diagnostic Center for an MRI or for consultation with a neurosurgeon, I have lain exactly here since I came down off the ladder a month and a half ago.

From the bed where I am lying, I look through windows that open to the southwest. I can see a forested ridge that rises from the grassy field where the house is situated. Today, the ridge is shrouded in gray with snow blowing through the trees. Gusts of cold wind shoulder in against the house, causing the snow to whirl about the windows, and, through this gauzy dimness, I can see the trees thrashing on the ridge above. I can see all this, lying on my back with my knees elevated on two pillows to ease the pain which is perpetually with me and with one pillow beneath my head. I can also see from here five little apple trees which my wife, Karen, and I have planted and the vegetable garden with its neat little plots all laid out and carefully fenced against the wind and the browsing deer.

It was on a day such as this a couple of weeks ago that the window birds came. My wife had gone to town for supplies and I was alone in the house. It was about three in the afternoon, and the pain had come on me in a hard way. I had taken a tablet of Vicodin, a narcotic prescribed for severe pain, and I was lying right here, as I am now, trying to resist the futility of squirming about, and concentrating instead on holding perfectly still, breathing as calmly as I could in the pain and waiting for some degree of relief to come. I was exhausted and forlorn, and the best that could be said was that, if hope had collapsed for the time, I was still holding on. And then great wet tears formed and overran the sockets of my eyes and spilled down the sides of my face. And the tears seemed the most neutral I have known, seeming to arise in the absence of any personal sorrow, seeming to have little to do with even the act of crying itself. And through the smeared senses of my eyes, beyond the window, I could see the snow turning on the wind of a darkening sky.

And then there fluttered up into the window space, their wings brushing the very glass itself, the silhouettes of a small flock of sparrows. They seemed blown up against the window, carried like the snow on the force of the wind. And then they dropped out of sight beneath the level of the sill and then rode up again into view where the wind swung them through the apple trees and they grabbed perches on the winter bared limbs that pitched and shuddered beneath them. As they clung there for a second, I could make out the darkened hoods of the Juncos among them and the lateral crown stripes of a few white-crowned sparrows. There were perhaps a dozen of them gripping the tossing branches of the little trees, their feathers blown backward, and then, as one, they all let go and disappeared in the darkness up the ridge.

But even before they were lost to sight, while they could still be seen bobbing in the wind, where the little flock receded in the distance, I recognized that joy had come. And before this recognition, before the joy had been framed as a separate thought and thus set apart as an experience, I knew that I had simply been joy, the whole of me, without reservation, without anything set aside, so that I had not felt joy in addition to or in spite of my circumstances but rather that the whole of my circumstances had simply become joy. Joy is an act of love. My eyes were loving the little birds and the wind and the trees; the tears that blurred these same eyes were loving the birds and the wind and the trees; the wet skin on my face was loving them, the breath that moved in me was loving them; my whole body where it lay injured with its useless legs propped up on pillows was loving them; the very pain itself where it rolled out in waves from my injured spine was loving the little birds and the wind and the trees.

As I lie here today, the window birds are a memory now. Beyond the window, I see the garden, with clover dug under and compost. Beneath its winter mulch, the garden lies fallow and waits, and I lie here fallow and wait, and everywhere, in all places, at all times, and in all beings, joy lies fallow and waits. (Jensen, 1996)

The sight of, and involvement with, the window birds altered Jensen's experience and management of pain. It also brought about an attitudinal shift allowing him the understanding that joy could simply lie fallow, waiting to again be experienced. From this point too, there was a continuing progress with regard to his journey of recovery. He subsequently wrote: "I am recovering well, and can already walk four miles without stop." Unfortunately, his surgeon advised that he no longer go backpacking, engage in sustained carpentry, dig in the garden, or lift bales of hay. It was with reluctance and sadness that he and his wife placed their 20 acres, along with the home they had built themselves and their dreams for retirement, on the real estate market. But it was not long before he was discovering some of the joy that had lain fallow. In a subsequent essay titled "Maintenance," he wrote of how he joined a small group of local residents on a wildflower outing near his new home.

> On the mountain, we walked with the others on a windswept plateau where tiny flowers of yellow and blue hugged the rocky earth. [My wife] and the other women were talking among themselves and, when they turned down along a little stream towards a falls, I was drawn uphill to see what species of sparrow it was that moved so low among the grasses. The sparrows turned out to be lark sparrows and, in my trailing after them, I found myself brought out upon a prominence that lay an unobstructed horizon about me on all sides. I turned slowly, 360°. I felt a little anxious to know that I could, at least at that moment, walk in any of all possible directions. (Jensen, 1996)

The case of Selina and the personal account by Jensen illustrate both the stages of the ecopsychobiological model (see Figure 15.1) and the stages at which the therapeutic interventions can be made to influence the process of health and healing.

THERAPEUTIC APPLICATION OF THE STAGES IN THE ECOPSYCHOBIOLOGICAL MODEL

The Individual's Initial State

At this first stage in the ecopsychobiological process, both the selection of and the response to natural stimuli will be influenced by the person's initial affective and cognitive state when entering the natural environment. Given the fact that Jensen is a "birder," or amateur ornithologist, his initial state in perceiving the window birds was likely to include both interest and expectations. Already there was some rationale for observing the stimuli outside of the window.

For Selina, that initial state was created in therapy. She was asked, during hypnosis, to recall a place where she had experienced both happiness and health. She was then provided with a therapeutic rationale that if such experiences of the past had facilitated well-being, it was likely that re-creating similar experiences would elicit similar states of well-being.

The example given in Exercise 16.1 is another means by which the therapist can help influence the client's initial expectations about the therapeutic assignment. I may recount such examples from my own experience as a means of helping to set an expectancy for the client or provide a metaphor for change.

> *Exercise 16.4:* Imagine the most health-conducive environment in which you could possibly live. Without regard to finance, employment, education, and so forth, define the essential characteristics of that health-conducive environment.
>
> Where do you know that comes closest to this ideal?
>
> It may not be possible to live there, but it may be possible to visit, spend some time in that environment, and enjoy.

Natural Environmental Stimuli

At this stage, the therapist may assign the therapeutic tasks that are considered likely to help the client move toward her or his goal of health and healing. The nature-guided strategies presented in Chapters 6 through 10, along with the exercises offered in this chapter, may be beneficial in creating exposure to and interactions with natural stimuli. Selina, for example, was given an imagery-type sensate focusing exercise during hypnosis. She was also presented with nature-based assignments to help her recapture her former experiences of health and happiness. Jensen spontaneously engaged in a sensate focusing task while becoming totally absorbed in watching the window birds.

Initial Affective Reaction

Jensen illustrates clearly the direct influence that natural stimuli have on our emotional reactions. This primary process bypasses conscious thinking in eliciting a change of feeling. For Jensen, it was a shift from pain to joy. He said, "Before the joy had been framed as a separate thought and thus set apart as an experience, I knew that I had simply been joy."

Therapeutic interventions in ecotherapy are designed to create such a context for emotional change. That a change takes place at all or that it takes place in the therapeutically desired direction cannot be guaranteed. The art of nature-guided therapy is to create that context which, in all probability, is likely to bring about a therapeutically oriented state of emotional and physical well-being.

Secondary Responses

Some of the secondary filters of environmental stimuli might also be influenced therapeutically. Little may be done about culturally based attitudes toward the environment, but a client's past learnings and experiences can be converted into current therapeutic gain. By asking Selina to go back to her experiences of a place of well-being, we were looking at past, positive learnings and experiences of interactions with nature. These (as they were in this case) may then be used in the current therapeutic context.

Therapeutic rationale such as that offered to Selina can influence a person's current cognitions or attitudes about the given nature-guided strategy and, consequently, ways that this then activates in-built resources.

It is in these first four areas of the ecopsychobiological model that the therapist can present nature-guided interventions. The positive activation of inner resources is likely to ensure limbic-hypothalamic transduction of health-related information to the autonomic nervous system, the endocrine system, and the immune system regarding the maintenance and/or restoration of health.

> *Exercise 16.5:* After engaging in each of the preceding exercises, ask yourself the following questions:
>   How did I feel during and after that exercise?
>   What difference has it made to me physically?
>   What changes can I observe in my heart rate, respiration, muscle tone, and general sense of well-being?
>   How might I again capture such feelings of health and happiness?

In personal correspondence, Jensen concluded, "Unless we humans recognize that our health depends on harmony with the natural world, we shall never be truly well."

A STORY OF NATURE-GUIDED HEALING

As I wrote I wondered how I might conclude this work. Would I write in summation of the many things discussed here? Would I argue for the preservation of nature for the preservation of our own well-being? Would I quote from the ecstasy of a poet reaping the enjoyments of a natural interaction? Would I find sagacious words in the traditional wisdom of Buddhism, American Indians, Taoism, or Australian Aborigines? Would I quote facts or data in the field of research?

I am drawn more to a Tibetan folktale. It is the story of a man who was a great traveler. He had adventured into many parts of the world, enjoying wonderful experiences and seeing many glorious sights. It was in his homeland of Tibet, however, that he had his greatest experiences of all.

Traveling through a forest, he came to a very large and beautiful tree. The branches spread out, umbrella-like, around the surrounding land. He decided to rest in the shade of this comfortable tree. Nestling into its exposed, comfortable roots, he rapidly fell asleep.

During the night, he was suddenly awakened by a strange commotion. It was pitch black. Without making a sound, he peered around the large trunk of the tree to see in the darkness the light of hundreds of small eyes of many different animals. Carefully, noiselessly, he climbed up into the branches of the tree to look down onto this strange gathering. It seemed that every species of animal from the forest had sent a representative to this great meeting. They formed a circle around their obvious leader, a proud and confident-looking snow lion. In turn, the snow lion asked after the welfare of each species in the forest. He smiled with their humor, joined in their sadness, nodded in agreement, and at times offered his wisdom.

Just when it seemed that all of the animals had had their turn and a quietness began to fall over the meeting, an old, frail monkey spoke quietly from the back of the crowd. "I have a sad story to tell," said the monkey. "It is about the stupidity of humans."

The lion encouraged him to continue.

"I wish I could become a human," said the monkey. "If I was I would do so much to make all the creatures of this world happy. As I am, no matter how much I try to offer them my advice, they just ignore the chatterings of an old monkey."

"Down by the river," he continued, "is a family whose only daughter is very ill. She injured her leg and for the last three months she has been suffering with pain and fever. Her parents are distressed, but they don't know how to make it better."

"I would tell them how to heal their daughter's leg," said the old monkey, "if only I was human, if only I could speak their language."

At the snow lion's prompting he went on to offer his remedy. "Under a large rock near the front of their house lives a frog. The frog too is very ill. Suffering dehydration, it can't move or search for water to prevent it from dying. If only the girl's parents would take the golden tray from their household altar, gently remove the rock, and place the frog on the tray, they could carry it to the river, where it would be rejuvenated. Then the daughter's leg would heal. Her pain and fever would disappear."

The snow lion reflected on the monkey's sadness, sat for a moment in contemplation, and replied, "You are right, you know the cure for this human suffering. You see how they have become detached from the rest of the universe and how, for the well-being of all, that caring relationship needs to be reestablished. But, as much as we have tried to communicate with them before, they will not listen to us. We must leave them to find their own solutions" (adapted from Hyde-Chambers & Hyde-Chambers, 1995).

REFERENCES

Achterberg, J. (1985*). Imagery in healing.* Boston: Shambala.

Achterberg, J., & Lawlis, G. (1984). *Imagery and disease.* Champaign, IL: Institute for Personality and Ability Testing.

Amedeo, D. (1993). Emotions in person-environment-behaviour episodes. In T. Garling & R. G. Colledge (Eds.), *Behaviour and environment: Psychological and geographical approaches.* Amsterdam: Elsevier.

Anderson, L. M. (1981). Land use designations affect perception of scenic beauty in forest landscapes. *Forest Science, 27,* 392–400.

Australian Bureau of Statistics. (1988). *Information paper: Time use pilot survey, Sydney, May–June 1987.* Sydney: Author.

Bateson, G. (1980). *Mind and nature: A necessary unity.* New York: Bantam.

Baum, A. (1991). A psychological perspective, with emphasis on relationships between leisure, stress, and well-being. In B. Driver, P. Brown, & G. Peterson (Eds.), *Benefits of leisure.* State College, PA: Venture.

Baum, A., Singer, A. E., & Baum, C. S. (1982). Stress and the environment. In G. W. Evans (Ed.), *Environmental stress* (pp. 15–44). New York: Cambridge University Press.

Beck, A. T. (1967). *Depression: Clinical, experimental and theoretical aspects.* New York: Hoeber.

Bookchin, M. (1988). *The ecology of freedom: The emergence and dissolution of hierarchy.* Palo Alto, CA: Cheshire Books.

Borkan, J., & Quirk, M. (1992). The meaning of hip fracture for the hardy elderly: A new look at psycho-social prognostic factors. *International Journal on Aging and Human Development, 34,* 339–350.

Borkan, J., Quirk, M., & Sullivan, M. (1991). The meaning of hip fracture for the hardy elderly. *Social Science and Medicine, 33,* 947–957.

Bowden, S., Dovers, S., & Shirlow, M. (1990). *Our biosphere under threat: Ecological realities and Australia's opportunities.* Melbourne: Oxford University Press.

Bowers, K. (1977). Hypnosis: An informational approach. *Annals of the New York Academy of Sciences, 296,* 223–237.

Burns, G. W. (1974, June). Reinforcement preferences of a Western Australian prison sample. *Department of Corrections Research Bulletin.*

Burns, G. W. (1995). Psychoecotherapy: A hypnotic model. In G. D. Burrows & R. O. Stanley (Eds.), *Contemporary international hypnosis* (pp. 279–284). London: Wiley.

Burns, G. W. (1997). Making brief therapy an ordeal. *Psychotherapy in Australia,* 4, 1, 44–47.

Clifford, T. (1984). *The diamond healing: Tibetan Buddhist medicine and psychiatry.* Wellingborough, England: Crucible.

Cooper-Marcus, C. (1992). Environmental memories. In I. Altman & S. M. Low (Eds.), *Place attachment.* New York: Plenum.

Davis, M., & Severinsen, D. (1974). Stop and smell the roses. In *Leeds hits of our time No. 35.* London: Leeds Music.

Dell, T. F. (1985). Understanding Bateson and Maturana: Toward a biological foundation for the social sciences. *Journal of Marital and Family Therapy, 11,* 1–20.

de Mello, A. (1987). *The song of the bird.* Anand, India: Gujarat Sahitya Prakach.

Demick, J., & Andreoletti, C. (1995). Some relations between clinical and environment psychology. *Environment and Behaviour, 27,* 56–72.

de Shazer, S. (1985). *Keys to solution in brief therapy.* New York: Norton.

Dobbs, H. (1987). Dolphins—Can they dispel the blues? *World Magazine.*

Dobbs, H. (1988). Dolphins and the blues: Can dolphins help humans suffering from depression? *Caduceus,* p. 4.

Donden, Y. (1986). *Health through balance: An introduction to Tibetan medicine.* New York: Snow Lion.

Durning, A. T. (1995). Are we happy? In T. Roszak, M. E. Gomes, and A. D. Kanner (Eds.), *Ecopsychology: Restoring the earth, healing the mind.* San Francisco: Sierra Club Books.

Eliade, M. (1959). *The sacred and the place: The nature of religion.* Chicago: Harcourt, Brace & World.

Eliade, M. (1989). *Shamanism: Archaic techniques of ecstasy.* London: Arkana.

Esquivel, L. (1993). *Like water for chocolate.* London: Black Swan.

Garrett, L. (1994). *The coming plague: Newly emerging diseases in a world out of balance.* London: Virago.

Gibson, E. J. (1969). *Principles of perceptual learning and development.* New York: Appleton-Century-Crofts.

Gibson, J. J. (1966). *The senses considered as perceptual systems.* Boston: Houghton Mifflin.

Gibson, J. J. (1979). *The ecological approach to visual perception.* Boston: Houghton Mifflin.

Gold, P. (1988). *Tibetan pilgrimage.* New York: Snow Lion.

Greeno, J. G. (1994). Gibson's affordances. *Psychological Review, 101,* 336–342.

Greenway, R. (1995). The Wilderness Effect and Ecopsychology. In T. Roszak, M. E. Gomes, and A. D. Kanner (Eds.), *Ecopsychology: Restoring the earth, healing the mind.* San Francisco: Sierra Club Books.

Haley, J. (1969). The art of being a failure as a therapist. *American Journal of Orthopsychiatry, 39,* 691–695.

Haley, J. (1973). *Uncommon therapy: The psychiatric techniques of Milton H. Erickson, M.D.* New York: Norton.

Haley, J. (1984). *Ordeal therapy: Unusual ways to change behavior.* San Francisco: Jossey-Bass.

Haley, J., & Richeport, M. (1993). *Milton H. Erickson, M.D.: Explorer in hypnosis and therapy* [videotape]. Rockville, MD: Triangle Productions.

Hammond-Tooke, D. (1989). *Rituals and medicine.* Cape Town: Ad Donker.

Hartig, T., & Evans, G. W. (1993). Psychological foundations of nature experience. In T. Garling & R. D. Golledge (Eds.), *Behaviour and environment: Psychological and geographical approaches.* Amsterdam: Elsevier.

Hartig, T., Mang, M., & Evans, G. W. (1990). Perspectives on wilderness: Testing the theory of restorative environments. In A. T. Easley, J. Passinear, & B. L. Driver (Eds.), *The use of wilderness for personal growth, therapy and education.* Ft. Collins, CO: USDA Forest Service.

Harvey A. (1983). *A journey in Ladahk.* London: Picador.

Henry, J. P., & Meehan, J. P. (1981). Psychosocial stimuli, physiological specificity, and cardiovascular disease. In H. Weiner, M. A. Hofer, & A. J. Stunkard (Eds.), *Brain, behavior, and bodily disease.* New York: Raven Press.

Heywood, L. A. (1978). Perceived recreational experience and the relief of tension. *Journal of Leisure Research, 10,* 86–97.

Hillman, J. (1995). A psyche the size of the earth. In T. Roszak, M. E. Gomes, & A. D. Kanner (Eds.), *Ecopsychology: Restoring the earth, healing the mind.* San Francisco: Sierra Club Books.

Hills, B. (1989). *Blue murder.* Melbourne: Sun Books.

Hodgson, B. (1995). Grand Teton. *National Geographic, 187*(2), 116–140.

Hoffmann-Williams, K. J., & Harvey, D. H. P. (1995). *Beliefs about a natural forest: A preliminary exploration of the relationship between forest ethics and forest aesthetics.* Paper presented at the 1st Annual Conference of the Society of Australasian Social Psychologists, Hobart, Australia.

Huxley, A. (1984). *Beyond the Mexique.* London: Triad/Paladin.

Hyde-Chambers, F., & Hyde-Chambers, A. (1995). *Tibetan folk tales.* Boston: Shambala.

Ittelson, W., Franck, K., & O'Hanlon, T. (1976). The nature of environmental experience. In S. Wapner, S. Cohen, & B. Kaplan (Eds.), *Experiencing the environment* (pp. 187–206). New York: Plenum.

Ittelson, W. H., Rivlin, L. G., Proshansky, H. M., & Winkel, G. H. (1974). *An introduction to environmental psychology.* New York: Holt, Rinehart & Winston.

Jensen, L. (1996). Window birds and maintenance. In L. Jensen & E. Roberts (Eds.), *Bowing to the mountain.* Carmel, CA: Sun Flower Ink.

Jerstad, L., & Stelzer, J. (1973). Adventure experiences as treatment for residential mental patients. *Therapeutic Recreation Journal, 7*(3), 8–11.

Jung, C. (1960). *The structure and dynamics of the psyche. Vol. 3. The collected works of Carl G. Jung* (R. F. C. Hull, Trans.). Princeton, NJ: Princeton University Press.

Kanner, A. D. and Gomes, M. E. (1995). The All-Consuming Self. In T. Roszak, M. E. Gomes, and A. D. Kanner (Eds.), *Ecopsychology: Restoring the earth, healing the mind.* San Francisco: Sierra Club Books.

Kaplan, R. (1973). Some psychological benefits of gardening. *Environment and Behavior, 5,* 145–165.

Kaplan, R. (1974). Some psychological benefits of an outdoor challenge program. *Environment and Behavior, 6,* 101–116.

Kaplan, R. (1983). The role of nature in the urban context. In I. Altman & J. F. Wohlwill (Eds.), *Human behavior and environment: Advances in theory and research* (Vol. 6, pp. 127–161). New York: Plenum.

Kaplan, R. (1984). Wilderness perception and psychological benefits: An analysis of a continuing program. *Liesure Sciences, 6,* 271–289.

Kaplan, R. (1985). Nature at the doorstep: Residential satisfaction and the nearby environment. *Journal of Architectural and Planning Research, 2,* 115–127.

Kaplan, R., & Kaplan, S. (1989). *The experience of nature: A psychological perspective.* Cambridge, England: Cambridge University Press.

Kaplan, S., & Talbot, J. F. (1983). Psychological benefits of a wilderness experience. In I. Altman & J. F. Wohwill (Eds.), *Human behavior and environment. Vol. 6: Behavior and the natural environment* (pp. 163–203). New York: Plenum.

Kellogg, J. H. (1907). *The home book of modern medicine.* London: Modern Medicine.

Kesner, R. (1984). The neurobiology of memory: Implicit explicit assumptions. In G. Lynch, J. McGaugh, & N. Weinberger (Eds.), *Neurobiology of learning and memory* (pp. 111–118). New York: Guilford Press.

Khangkar, L. D. (1991). *Lectures on Tibetan medicine.* Dharamsala, India: Library of Tibetan Works and Archives.

Kiefer, C., & Cowan, A. (1979). State-context dependency and theories of ritual. *Journal of Psychological Anthropology, 2*(1), 53–58.

Knopf, R. C. (1987). Human behaviour, cognition, and affect in the natural environment. In D. Stokols & I. Altman (Eds.), *Handbook of environmental psychology* (Vol. 1, pp. 783–825). New York: Wiley.

Knudtson, P., & Suzuki, D. (1992). *Wisdom of the elders.* Sydney: Allen & Unwin.

Krippendorf, J. (1992). Towards new tourism policies: The importance of environmental and sociocultural factors. *Tourism Management, 3,* 135–148.

Lankton, S. R., & Lankton, C. H. (1983). *The answer within: A clinical framework of Ericksonian hypnotherapy.* New York: Brunner/Mazel.

Leopold, A. (1949). *Sand County Almanac.* New York: Oxford University Press.

Levitt, L. (1991). Recreation for the mentally ill. In B. L. Driver, P. J. Brown, & G. L. Peterson (Eds.), *Benefits of leisure.* State College, PA: Venture.

Le Winn, E. B., & Dimancescu, M. D. (1978). Environmental deprivation and enrichment in coma. *Lancet, 2,* 156–157.

Lewis, M., Mishkin, N., Bragin, E., Brown, R., Pert, C., & Pert, A. (1981). Opiate receptor gradients in monkey cerebral cortex: Correspondence with sensory processing hierarchies. *Science, 211,* 1166.

Locke, S., Kraus, L., Leserman, J., Hurst, M., Heisel, S., & Williams, R. (1984). Life change stress, psychiatric symptoms, and natural killer-cell activity. *Psychosomatic Medicine, 46,* 441–453.

Low, S. M. (1992). Symbolic ties that bind: Place attachment in the plaza. In I. Altman & S. M. Low (Eds.), *Place attachments.* New York: Plenum.

Lowry, T. P. (1974). Camping as a short term private psychiatric hospital. In T. P. Lowry (Ed.), *Camping therapy: Its uses in psychiatry and rehabilitation.* Springfield, IL: Charles C Thomas.

Mason, J. (1993). *An unnatural order: Uncovering the roots of our domination of nature and each other.* New York: Simon & Schuster.

Maturana, H. R. (1983). What it is to see? *Archivos de Medicina y Biologia Experimental, 16,* 255–269.

Maturana, H. R., Mpodozis, J., & Letelier, J. C. (1995). Brain language and the origin of human mental functions. *Biological Research, 28,* 15–26.

Maturana, H. R., & Varela, F. J. (1987). *The tree of knowledge: The biological roots of human understanding.* Boston: New Science Library.

Mazumdar, S., & Mazumdar, S. (1993). Sacred space and place attachment. *Journal of Experimental Psychology, 13,* 231–242.

McAndrew, F. T. (1993). *Environmental psychology.* Pacific Grove, CA: Brooks/ Cole.

McDonald, B. L. (1991). Spiritual benefits of leisure participation and leisure settings. In B. Driver, P. Brown, & G. Peterson (Eds.), *Benefits of leisure.* State College, PA: Venture.

McIntyre, N. (1990). *Recreation involvement: The personal meaning of participation.* Unpublished doctoral dissertation, University of New England, Australia.

McNeilly, R., & Brown, J. (1994*). Healing with words.* Melbourne: Hill of Content.

McRae, M. (1997). Wilderness rafting Siberian style. *National Geographic, 192*(5), 32–45.

Meares, A. (1960). *A system of medical hypnosis.* New York: Julian Press.

Meares, A. (1970). *Relief without drugs.* Glasgow: Fontana.

Meares, A. (1978). *The wealth within.* Melbourne: Hill of Content.

Meares, A. (1982–1983). A form of intensive meditation associated with the regression of cancer. *American Journal of Clinical Hypnosis, 25*(2–3), 114–121.

Meares, A. (1985). *A way of doctoring.* Melbourne: Hill of Content.

Mehrabian, A., & Russell, J. A. (1974). *An approach to environmental psychology.* Cambridge, MA: MIT Press.

Mercer, D. (1991). *A question of balance: Natural resources conflict issues in Australia.* Sydney: Federation Press.

Messner, R. (1980). Letter from Nanga Parbat. In B. Motravetz, *The big book of mountaineering* (p. 6). Woodbury, NY: Barron's.

Moore, E. O. (1982). A prison environment's effect on health care service demands. *Journal of Environmental Systems, 11,* 17–34.

Murray, E., & Mishkin, M. (1985). Amygdalectony impairs osmodal association in monkeys. *Science, 228,* 604–606.

Nelson, R. K. (1983). *Make prayers to the raven.* Chicago: University of Chicago Press.

Nesse, R. M., & Williams, G. C. (1996). *Evolution and healing: The new science of Darwinian medicine.* London: Phoenix.

Newman, R. S. (1980). Alleviating learned helplessness in a wilderness setting: An application of attributional theory to outward bound. In L. J. Fryans, Jr. (Ed.), *Achievement motivation: Recent trends in theory and research* (pp. 312–345). New York: Plenum.

O'Hanlon, W. H., & Weiner-Davis, M. (1989). *In search of solutions: A new direction in psychotherapy.* New York: Norton.

Ornstein, R., & Ehrlich, P. (1989). *New world new mind: Changing the way we think to save our future.* London: Methuen.

Parsons, R. (1991). The potential influences of environmental perception on human health. *Journal of Environmental Psychology, 11,* 1–23.

Pert, C. (1985). Neuropeptides, receptors, and emotions. *Cybernetics, 1*(4), 33–34.

Pert, C. (1987). Neuropeptides: The emotions and body-mind. *Noetic Sciences Review, 2,* 13–18.

Pert, C., & Ruff, M. (1987). AIDS research: A leading edge at NIMH. *Psychological Perspectives, 18,* 105–112.

Peterson, D. (1989). *The deluge and the ark: A journey into primate worlds.* Boston: Houghton Mifflin.

Pigram, J. J. (1993). Human nature relationships: Leisure environments and natural settings. In T. Garling & R. G. Golledge (Eds.), *Behaviour and environment: Psychological and geographical approaches.* Amsterdam: Elsevier.

President's Commission on America's Outdoors. (1986). *Report and recommendations to the president of the United States.* Washington, DC: U.S. Government Printing Office.

Purcell, A. T., Lamb, R. J., Perin, E. M., & Falchero, S. (1994). Preference or preferences for landscape. *Journal of Environmental Psychology, 14,* 195–209.

Quirk, M., & Wapner, S. (1995). Environmental psychology and health. *Environment and Behaviour, 27,* 90–99.

Rapoport, A. (1982). *The meaning of the built environment: A nonverbal communication approach.* Beverly Hills, CA: Sage.

Reanney, D. (1994). *Music of the mind: An adventure into consciousness.* Melbourne: Hill of Content.

Reitman, E. E., & Pokorny, A. D. (1974). Camping at a psychiatric day center. In T. P. Lowry (Ed.), *Camping therapy: Its uses in psychiatry and rehabilitation.* Springfield, IL: Charles C Thomas.

Relph, E. (1976). *Place and placelessness.* London: Pion.

Rickard, H. C., Serum, C. S., & Forehand, R. (1975). Problem-solving attitudes of children in a recreation camp and in a therapeutic camp. *Child Care Quarterly, 4,* 101–107.

Rickard, H. C., Serum, C. S., & Wilson, W. (1971). Developing problem solving attitudes in emotionally disturbed children. *Adolescence, 6,* 451–456.

Rolston, H. (1991). Creation and recreation: Environmental benefits of leisure. In B. Driver, P. Brown, & G. Peterson (Eds.), *Benefits of leisure.* State College, PA: Venture.

Roseman, M. (1991). *Healing sounds from the Malaysian rainforest: Temair music and medicine.* Berkeley: University of California Press.

Rosen, S. (1982). *My voice will go with you: The teaching tales of Milton H. Erickson, M.D.* New York: Norton.

Rossi, E. L. (1986). *The psychobiology of mind-body healing: New concepts of therapeutic hypnosis.* New York: Norton.

Rossi, E. L. (1993). *The psychobiology of mind-body healing: New concepts of therapeutic hypnosis* (2nd ed.). New York: Norton.

Rossi, E. L., & Cheek, D. B. (1988). *Mind-body therapy: Methods of ideodynamic healing in hypnosis.* New York: Norton.

Roszak, T. (1992). *The voice of the earth.* New York: Simon & Schuster.

Roszak, T., (1995). Where psyche meets gaia. In T. Roszak, M. E. Gomes, and A. D. Kanner (Eds.), *Ecopsychology: Restoring the earth, healing the mind.* San Francisco: Sierra Club Books.

Roszak, T. (1996). The nature of sanity. *Psychology Today, 29,* 22–24.

Russell, J., & Mehrabian, A. (1976). Some behavioral effects of the physical environment. In S. Wapner, S. Cohen, & B. Kaplin (Eds.), *Experiencing the environment.* New York: Plenum.

Sakya, K., & Griffith, L. (1980). *Tales of Kathmandu: Folk tales from the Himalayan kingdom of Nepal.* Brisbane: House of Kathmandu.

Sartorius, N., & Ban, T. (1986). *Assessment of depression.* Berlin: Springer-Verlag.

Scherl, L. M. (1987). Our need for wilderness: A psychological view. *Habitat, 15*(4), 32–35.

Scherl, L. M. (1989). Self in wilderness: Understanding the psychological benefits of individual-wilderness interaction through self-control. *Leisure Sciences, 11,* 123–135.

Scherl, L. M. (1990). *Wilderness values and management.* Paper presented at the Institute of Tropical Rainforests workshop, Townsville, Australia.

Scholes, K. (1995). *We of the earth.* Melbourne: Hill of Content.

Schreyer, R., Williams, D. R., & Haggard, L. (1990). Periodic versus continued wilderness participation—Implications for self-concept enhancement. In A. T. Eastley, J. F. Passineau, & B. L. Driver (Eds.), *The use of wilderness for personal growth, therapy and education* (General Technical Report RM-193, pp. 23–26). Fort Collins, CO: U.S. Department of Agriculture, Forest Service, Rocky Mountain Forest and Range Experiment Station.

Sebba, R. (1991). The landscapes of childhood: The reflection of childhood's environment in adult memories and in children's attitudes. *Environment and Behavior, 23,* 395–442.

Seligman, M. E. P. (1975). *Helplessness: On depression, development and death.* San Francisco: Freeman.

Seligman, M. E. P. (1990). *Learned optimism.* New York: Alfred A. Knopf.

Shakespeare, W. (n.d.). Troilus and Cressida. In *The complete works of William Shakespeare.* London: Abbey Library.

Siegel, B. S. (1986). *Love, medicine and miracles.* New York: Harper & Row.

Simonton, O., Simonton, S., & Creighton, J. (1978). *Getting well again.* Los Angeles: Tarcher.

Smith, G., McKenzie, J., Marmer, D., & Steele, R. (1985). Psychological modulation of the human immune response to varicella zoster. *Archives of Internal Medicine, 145,* 2110–2112.

Smith, P. (1994). Inner Japan. *National Geographic, 186*(3), 65–95.

Spiegel, D. (1993). *Living beyond limits: New hope and help for facing life-threatening illness.* London: Vermilion.

Stokols, D. (1992). Establishing and maintaining health environments: Towards a social ecology health promotion. *American Psychologist, 47,* 6–22.

Stone, N. J., & Irvine, J. M. (1994). Direct and indirect window access, task type and performance. *Journal of Environmental Psychology, 14,* 57–63.

Strongman, K. T. (1987). *The psychology of emotion.* New York: Wiley.

Suzuki, D. (1990). *Inventing the future: Reflections on science, technology and nature.* Sydney: Allen & Unwin.

Swan, J. (1988). Sacred places in nature and transpersonal experiences. *ReVision, 10,* 21–26.

Theroux, P. (1985). *Sunrise with sea monsters.* Suffolk, England: Penguin.

Thoreau, H. (1987). In C. Bode (Ed.), *The portable Thoreau.* New York: Penguin.

Tsui-po, P. (1994). *Healing secrets of ancient China.* Melbourne: Hill of Content.

Ulrich, R. S. (1981). Natural versus urban scenes: Some psychophysiological effects. *Environment and Behavior, 13,* 523–556.

Ulrich, R. S. (1983). Aesthetic and affective response to natural environment. In I. Altman & J. F. Wohlwill (Eds.), *Human behavior and environment: Advances in theory and research* (Vol. 6, pp. 85–125). New York: Plenum.

Ulrich, R. S. (1984). View through a window may influence recovery from surgery. *Science, 224,* 420–421.

Ulrich, R. S., Dimberg, U., & Driver, B. (1991). Psychophysiological indicators. In B. Driver, P. Brown, & G. Peterson (Eds.), *Benefits of leisure.* State College, PA: Venture.

Ulrich, R. S., & Simons, R. F. (1986). Recovery from stress during exposure to everyday outdoor environments. In J. Wineman, R. Barnes, & C. Zimring (Eds.), *Procedings of the Seventeenth Annual Conference of the Environmental Design Research Association* (pp. 115–122). Washington, DC: EDRA.

Valentine, P. S. (1984). Wildlife and tourism: Some ideas on potential and conflict. In B. O'Rourke (Ed.), *Contemporary issues in Australian tourism* (pp. 29–54), Sydney: Department of Geography, University of Sydney.

Vernon, E. (1982). *Aphrodisiacs: An owner's manual.* London: Enigma Books.

Walters, C., & Havens, R. A. (1993). *Hypnotherapy for health, harmony, and peak performance: Expanding the goals of psychotherapy.* New York: Brunner/ Mazel.

Wapner, S. (1995). Toward integration: Environmental psychology in relation to other sub-fields of psychology. *Environment and Behavior, 27,* 9–32.

Watzlawick, P. (1978). *The language of change.* New York: Basic Books.

Watzlawick, P. (1983). *The situation is hopeless, but not serious: The pursuit of unhappiness.* New York: Norton.

Watzlawick, P. (1984). *The invented reality.* New York: Norton.

West, M. J. (1986). *Landscape views and stress response in the prison environment.* Unpublished master's thesis, University of Washington.

White, L., Tursky, B., & Schwartz, G. (1985). *Placebo: Clinical implications and insights.* New York: Guilford Press.

Wilby, S. (1992). *Across the top.* Sydney: Pan Macmillan.

Wordsworth, W. (n.d.). *Healing nature.* London: Thomas Nelson & Sons.

Wordsworth, W. (n.d.). *My heart leaps up.* London: Thomas Nelson & Sons.

Wright, A. N. (1983). Therapeutic potential of the outward bound process: An evaluation of a treatment program for juvenile delinquents. *Therapeutic Recreation Journal, 17*(2), 33–42.

Yapko, M. (Ed.). (1989). *Brief therapy approaches to treating anxiety and depression.* New York: Brunner/Mazel.

Yapko, M. (1992). *Hypnosis and the treatment of depressions: The strategies for change.* New York: Brunner/Mazel.

Yapko, M. (1997). *Breaking the patterns of depression.* New York: Doubleday.

Yates, A. J. (1970). *Behavior therapy.* New York: Wiley.

Zeig, J. (1980). *Teaching seminar with Milton H. Erickson, M.D.* New York: Brunner/Mazel.

AUTHOR INDEX

SUBJECT INDEX